Amber Waves of Grain

Amber Waves of Grain

American Macrobiotic Cooking

By Alex and Gale Jack

Foreword by Michio and Aveline Kushi
Illustrated by Rod House

Japan Publications, Inc.

To our mothers, Dessie and Esther, with love

Published by Japan Publications, Inc., Tokyo & New York

Distributors:
UNITED STATES: Kodansha America, Inc., through Farrar, Straus & Giroux, 19 Union Square West, New York 10003. CANADA: Fitzhenry & Whiteside Ltd., 91 Granton Drive, Richmond Hill, Ontario L4B 2N5. BRITISH ISLES AND EUROPEAN CONTINENT: Premier Book Marketing Ltd., 1 Gower Street, London WC1E6HA. AUSTRALIA AND NEW ZEALAND: Bookwise International, 54 Crittenden Road, Findon, South Australia 5023. THE FAR EAST AND JAPAN: Japan Publications Trading Co., Ltd., 1-2-1, Sarugaku-cho, Chiyoda-ku, Tokyo 101.

First Edition: September 1992

LCCC No. 92-070445
ISBN: 0-87040-877-1

Printed in the United States of America

Contents

Foreword

"O beautiful for spacious skies,
For amber waves of grain . . ."
— America the Beautiful

For the last forty years, we have lived in America and consider this beautiful country our home. There are many healthful whole grains, beans, vegetables, seaweeds, seeds and nuts, fruits, and other foods that naturally grow here, and many others have been brought to America by families from around the world. *Amber Waves of Grain* is a wonderful celebration of traditional cooking in America and of a balanced style of macrobiotic cooking that is emerging in harmony with the natural environment from New England to California, from the Great Lakes to the Desert Southwest.

This book may surprise you about the origin and widespread use of some foods in the modern macrobiotic diet. For example, you will learn that brown rice is as American as Amerigo Vespucci, who arranged for its first shipment to the New World, and Ben Franklin and Thomas Jefferson, who lived on brown rice as their staple food, gave up animal food at different times in their lives. Ginger, mugwort, and other medicinal plants associated with Far Eastern healing, have long been used as home remedies in North America. Sea vegetables, associated today exclusively with Oriental cooking, were used by native peoples on both the East and West Coasts, by the early colonists, and in New Orleans and other parts of the deep South. The notion you are what you eat is found in *Moby Dick, Huckleberry Finn,* and

"You tell me whar a man gets his corn pone, en I'll tell yu what his 'pinions is."
— Mark Twain

7

Early American Rice Dishes

Boiled rice
Rice 'n beans
Rice croquettes
Rice dumplings
Parched rice
Rice pilou
Rice fritters
Deep-fried rice
Soft rice
Rice gruel
Rice cream
Rice bread
Rice soup
Rice milk
Rice cream
Rice custard
Rice pudding
Rice cakes
Rice jelly
Rice waffles
Rice balls

other great American novels.

Alex and Gale Jack have been our associates for many years and have been pioneers in the spread of modern macrobiotics in the United States and abroad. Alex has written books with us on macrobiotic philosophy and health care, including *Aveline Kushi's Complete Guide to Macrobiotic Cooking*, which has been translated into several languages. Gale has taught cooking in her native Texas and at the Kushi Institute and has given private instruction to families around the country. During the last several years, Alex and Gale have managed our principal educational center in Becket, Massachusetts, and coordinated the One Peaceful World international information network and friendship society.

The recipes in this book—drawn from all regions of the continent—are enlivened by a wealth of cultural and historical information, quotations from famous American literary and historical figures, cooking tips and notes on health and ecology, and graceful drawings by Rod House. Through these pages, we hope that many readers will rediscover the macrobiotic heritage of their ancestors and come closer to the natural spirit of the land.

As we have taught for the last forty years, modern civilization is now ending. Cancer, heart disease, AIDS, and other degenerative diseases are sweeping the world. No family is immune from this present-day Noah's Flood. Led by America, modern society is now reawakening to principles of natural order and the imperative of living and eating in harmony with the environment. Personal illness, family disunity, community violence, economic decline, war and social disorder, and destruction of the global environment—all of these can be reduced and ultimately reversed, beginning with the daily preparation of healthful, blanced meals at home. Together we can save America. We can save the planet.

Amber Waves of Grain is an insightful look at America's golden grain-centered past, a valuable contribution to present East West harmony, and a steady guide to a future world of enduring health, happiness, and peace.

Michio and Aveline Kushi
Brookline, Massachusetts
February 29, 1992

Preface

America is a land of immigrants. From around the globe, families have come to the New World to flee religious persecution and economic and political oppression, to till the soil and create a better future for their children, to enjoy life, liberty, and the pursuit of happiness. According to their myths and legends, the earliest inhabitants of the continent also came from across the seas to settle and cultivate the land. Present-day Americans are made of all different colors, races, religions, and ethnic backgrounds. The nation traditionally has referred to itself as a Melting Pot—a vessel in which nourishing food is cooked and from which flows the clarity and strength to realize its dreams.

New arrivals to the continent also included the whole cereal grains, the staff of life and main ingredient in the family cauldron for endless generations. Maize—or Indian corn—came originally from South and Central America and made its way along the Gulf Shore, up the Mississippi River Valley, and to the edge of the Eastern Waters. Barley, wheat, oats, and rye were brought over by the first Europeans and spread from New England to the Mid-Atlantic, Midwest, and Great Plains. Rice came to the New World from Africa after an earlier voyage from the Far East. Millet and sorghum also journeyed across the Atlantic Ocean from Africa, and quinoa and amaranth traveled north from South and Central America.

For millennia, wild grasses such as goosefoot, served as principal foods. Wild rice, the continent's main native grain, is an aquatic seed-bearing grass that grows near Lake Superior in the heartland of the country. But even this grain may be an immigrant from China or Tibet, where strains of wild rice are also found and which may have migrated in a distant geological era.

"Then Kitche Manitou made the plant beings. These were four kinds: flowers, grasses, trees, and vegetables. To each he gave a spirit of life, growth, healing, and beauty. Each he placed where it would be the most beneficial, and lend to earth the greatest beauty and harmony and order.

"After plants, Kitche Manitou created animal beings conferring on each special powers and natures. There were two-leggeds, four-leggeds, wingeds, and swimmers.

"Last of all he made human beings. Though last in the order of creation, least in the order of dependence, and weakest in bodily powers, human beings had the greatest gift—the power to dream."
— Ojibway Creation Myth

9

The Seven Waves
of Macrobiotic Tradition

"*Upon this may be founded dietetic rules and a medical mode of treatment for preserving life; and hence arises a particular science, the Macrobiotic, or the art of prolonging it . . .*"
— *C.W. Hufeland, M.D., Macrobiotics or the Art of Prolonging Life 1796*

Whole grains—including porridge, cereal, bread, noodles, dumplings, and pasta—formed the foundation of all previous civilizations and are intertwined with America's origin and destiny. The rediscovery of whole grains in the last generation has been due largely to the macrobiotic community. The modern founders, George and Lima Ohsawa and Michio and Aveline Kushi, hailed from the Far East, and there is a unique Japanese flavor to their teachings and expression. But as they would be the first to explain, macrobiotics is a universal philosophy and way of life found in all cultures, climates, and countries. Indeed, the term itself—*makrobios* or "long life"—originated in ancient Greece with Hippocrates, the Father of Medicine who taught, "Let food be thy medicine and thy medicine be food." From the classical world of Greece and Rome and the ancient Holy Land, the term *macrobiotics* spread around the world. In the late eighteenth century, it was revived by Christolph Hufeland, a German medical doctor who advocated returning to a natural way of life, centered around whole grains and vegetables, and who influenced Goethe and the Bohemian community of artists and writers. In the 1950s and early 1960s, the term *macrobiotics* was rediscovered and adopted by the Ohsawas and Kushis and applied to the traditional natural philosophy and healing practices of the East, which shared a similar dietary approach.

In North America, we can identify seven waves of macrobiotic tradition and influence.

1. Native Americans—For thousands of years the Algonquins, Iroquois, Chippewa, Cherokee, Hopi, and other native peoples of the continent ate primarily corns, beans, and squash. This wholesome food was supplemented with wild rice and other wild grasses, greens and other vegetables, acorns (from which flour could be made), fruits, nuts, and seeds, seaweed, and a small amount of fish, seafood, or wild game.

2. The Colonial—With the modern discovery of the New World, settlers came from England, France, Spain, Holland, and other European countries. They adopted many native foods, especially corn, beans, and pumpkins, as well as introducing barley, wheat, oats, rye, and other staples from their homelands. From the early 1600s through the Revolutionary War, the way of eating that prevailed in New England, the Mid-Atlantic, and the South was based predominantly on grains and vegetables. Benjamin Franklin, George Washington, Thomas Jefferson, and other leaders of the American Revolution were especially committed to a grain-based way of eating and agriculture as the foundation of the new Republic.

3. The African—The African contribution to American culture and history includes the development of rice farming in the South and the introduction of millet, okra, sesame seeds, and other valuable plants. The fabled cuisine of the South is largely the creation of black cooks and farmers who served for nearly three centuries as slaves before winning their freedom. In sharp contrast to the gourmet cookery of the aristocracy, the way of eating of ordinary families—both black and white—in the South centered primarily on corn and rice, black-eyed peas, red beans, and peanuts, collards and other greens, and other seasonal produce. Fish and seafood from rich coastal and inland waters supplemented this essentially healthful fare.

4. Health Reform—As the infant nation began to expand and industrialize, animal food became increasingly available, along with sugar, spices, and other harmful foods integral to the slave trade. Influenced by Dr. Hufeland, the macrobiotic physician and founder of the modern health food movement, Rev. Sylvester Graham, Bronson Alcott, Mary Gove Nichols, Henry David Thoreau, Ralph Waldo Emerson, Ellen Harmon White, John Kellogg, John Muir, and other social leaders and health reformers counseled a return to a simple grain-based way of eating. Many utopian communities and religious sects of this era including the Shakers, Mormons, Transcendentalists, and Seventh Day Adventists incorporated vegetarian or semi-vegetarian regimens into their practice.

5. The Pioneer—As the country moved westward, families set off in covered wagons to Iowa, the Oregon Territory, the Oklahoma Territory, and other sparsely settled areas. The frontier cuisine that developed combined a degree of animal food appropriate for a nomadic trek and lifestyle along with familiar grains and beans that could be planted once the land was cleared.

6. The Ethnic—Beginning in the mid-nineteenth century, waves of immigrants arrived from the British Isles, Central Europe, and Scandinavia. These were followed by families from Eastern Europe and Russia, laborers and cooks from China and the Far East, and in the twentieth century by people from every land and nation including Central and South America, South and Southeast Asia, and the Middle East. The new arrivals brought with them their traditional cuisines and cooking methods based primarily on whole, unprocessed foods.

7. The Ecological—Modern macrobiotics and organic agriculture developed in the 1960s, spearheading the emerging

"As far as we could see, the miles of copper-red grass were drenched in sunlight that was stronger and fiercer than at any other time of the day. The blond cornfields were red gold, the haystacks turned rosy and threw long shadows. The whole prairie was like the bush that burned with fire and was not consumed."
— Willa Cather, My Antonia

ecology movement. Michio and Aveline Kushi, Frances Moore Lappé, Robert Rodale, Wendell Barry, Gary Snyder, Robert Bly, and other educators, authors, and poets taught that modern civilization must return to its roots, including a more vegetable-quality diet, to ensure the survival of the species and the planet.

Increasingly, the simple grain-based way of eating of the counterculture has moved into the mainstream. But it would be an exaggeration to describe American cooking as a whole over the last five centuries as macrobiotic. The nation's romance with cattle—particularly with beef in the form of steak and hamburger and dairy food in the form of milk and ice cream—is a major theme in the development of the country. However, beneath the triumph of the standard modern way of eating—high in meat, poultry, eggs, dairy food, sugar, refined flour, canned foods, and foods grown or treated with chemicals and other additives—the seven streams of whole foods tradition in America endure. They run deeply in the national psyche waiting to revive the land.

The Art of Cooking

Cooking is the supreme art, creating life itself. As Antoine Brilliat-Savaran, the eighteenth century French authority on dining wrote before emigrating to America, "Tell me what you eat, and I will tell you what you are." The values we identify with the American character—fairness, plain-dealing, inventiveness, hard-work, generosity, and optimism—are qualities traditionally associated with eating whole cereal grains.

Composed primarily of complex carbohydrates, grains give a slow, steady, dependable source of energy. In contrast, meat and sugar, as well as many refined and artificial foods, give a strong burst of initial power but wear off quickly, requiring frequent refueling. The end result is constant dissatisfaction and snacking, leading to hypoglycemia, a condition affecting an estimated 80 percent of the current American population and one characterized by sharp mood swings and other physical, mental, and spiritual imbalances. Returning to whole grains, many people are surprised to find how much calmer and more peaceful they feel. They also find they develop the perseverance necessary to carry out their goals.

In macrobiotic cooking, there is no standard diet appropriate for everyone. Rather there is a standard dietary approach based on universal principles that can be applied to different climates and environments and which takes into account different activity levels and personal needs. When modern macrobiotics first

"The secret for health and wisdom, freedom and happiness—all physical, mental, and spiritual as well as all social well being—is in front of us, day to day, lying in every dish we consume. How to choose, how to prepare, how to eat are the most central answers to the questions of the destiny of human beings."
— Michio Kushi
The Book of Macrobiotics

came to America, cooking was primarily Japanese. As temperate four-season countries, Japan and America broadly share the same traditional way of eating—whole grains, beans, vegetables from land and sea, and a small amount of animal food. However, there are significant differences in the types of foods used, the amounts of seasonings, and the styles of cooking and food preparation.

Though not tuned finely to the climate and environment of North America, George Ohsawa's "Zen Macrobiotic Cooking" served to wake up Americans from several generations of dietary slumber. In a time when the leading scientific and medical authorities scoffed at any connection between nutrition and health besides scurvy and other rare vitamin-deficiency diseases, Ohsawa's strong samurai style of teaching and cooking served to show that the emperors of modern medicine and nutritional science had no clothes. Further, the America he visited in the late 1950s and early 1960s consumed the largest amount of meat, sugar, refined foods, and chemicals of any era in human history. Supreme excess in the form of hamburgers, French fries, Coke, and ice cream inevitably attracted its opposite in the supreme simplicity of brown rice and *gomashio*. Ohsawa delighted in outraging the high priests of religion and science by declaring that the way from biological degeneration to spiritual enlightenment led through the kitchen.

In the late 1960's and 1970's, Michio and Aveline Kushi developed the standard macrobiotic dietary approach, considerably widening the diet to include more variety and flexibility. They also substantially reduced the amount of salt, miso, soy sauce, and other seasoning used in cooking. In Japan, largely a warm, humid country, people traditionally balance the moisture in the air with more salt than in America, which is considerably drier and less humid. In addition, Japanese have eaten less animal food than their Western counterparts and are thus able to take in more salt and other seasonings.

By the early 1980s, adjustments taking into account these factors began to appear in the Kushis' cookbooks and in cooking classes taught around the country by Kushi Institute teachers. The macrobiotic community considerably lightened up. There were less tightness, rigidity, and arrogance—qualities associated with excess salt consumption, excessive pressure cooking, and lack of variety in meals—and many ordinary middle-class Americans found they could adjust more easily to the new way of eating.

Meanwhile, a cornucopia of new foods became available—sourdough and other whole grain breads, whole wheat noodles and pasta, and ready-made tofu and tempeh, to name a few—as

"The idea of principal food, the basis of which is primarily biological and physiological and only secondarily economic, geographic, and agricultural, is one of the most important discoveries of human beings—fully as fundamental as the discovery of fire."
— *George Ohsawa*

organic and natural foods manufacturers, distributors, and retail stores and co-ops multiplied around the country. As Michio and Aveline often noted, in the beginning they imported Japanese foods and specialty items since organically grown grains, beans, and other healthful foods were no longer available in this country. In the 1960s, they set up Erewhon Trading Company to make native American grown foods available. Today macrobiotic quality foods grown and naturally processed primarily in America are available in many supermarkets and restaurants, in schools and hospitals. The Kushis succeeded in launching a dietary revolution beyond their original expectations, realizing Columbus' dream of unifying East and West.

Some of the recipes in this volume are drawn from the hearty pioneer cuisine that her grandparents prepared when they arrived by covered wagon in the Oklahoma Territory, from the foods native to the Cherokee side of her family, and from recipes we prepared when we were running the Heart-of-Texas Macrobiotic Center out of our home in Dallas.

In the pages that follow, we hope to present macrobiotic cooking in a way that is inviting and easy to follow, using familiar foods and common language. In addition to helping you create delicious, attractive, healthful meals, we hope that this book will inspire you to rediscover your own family's macrobiotics roots in the soil and stars of this beautiful land.

In writing this book, we are grateful to Michio and Aveline Kushi for their inspiration and guidance; to the spirit of our parents, grandparents, and ancestors (including Gale's forebears in the South who arrived by covered wagon in the Oklahoma Territory and Alex's family from the North who were farmers, clergymen, and artisans); and to Edward and Wendy Esko, Charles Millman, Michael and Alice Joutras, Lynda Shoup, and our associates at the Kushi Institute and One Peaceful World. We are grateful to Esther Jack, Alex's mother, for help with proofreading and to the Mr. Iwao Yoshisaki and Mr. Yoshiro Fujiwara, the publishers, for their support and encouragement. To our son, Jon, goes the credit for many of the recipes in the dessert chapter. To our daughter, Masha, whose anticipated arrival from her native Russia this winter, we owe meeting our deadline. As the newest American, may she grow up in health and harmony in this beautiful country nourished on amber waves of grain.

Alex and Gale Jack
Becket, Massachusetts
March 1, 1992

"I wish to leave for another very large island, which I believe must be Cipangu [Japan]."
— Columbus, Journal, October 21, 1492

Part I

Our Common Dream

1
Getting Started in the Kitchen

As the staff of life, whole grains were the basis of traditional weights and measures. Originally, the inch was defined as three grains of barley laid end to end. The foot, the yard, and standards of volume such as the cup, pint, and quart also originated with units of cereal grain.

The first cookbooks did not give measurements. They listed the kinds of foods, but did not specify how many teaspoons, tablespoons, and cups to use. This was partly because eating utensils and cookware were made by hand and not manufactured in uniform sizes. But also, people's intuition was sharper then. They let the grain, the dough, and the water cook themselves.

They used a pinch of this and a smidgin of that. They listened for the tell-tale sizzle and distinctive aroma of the cooking food without glancing at a clock or timer. They also cooked according to the changing seasons and to the day's weather. It was rare to plan the menu for an entire day ahead—much less for an entire week. Even with the *Farmer's Almanac* in hand or using Nine Star Ki (traditional Oriental astrology), you couldn't be sure a heat wave wouldn't set in and you might want something cooling rather than warming. Besides, the turnips in the garden might be just right for pulling up by suppertime, while the bok choy would have wilted.

Then there was the prospect that the corn would ripen early, and everybody would go into the fields for several days to reap the harvest. Gathering the grain, threshing it, and storing it for the long winter was hard work. But it was also satisfying. Scything the fields was better exercise than stickball or *tai ch'i*,

"Jim he got some corn-dodgers . . . and cabbage and greens—there ain't nothing in the world so good when it's cooked right."
— Mark Twain, Huckleberry Finn

and it kept the young people out of mischief. Afterwards, everyone would go to the local community center called a church, temple, or shrine to give thanks to the eternal process of creation and then enjoy a wonderful harvest festival. For the fieldwork and celebration, there would be bread to bake or rice balls to make, vegetable knishes or seaweed patties to fry, beer or sake to brew, and special dishes to prepare for the children and grandparents.

Around the world, the human family followed this timeless, seasonal way of living for thousands of years. Today, of course, all traditional standards have vanished. Most of us are celestial illiterates—unable to read the stars in the sky, remember the phases of the moon, or know the time of day the sun rises and sets. Almost completely removed from the cycles and rhythms of the natural world, we measure our days and hours by the payroll deadline and the VCR, we cook in programmed microwave ovens, and we celebrate our festivals not on the anniversary they fall but on the nearest weekend.

Yin and Yang

Modern macrobiotics is partly a reaction to the artificiality of modern life. But it is not old-fashioned. Unlike members of various sects and cults who withdraw from modern society, macrobiotic individuals and families continue to live in a world of constant change. They make use of technological advances, but reduce their reliance on excessive mechanical and electronic conveniences that may hinder their health or the environment. In order to remain balanced within the field of opposites, a reliable compass is needed. That compass is *yin* and *yang*—the two fundamental energies or forces that make up all phenomena.

The terms *yin* and *yang* come from the Far East, but they are not Oriental. They are universal categories of experience and, under various names and forms, have been used in every civilization. In Greece, Empedocles knew them as *activity* and *love*. In the ancient holy land, Jesus called them *movement* and *rest*. Though it lacks a true unifying principle, modern science knows them as *centripetal* and *centrifugal force*, *time* and *space*, *anode* and *cathode*, and other pairs of complementary opposites. Popular culture today knows them as *hard* and *soft*, *tough* and *tender*, *macho* and *fem*, *hip* and *straight*, *hawk* and *dove*, *Type A* and *Type B*, and other common polarities.

Modern macrobiotics uses yin and yang as a tool to understand life as a whole (*see list in the margin*). As an example, let's look at cars—the archetypal American invention and icon.

Yin
Expansive
Dispersive
Separating
Inactive
Slow
Vertical
Outward
Light
Cold
Dark
Wet
Thin
Large
Long

Yang
Contractive
Asssimilative
Gathering
Active
Fast
Horizontal
Inward
Heavy
Hot
Bright
Dry
Thick
Small
Short

We can learn a lot about ourselves and other people by observing their cars and driving habits. Relative to walking, horseback riding, or bicycling, automobiles are yang—faster and more active. By the same token, someone who habitually drives a car in the left-hand lane is more yang—active, faster, more aggressive. In comparison, someone who tends to drive in the right-hand lane is more yin—passive, slower, weaker.

Driving in the middle lane is more balanced. Our goal in macrobiotics is moderation. Extreme behavior usually leads to its opposite. Living in the fast lane leads to a short life. Living in the slow lane may result in never reaching our destination. To be truly balanced, we must be able to shift lanes at will, sometimes driving in the fast lane when necessary, other times in the slow lane, but generally sticking to the center of the road.

We can also classify cars by color, size, speed, and other characteristics. A small red sports car is very yang, while a large blue sedan is more yin. Race-car drivers and sports car owners are usually very yang and aggressive in their lifestyles, while those who drive large cars are more yin and prudent. Red and black, the most yang colors, are naturally preferred for speedier cars, while earth and sky tones are popular for more basic transportation. In this way we can begin to understand people by their cars. Those who drive compact or more medium-size cars, especially those that are more beige, amber, yellow, or silver (half black/half white) are often more balanced.

In the Far East, the ability to balance yin and yang is called following the Middle Way. In the West, it was called observing the Golden Mean. It turns up over and over again in folklore, fairy tales, and nursery rhymes. In the story of the three bears, Goldilocks prefers her porridge neither too hot (too yang) nor too cold (too yin) but just right (balanced).

Essentially the goal of macrobiotic cooking is to prepare balanced meals. This takes into account the proper choice of foods—including their balance of energy and nutrients—in addition to their color, shape, size, and texture and the way in which they are cut, processed or cooked, combined with other ingredients, served and displayed, blessed and consumed.

All of these factors, and doubtless others, go into creating a balanced meal. And that meal—whether balanced or not—becomes us. Goldilocks' hair, her most striking feature, was so beautiful because she ate essentially balanced food, including golden grain. If she had been eating curds and whey like Little Miss Muppet, she would have become too yin, attracted a spider to sit down beside her, and been frightened away. If she had been eating stronger animal food, she would have become too yang, repelled the bears, and been attacked like the three mice

"My kitchen is a mystical place, a kind of temple for me. It is a place where the surfaces seem to have significance, where the sounds and odors carry meaning that transfers from the past and bridges to the future."
— *Pearl Bailey*

"A good cook is like a sorceress who dispenses happiness."
— *Elsa Schiaparelli*

*Heap high the farm-
er's wintry hoard!
Heap high the golden
corn!
No richer gift has Au-
tumn poured
From out her lavish
horn.*

*Let other lands exult-
ing glean
The apple from the
pine,
The orange from its
glossy green,
The cluster from the
vine.*

*But let the good old
corn adorn,
The hills our fathers
trod;
Still let us for His
golden corn,
Send up our thanks to
God.*
*— John Greenleaf
Whittier*

whose tails were cut off with a carving knife.

No wonder cooking is the supreme art. Mastery of earth (the foods), water (the cooking water), air (cookware), and fire (the flame) are essential to creating balanced meals. The fifth and most important ingredient—love—is not listed in any recipe. But it is the cook's mind or spirit that determines whether the meal is peaceful and harmonious or the dietary equivalent of war. Let's look more closely at each of these elements.

Cooking According to the Seasons

In most parts of North America, we experience the change of seasons, from warmer to colder and colder to warmer. In nature, bears, eagles, foxes, and deer, as well as oak trees, maple trees, bluebonnets, and wild roses change their qualities and numbers according to the seasons. For optimal health and adaptability to our environment, as human beings we need to observe the natural order of spring, summer, fall, and winter. If we eat thick, warming soups and stews, heavy casseroles, salty main dishes, and animal food in the summer, we become overheated and seek out artificial air-conditioned surroundings or take too much yin to make balance. Conversely, if we eat strawberries and watermelon in the winter, we soon become imbalanced in the other direction and require overheated homes. Modern food storage and transportation has enabled us to enjoy foods from all seasons and climates. By violating natural ecological and seasonal boundaries, however, our natural immunity to disease is beginning to decline.

Nature produces different grains, beans, vegetables, fruits, seeds and nuts, and other crops in different seasons. Ideally, fresh produce should be consumed as much as possible in the month or season in which it is harvested. Grains and beans, nuts and seeds, seaweed and salt, and other foods that keep naturally are suitable for eating all year long. During the winter, when little could be grown, our ancestors for thousands of years consumed foods that were stored and preserved by simple methods. Grains, beans, nuts and seeds, root and round vegetables, and many green vegetables such as cabbage will keep easily for use throughout the colder months. In the modern macrobiotic home, we try to follow this traditional way of eating as much as possible. We use foods that are processed and stored according to traditional methods, including pickling, drying, and smoking, and avoid foods preserved by canning, freezing, and other artificial and chemical methods.

In the spring, when the rising energy of the earth is released after the long, cold winter, we add fresh greens to our meals, have more lightly boiled vegetables and pressed or boiled salads, and begin to use lighter cooking methods. We begin to reduce the amount of salt and other seasonings slightly and use pickles that have aged less and condiments of milder strength. Barley, wheat, and other grains that have ripened over the winter may be used more frequently. Sprouts, scallions, chives, and condiments made with miso and oil are used often to help release the stagnated energy of the winter.

In summer, when the foliage reaches its zenith, we use foods that have more outward, active energy, including collards and other broad leafy greens, sweet corn, yellow squash and zucchini, and strawberries, cantaloupe, and other locally grown fruits. Fresh salads are enjoyed frequently, often with grains, noodles, beans, and seaweed. Boiling, steaming, stir-frying, and other lighter cooking methods are used more frequently. Salt and seasoning is generally light, but because of perspiration and loss of minerals in hot weather, strong condiments are prepared in small volume. Umeboshi are particularly good for cooling the body and can be used in beverages and seasoning. Fresh tofu, cool or chilled noodles, fresh cucumbers, and other cooling foods are very refreshing during this season.

In the autumn, the energy of the sky and earth begins to reverse direction and turn down and inward. To adjust to the change from hot to cool, we begin to include more buttercup, butternut, acorn, and other fall-season squashes and other root vegetables in our menus. Many colorful foods are harvested at this season, including millet, cabbage, onions, and other round vegetables that can be used slightly more frequently at this time of the year. Cooking styles begin to emphasize richer tastes and stronger methods, including hearty soups and stews, fried and deep-fried dishes, and preparations featuring mochi, sweet rice, dried tofu, tempeh, and other energizing foods. Slightly more salt and seasoning can be used, dried fruits can begin to replace fresh fruit, and the amount of raw foods can be reduced.

In winter, as the earth's energy recedes, cold weather arrives, and many parts of the land are covered with deep snow, we begin serving warm, strengthening food. We use proportionately more seitan, tempeh, mochi, fried rice and noodles, tempura, and strongly seasoned seaweed during this season. *Nishime*-style boiling, deep-frying, *kimpira*-style sautéing, and other longer, stronger cooking methods are used regularly, and slightly more salt and seasoning are used. Fresh grated ginger root gives warming energy and can be used frequently in stews.

By enjoying the produce of the good earth in season we can maintain our health and vitality throughout the year.

"The discovery of a new dish does more for human happiness than the discovery of a new star."
—Brillat-Savarin,
The Physiology of Taste 1825

Color, Texture, and Taste

"The true cook is the perfect blend, the only perfect blend, of artist and philosopher. He knows his worth: he holds in his palm the happiness of mankind, the welfare of generations yet unborn."
— *Norman Douglas, An Almanac*

Alex likes to tell the following story. "I first realized that cooking was an art when Gale and I married. Her food was fantastic. It was so much more delicious, satisfying, and attractive than my cooking. However, one thing irritated me. Afterward when I went to clean up, there would be half an onion left on the cutting board all diced up. Next to it would be two or three pieces of carrot, and then on the counter there would be small bowls and cups of partially soaked grains or beans, an inch of kuzu cream with soy sauce in the measuring bowl, several slices of umeboshi plum, a half grated piece of daikon, and bits and pieces of other foods. My Puritan New England conscience rebelled at this evident waste, even though Gale used up all the ingredients very creatively in future meals. I wondered whether this was the way they did things in Texas. Why couldn't she just carefully measure out everything she needed beforehand?

"After several incredible meals, it dawned on me that Gale was an artist. The cutting board was her palette, the knives and cookware her brushes, and the various foods, sauces, and seasonings her colors. I have never regretted cleaning up the kitchen since. Who would fault Rembrandt or Cézanne for leaving so many pigments by their easel?

"Since then I have come to appreciate that each cook, like each painter, has his or her own style. Some, like Gale, do portraits—homestyle food personally suited to each family member. Others do landscapes—more restaurant or gourmet-style food with a profusion of dishes and delights from which everyone can freely choose. Some are like Zen calligraphers or miniaturists, adding just a touch of color or texture: A garnish of green scallions on a bowl of noodles, a pinch of brown or black sesame salt on a bowl of rice, a ribbon of purple dulse in a salad. Others are muralists, preparing a panorama of courses and special dishes in a motif of seasonally-coordinated serving dishes and pressed maple leaves, sprigs of holly, or other natural decorations by the table. The range of styles and compositions is limitless. Of course, not every meal is a masterpiece. But each dish can be attractively prepared, and each cook leaves her unique signature in every meal she prepares."

Grains and vegetables are our primary foods in macrobiotic cooking, so the principal colors at the table are usually amber, yellow, orange, or light brown. Complementing these moderate, peaceful hues are the more calming bright greens and whites of leafy vegetables and the more energizing reds and blacks of beans, seaweeds, and seasonings. Not every color, texture, and taste needs to be represented at the table, but each meal should reflect a harmonious balance of contrasting colors as a whole.

The Art of Cutting

Food is alive, and the way we handle it contributes to the energy and vitality we receive. For most Americans, the knives found in a macrobiotic kitchen are very different from the knives with which we grew up. Paring and carving knives, butcher knives, and cleavers are designed to cut meat, poultry, and other animal food. Vegetables and other plants require a finer, more delicate blade and one that is squarer or more rectangular in shape. The manner of cutting, too, is strikingly different. Animal foods are chopped, split, and dismembered, while vegetable foods are sliced, diced, minced, and shredded. The way the knife is held, the direction in which it is angled, and the force of cutting also differ.

Cutting vegetables is a lost art. There are a dozen basic cuts including rounds, diagonals, half moons, quarters, matchsticks, cubes, irregular or rolling style, rectangles, dicing, shaving, flower shapes, and chrysanthemums (see illustrations). The method we select will depend on the overall number and type of different dishes in the meal, the natural energy of the plant itself, and the way of cooking and time available for meal preparation. Thickly sliced vegetables take more time to cook than thinly sliced ones. Vegetables cut into smaller pieces often give a sweeter taste than those cut in larger pieces. But large pieces give more initial energy. Greens tend to lose shape and volume in cooking, while root and round vegetables keep their appearance and may be cut in many ways. The meal as a whole should include a complement of shapes, sizes, and thicknesses. If we use large rounds in a soup or stew, we should use thin slices or cubes in a side dish. Each individual carrot or onion in each dish, however, should be cut the same way to allow even cooking.

Taking cooking classes with an experienced macrobiotic cook is recommended to learn the basic methods. However, beyond technique, the ideal is to let the vegetables cut themselves. This sometimes involves asking (mentally or aloud) the carrots and onions how they would like to be prepared. You will be surprised at the answers you receive. It also includes cutting in a peaceful, harmonious motion in which the whole blade slides effortlessly through the plant without conscious exertion.

This may sound esoteric like Zen or the Tao, but it's really just the care and skill traditionally given to any art or craft. In

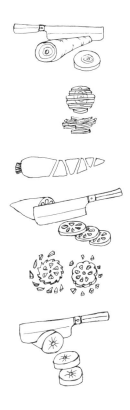

Cutting Tip
Cut vegetables just before cooking to prevent loss of energy and nutrients.

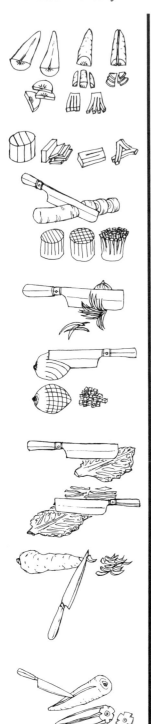

the past, woodsmen in New England or British Columbia, for example, used to go into the forest and ask the tree's permission to cut it down. They would explain to the tree what its wood would be used for—to make a house for the family, a bench for the church, a boat for the fishermen, spinning wheels for the ladies, paper for the printer, toys for the children. The tree would then be happy to give its life. The woodsman would cut it down respectfully and then plant a seedling on its site. The same with food and the other fruits of nature. Like the forester and the tree, the captain and his ship, and the cook and her vegetables, everything proceeds smoothly when we reverence life around us and honor our tools. Heaven and earth support us, and we become one with whatever we are doing.

Our Daily Water

The Southwestern desert is the oldest continuously inhabited part of the continent. People often ask the Hopi and other native peoples why they settled there where there is so little water. The answer they give is that their ancestors had such faith that they deliberately sought out the most inhospitable climate. If they were pure of heart, they reasoned that the Great Spirit would provide them with all they truly needed. In the desert, they discovered amazing ways to locate water and grow maize.

Corn and water. Bread and water. Grain and water. Yang and Yin—the essentials of life. The source of our water is of supreme importance, yet today many of us do not know where our water comes from. Watershed is an ecological term for an entire area of a valley that is drained by water, from the ridgetop on one side to the ridgetop on the other. Nearly everyone lives in a watershed, so getting to know the source of our water is a basic step to both personal and community health. Here in the Berkshires, we discovered that we live in the Farmington watershed which begins in western Massachusetts and flows South into Connecticut. There is a Farmington River Association devoted to preserving the quality of the water in the valley, as well as organizing community events and outings.

Within this small ecosystem, our daily water comes from the well in our house and is very good quality. Before when we were living on the main road, salt from town trucks and road crews would seep into our well in the winter, and we would have to get water from a natural spring several miles away or buy spring water at the supermarket (imported from Maine, New Hampshire, and Connecticut). The water at the nearby Kushi Institute also comes from a well and is fine for daily use. On the ridge behind the K.I., however, there is an old reservoir which used to be connected to the Main House by an underground pipe. That water—from natural springs and rain—was the most refreshing water that we had ever had. We hope that one day soon it can be reconnected and used for daily cooking and drinking again. There are many mountain springs, waterfalls, and other highly charged places like this around the country whose water has a special quality and was viewed as holy or sacred by native peoples.

In many parts of the country, good water is hard to find. Pesticides are the major source of water pollution in America, but there are many others including industrial wastes, nuclear by-products, and untreated sewage. For those without a clean source of running water, there is no easy solution. Many macrobiotic households have bottled spring water delivered or buy it at the natural foods store or co-op. Others use water purifiers. Our general advice is to obtain the best quality of water you can comfortably afford—financially or in your own time and labor.

For daily cooking and drinking, natural spring or well water is best. Chemically treated or distilled water should be avoided. Water contributes to the sweetness, bitterness, or other taste of the food. Water that is neither too hard nor too soft is ideal. If your water is too hard, soften it by boiling. If it is too soft, add a little more salt or seasoning in cooking. Besides plain water, the water that foods are cooked in may be saved. Noodle water, vegetable water, and sometimes soaking water for grains, beans, and sea vegetables that is not used in cooking can be preserved and used in some other dish, though using too much leftover water makes food too yang. Better give it to the cat or the geraniums. Treating water as a precious friend will contribute immeasurably to our health and happiness.

"The noise made by a pot when struck or when simmering on the fire is supposed to be the voice of its associated being. The clang of a pot when it breaks or suddenly cracks in burning is the cry of this being as it escapes or separates from the vessel."
— Frank Hamilton Cushing, Zuni Breadstuffs

Cookware and Utensils

Roasting trays, water jugs, baking surfaces, bowls, and other cooking vessels are traditionally made of gourds, bark, clay, earthenware, wicker, stone, wood, metal, glass, and other natural materials. Among other things, cookware serves to protect and preserve food from deteriorating when exposed to the open air. Sometimes, as in the case of the birch bark which the Algonquins and other native peoples used, or bamboo in Oriental-style cooking, light mats, containers and cookware allow the food to breathe naturally without spoiling or attracting insects.

Today there are many types and styles of pressure cookers, frying pans, saucepans, crockpots, pickle presses, serving

Cooking Tip
Your cooking will go
more smoothly if you
gather all necessary
ingredients for the
meal before you begin
the first dish.

"I declare that a meal
prepared by a person
who loves you will do
more good than any
average cooing, and
on the other side of it
a person who dislikes
you is bound to get
that dislike into your
food, without intend-
ing to."
— Luther Burbank,
The Harvest of the
Years

bowls, and dinnerware available. Some are of excellent quality and if properly maintained will last a lifetime while extending your own. Aluminum, plastic, synthetics, and other materials that can be absorbed by the food should be avoided.

A pressure cooker is essential in a modern macrobiotic kitchen. Presssure cooking makes whole grains sweeter and easier to digest by keeping most of the hot steam inside the pot. Some pressure cookers are heavy and the covers are hard to screw down and release. We favor a lightweight model that is easy to carry around and open and close, and one with a release valve on the cover in addition to the steam nozzle. This is a safety feature which allows excessive hot air to escape if too much pressure builds up. There are also enamel-lined pressure cookers, which are more expensive and are said to give the food a better flavor. In our experience, cooking is not always even, so we prefer the ordinary stainless-steel variety.

For roasting grains and seeds, stainless frying pans are also ideal. Their temperature can be more easily adjusted than cast-iron, which takes longer to heat and longer to cool. While we don't recommend using cookware with aluminum surfaces that come into contact with the food, there are now stainless-steel frying pans and saucepans with heat-spreading aluminum on the outside bottom of the pans. These allow the food to cook more evenly without interacting with the food. However, there may still be some vibrational influence, so if you have health concerns these are not recommended.

The number and size of saucepans will of course depend somewhat on the size of your family, but generally it's handy to have a small one for sauces, kuzu and umeboshi drinks, and other medicinal preparations, and several medium and large saucepans for vegetables, beans, and boiled grains. You will also want to have a large kettle or saucepan for making noodles and pasta. Most of our saucepans and kettles are stainless, though we have one enamel-covered cast-iron pan with a heavy lid that is wonderful for beans, stews, and other hearty dishes.

Cast-iron skillets are nice for dishes that don't require a lot of oil. If we are sautéing vegetables with a moderate amount of oil we usually use stainless steel, but if we have to be careful about our oil intake we just lightly brush the skillet with oil and use cast-iron. Cast-iron is also excellent for cooking seaweeds, *su-kiyaki*-style vegetables, grain and vegetable burgers, and frying pancakes. We also use this type of skillet for pan-frying mochi, bread, and other foods without oil. We use two-sizes at home: a small and large one.

For steaming, we use a small perforated stainless steamer set inside a saucepan or a small collapsible model that can be unfolded and put inside a larger pot. Oriental-style bamboo steamers are also available, but tend to take longer to use.

You have to be careful when using glass for cooking. If it is natural it can crack, and if it is treated it can adversely affect the food. Pyrex pie plates are usually all right, but other pyrex cookware is treated. There are also glass baking dishes and other items that are combined with plastic and other synthetics which should be avoided. The one piece of glassware we use daily is our tea pot. Its transparency allows you to judge the strength of the tea, whether it is too dark (too strong, too yang) or too light (too weak, too yin). Glass lids are also handy for frying pans, letting the cook see how the food is doing without taking off the cover and letting valuable steam and pressure escape.

A variety of strainers is also essential. We have small bamboo strainers for tea, small flat stainless for deep-frying, medium cup-size for small amounts of rinsing and washing, and large bowl-size for preparing larger amounts of seeds, beans, and grains.

For cutting, we use several Oriental-style vegetable knives made of stainless or carbon-steel. A good cutting board and sharpening stone are a must. We like cherry or other soft wood to cut on, and use a rectangular stone for sharpening. The board should be rinsed lightly on both sides in cold water after use, and the knife's edge should be whetted daily or every other day. Like a good scythe or good pencil, a sharp edge makes the work go more smoothly, and taking care of your tools quickly becomes second nature.

For cooking utensils, we use primarily wood—spoons, paddles, and long cooking chopsticks. Wood has a calm, peaceful energy in comparison to metal implements. Finally, our basic kitchenware includes a ceramic mortar (known in Japanese as a *suribachi*) for making *gomashio* and other condiments, several graters (both enamel and stainless) for grating daikon and other vegetables, glass and metal measuring cups, and a large assortment of glass jars and bottles for storage.

At the table, we serve food in a wide variety of serving bowls and containers. Again, natural materials are preferred. For rice we have a lovely traditional wooden rice bucket from Japan. It keeps the freshly cooked rice warm and adds to the esthetic enjoyment of the meal. Different shapes are also very pleasing. Lovely circular, oblong, square, rectangular, butterfly, and other special shapes are available. For individual servings, we have a variety of bowls, dishes, cups, glasses, and plates. Regular dinner plates are generally more suitable for animal food that lays horizontally across the middle with potatoes, a vegetable, and a

"The white man had showed neither respect for nature nor reverence toward God, but, (the old chief of the Sac and Fox tribe) thought, tried to buy God with the byproducts of nature. He tried to buy his way into heaven, but he did not even know where heaven is.

"As for us," he concluded, "we shall still follow the old trail. If you should live long, and some day the Great Spirit shall permit you to visit us again, you will find us still Indians, eating with wooden spoons out of bowls of wood."
— Charles Eastman, From the Deep Woods to Civilization 1916

Storage Tip
Let cooked food cool completely before refrigerating.

roll to the side. We find small bowls and dishes more appropriate for grains, beans, and vegetables. For rice and other whole grains, we like Chinese or Japanese-style rice bowls. For noodles, we like larger, deeper bowls which hold more broth and can be held up and supped. For beans and casseroles, we sometimes use small round earthenware or glass dishes with a handle that are put in the oven and served directly to each person. For seaweed and greens, we like small half-size Oriental-style bowls. Often we serve a meal altogether and find medium-sized plates usually adequate.

For eating, we usually use chopsticks. Wood has a more peaceful vibration than metal. Interestingly, many American Indian tribes avoided metal spoons, forks, and knives when they were first introduced by Europeans, noting that they affected the quality and taste of the food. For drinking, we use small cups or juice-size glasses. Ordinarily, macrobiotic friends do not drink as much liquid as people eating the modern diet. Because of the strong yang energy of meat and other animal food, they customarily start the meal with a big glass of water and take plenty of juice, soft drinks, coffee, tea, and other beverages during the day. We enjoy tea and other beverages in much smaller volume. We enjoy regional cups, glasses, and mugs but usually fill them only half full.

Our Daily Fire

The use of fire sets human beings apart from other species, and through cooking, especially the preparation of whole cereal grains, humanity developed its upright (grain-like) posture, advanced intellect, and higher consciousness. Fire gives life energy, vitalizing all of our activities and allowing us to adapt to the ever-changing environment. The future of our species, our country, and our family all depends on our control and mastery of fire—for cooking, for technology, for household use.

"How to eat food and how to use fire in the preparation of food, are the matters of essence for the continual survival and development of the human species for millions of years in the future."
— Michio Kushi

The ideal fuel for cooking is wood. It gives a warm, natural heat, and food cooked over a wood flame is much more delicious, satisfying, and peaceful than any other method. Cooking with wood, however, is not practical in many modern households and in other communities may lead to deforestation or air pollution. The practical alternative is natural gas, which gives a clean, even heat, is easy to adjust, and respects the natural energy of the food. When we moved into our present house, it had an electric stove. The very first thing we did was have it replaced with a gas range. Electric—and microwave to an even greater extent—alter the natural structure of the foods, artificially speed up cooking, and overall are very weakening.

In our view, cooking with electric or microwave heat (now in 80 percent of American homes) is a major unrecognized cause of degenerative disease and loss of natural immunity. Several years ago Alex was teaching in Miami at the Macrobiotic Winter Conference. Afterwards he rented a car and drove down to visit his father and step-mother who were spending the winter in Key West. The house they were staying in had an electric stove, which Alex used to cook brown rice, millet, tofu, and other items from a nearby natural foods store. The morning he returned to Miami, he discovered that he was driving the wrong way down the road—a high-speed highway. This was the first time in his life he had ever made such a serious error in judgment while driving. Fortunately, there was almost no traffic, so he quickly changed direction before getting into an accident. Reflecting afterwards on how he became so imbalanced, Alex realized it was the electric cooking. The energy is very chaotic and disorienting—even when preparing good quality foods. In cooking classes and consultations, we strongly recommend that people switch from electric to gas, even if they are renting a house or an apartment. The cost of installing a new unit is a small price to pay for ensuring the health and safety of your family.

Finally, in our automotive age, a new and popular form of cooking is car cuisine—cooking on the engine of the family sedan, pick-up, or van. Every weekend, at football games and sporting events across the land, thousands of people are warming up their hamburgers and french fries before the big game in parking lots and fields. This craze has spawned a cookbook—*Manifold Destiny*. Like irradiation and other highly mechanized forms of food processing and preparation, "cooking with gas" in this way—even if it's brown rice and veggies on the hood of a Toyota—is best avoided.

Cooking Methods

The way we cook also contributes to our energy and balance. Generally, we use the quick, light upward energy of blanching, boiling, steaming, and stir-frying of vegetables to balance the long time cooking of pressure-cooked grains, which gives a heavier, more downward energy. Beans are ideally boiled or simmered so as not to be so yang. However, sometimes when time is a factor, we pressure cook beans, especially aduki beans. chickpeas, and other harder beans that can take hours to boil.

Boiling is the basic, most balanced way of preparing vegeta-

The Ten Most Common Mistakes in Macrobiotic Cooking

1. *Too much salt and other seasonings.*
2. *Too much oil.*
3. *Too much water*
4. *Too much fire.*
5. *Too much pressure cooking.*
6. *Too much flour and baked goods.*
7. *Too many snacks and desserts.*
8. *Too much stirring.*
9. *Overeating and not enough chewing.*
10. *Too little variety in meals, especially a lack of greens and other vegetables.*

bles and gives a slightly sweeter taste. But boiling in the macro-biotic kitchen is very different from the way most vegetables are boiled in modern society. Usually only a small amount of water—one-half to one inch—is needed to boil vegetables. The practice of submerging broccoli, carrots, onions, and other gar-den produce in water and overcooking them developed in a cul-ture in which animal food had substantially replaced grains and vegetables as principal fare. Many vegetables are done after only two to three minutes, others take five to ten minutes. This preserves their natural energy and texture, brightens their color, and brings out the natural taste or sweetness in the plant. Over-cooking in too much water makes for limp, tasteless, colorless vegetables deserving of their modern reputation.

In addition to short-time boiling, medium and long-time boil-ing are occasionally used, especially for root vegetables that take longer to prepare. In macrobiotic cooking, we often boil different vegetables together in large chunks over a low flame, along with seaweed, fu, or other ingredients. In the Far East, this is known as *nishime*-style and makes for a strong, warming dish, and also one that is very calming and relaxing, especially for the pancreas. In this method, water is added to the vegeta-bles until they are half covered.

Steaming is a nice light way to prepare vegetables and gives a slightly more bitter taste. There are several ways to prepare vegetables in a skillet, with and without oil. Basic sautéing with a little bit of oil and water, especially with carrots, onions, and burdock, is known as *kimpira*-style, after Sakata Kimpira, a leg-endary Japanese folk hero. We frequently cook without oil, add-ing a small amount of water to the skillet and water-sauté vege-tables or seaweed. Another method is pan-frying, in which the foods cook in the skillet for a longer period of time, with a little water or oil. Occasionally, as with mochi or bread, some foods may be pan-fried in a cast-iron skillet for a few minutes without oil or water without sticking or burning.

In general, we stir very little in macrobiotic cooking, even with stir-frying, sautéing, and other methods involving mixed foods. Again, this is the opposite of modern cooking in which foods are constantly stirred, turned over, and moved. This kind of cooking creates a chaotic vibration in the food and results from the cook eating too much animal food, especially eggs and poultry. In macrobotic cooking, we let the foods cook them-selves, stirring as little as possible. Then we stir or move them very gently with a wooden spoon or paddle. Metal is jarring and disturbs their vibration.

Baking is another popular way of cooking. It creates foods that are evenly cooked with radiant heat, giving a deep, warming energy and rich, delicious taste. We particularly enjoy baked squash in the autumn and winter and occasionally baked casseroles and baked apples and pears. Baked flour products, however, are a red flag in macrobiotic health care and medicine and need to be used within moderation. For those in usual good health, the standard macrobiotic dietary guidelines are two to three pieces of bread or baked goods a week. Baked flour products are very hard, dry, and tend to create mucus in the intestines. They tend to make the pancreas tight, giving rise to cravings for sweets and leading to indecision and frequent changes of mind as blood sugar levels fluctuate. Eating too many baked flour products—bread, muffins, biscuits, crackers, pretzels, bagels, cookies, cakes, pies, pastries, and other baked goods—is a major cause of modern disease, including a general rigidity and lack of flexibility in mind and spirit. Very delicious, good quality bread and other baked goods are enjoyed in macrobiotic cooking—but within moderation—not every meal and not every day.

Broiling, grilling, barbecuing, smoking, and other strong methods of cooking are also used sparingly.

The flame itself contributes to the energy of the dish and meal. A high flame or high heat gives a burst of strong, active energy. A medium flame or heat gives moderate, steady energy. A low flame or heat gives more slow, calming energy. For variety, all types of flame and heat may be used with an emphasis on a moderate to low fire.

Blenders, osterizers, food processors, toasters, and other electrical gadgets are avoided on a daily basis in the modern macrobiotic kitchen. Like electric and microwave stoves, they affect the quality of the food and give irregular energy. In our home, we don't use anything electric on a daily basis. Our one modern extravagance is a Belgian waffle iron which we use occasionally to make mochi waffles. Otherwise, we prefer the *suribachi*, a Foley food mill (turned by hand), and other traditional implements.

Cooking Tip
Though we don't use a blender or other electric gadgets on a daily basis, occasionally, for parties and special occasions when many guests are coming and a large quantity of food is prepared, we will use a blender for dips or desserts. In this case, we will let the food set for several hours before serving to allow the vibration to settle.

Cooking with Love

By eating together as family and friends, we create a similar mind and spirit. We begin to think and react in the same way, sharing a common dream. The modern way of eating includes not only food devoid of life energy and nourishment, but also the decline of eating together. Today families rarely share home-made food or eat at the same table. Most of the time, they eat by themselves or in front of television, congregate in twos or threes at irregular times around the refrigerator, and go out to a fast-food place or have a pizza delivered. The term "food contacts" has been coined by sociologists to refer to such practices as bumping into Mom or Dad while getting a snack in the kitchen or going out to McDonald's on the spur of the moment. No wonder families today cannot understand or talk to each other. They are no longer eating together and sharing the same view of life. The American Dream has fragmented into millions of tiny pieces.

By preparing food with a calm, peaceful mind, the cook creates health and happiness for her family. This in turn contributes to community health, to national health, and eventually to world health and world peace. This is the goal of macrobiotic cooking. What may initially appear to be a very restricted diet turns out to be an incredibly rich and diverse approach, synthesizing the traditional cuisine of all countries and cultures. The key is cooking according to universal principles and at the same time allowing for variety and personal needs. God's grace will surely shine on all who proceed in this simple, balanced way.

"Ma made the cornmeal and water into two thin loaves, each shaped in a half circle. She laid the loaves with their straight sides together in the bake-oven, and she pressed her hand flat on top of each loaf. Pa always said he did not ask any other sweetening when Ma put the prints of her hands on the loaves."
— Laura Ingalls Wilder, Little House on the Prairie

2
Macrobiotic Regional Cooking

Whenever someone observes that the modern macrobiotic diet is too Oriental, we like to tell the story of the Japanese edition of Michio and Alex's *The Cancer-Prevention Diet* (New York: St. Martin's Press, 1983). A big mainstream Tokyo publisher acquired the Japanese rights to this book and said that it wanted to introduce macrobiotics (which is very small and insignificant in the Far East) to modern Japan. The publisher asked permission, however, to make one small change. It said, "The menus and recipes are too American. Japanese don't know many of the foods and styles of cooking. Would you mind if we substituted more familiar foods?" Macrobiotics has truly become a marriage of East and West!

Foods that originated in the Far East form a small but essential part of the macrobiotic diet in North America. Once you master the twenty key Oriental foods (see list in the margin), you are well on your way to cooking healthy, satisfying meals. Imagine macrobiotic families in Japan and the Far East trying to learn and pronounce the twenty key Western foods (see second list), and you will appreciate how universal modern macrobiotics is.

The principles of macrobiotic cooking can be summarized as 1) eating according to the evolutionary spiral of biological life, 2) eating according to ancestral tradition, 3) eating according to climate and environment, and 4) eating according to personal health, activity level, and personal needs.

As human beings, we evolved consuming primarily cereal plants, just as monkeys and other early primates ate fruits and nuts. Mammals, birds, and reptiles further back on the evolutionary spiral developed on roots, tubers, seeds, eggs, and insects. Compact (small and dynamic), hardy (maturing through the change of seasons and all kinds of weather) and long-lived (capable of germinating after many centuries), grains are the perfect food for physical vitality, mental clarity, and spiritual development.

As we have seen, whole grains served as the core of the cuisine and culture of every previous civilization. In the Far East and Africa, grain tended to be eaten in whole form—in bowls of rice or pots of millet or sorghum. In the Middle East, people preferred grain in cracked form—bulghur, cracked wheat, couscous. In the West, grain was traditionally eaten in the form of flour—bread and baked goods. Of course, all three ways of eating grain can be found in all parts of the world. In the Far East, noodles, pasta and other softly prepared forms of flour are extremely popular. In the Middle East, the staff of life in ancient Egypt and Israel was round flat bread made of whole barley. In the West, oatmeal, Scotch oats, rye flakes, and other cracked or partially processed grains were customarily eaten along with whole grain porridges and dark whole wheat and rye bread. In the Americas, native peoples ate maize—their principal grain—in all three forms—as fresh ears of corn on the cob, as thin flat bread made from whole grain dough (tortillas), and as corn ground from coarse to fine meal (hominy, grits, suppone).

Grains in whole form give strong, steady energy and lead to a spirit of oneness. Grains in flour form, especially bread, give light to moderate energy and keen analytic abilities and attention to detail. Grains in partial form give moderate energy and practical insight. Traditionally, these patterns of eating have given rise to three slightly different ways of life and cultural expression emphasizing philosophy and religion in the East, science and industry in the West, and trade and commerce in between.

Beans and legumes form the natural dietary complement to whole grains. In the Americas, a variety of black, red, white, and spotted beans are eaten in tortillas or combined to form succotash. In Europe, household gardens grow dried pea beans and fava beans to eat with their rye and sourdough bread. In the Middle East and Africa, lentils, chickpeas, and falafel are eaten with main dishes. In the East, aduki beans and soybeans (usually in the form of tofu, tempeh, and other products) complement rice.

All of these wonderful grains and beans and their products are now available in America and have become part of the mod-

"Change takes place by eating. Each living thing selects something from the outside world and changes it in order to sustain life and grow. So it is by eating that we grow, that we develop and adapt to the environment."
— Michio Kushi

ern macrobiotic diet. At home, our family enjoys freshly cooked brown rice at least once every day (and often more). We find that rice is the most consistently satisfying grain for day to day vitality, focus on our dream in life, and feeling of unity with each other and other people. For extra vitality and creativity, we like millet, especially softly prepared or cooked together with rice. For calm, peaceful energy we like barley (cooked together with rice or in soups and stews) and whole oats (by itself or cooked with barley and lentils). Fresh corn we enjoy in season and cooked together with rice; also in the form of tortillas, grits (once a week), and chowder. All the other grains we enjoy from time to time, and several times a week we prepare noodles and like to have a piece of traditional sourdough or whole wheat bread every few days.

One secret we have discovered over the years and would like to share with you is: eat grain in whole form at every meal. Even if you are having noodles, bread, or cracked grains, eat a small bowl of rice, millet, or other whole grain (leftover is fine). This will help to center you. The same thing when you eat at a restaurant. Even if your main dish is tempura, croquettes, seafood, or some speciality, order a small bowl of plain rice or the grain of the day. You will be amazed at how balanced you stay just from observing this one simple principle.

Eating according to climate and environment is the third cornerstone of the macrobiotic nutritional pyramid. This means eating foods that grow in your local area and eating them in season as much as possible. North America spans all major climates—from cold arctic to hot tropical—but the vast majority of the continent and its people are situated in a broad temperate zone. Because of the modern centralization of agriculture and food distribution, locally grown food is often unavailable, while foods that grow in radically different environments are readily at hand. The modern American diet is a hybrid of foods that originate or are appropriate in a semipolar area—meat, cheese, ice cream ("Eskimo Pies")—and a tropical or subtropical zone—sugar, spices, tropical fruits and vegetables, coffee, soft drinks (made from equatorial cola nuts). Violating ecological boundaries is one of the major causes of degenerative disease in the world today. Returning to grains, beans, and vegetables that grow in a four-season climate is the most important step we can take to adapt to our environment and strengthen our natural immunity to disease. Practically speaking, this means eating foods that grow east or west of us (in the United States or Canada or imported from China, Japan, Europe, Russia) and avoiding foods that come from North or South (the Arctic, the Caribbean, Central and South America, South Asia, Africa, Southeast Asia,

"There is a certain class of unbelievers who sometimes ask me such questions as if I think that I can live on vegetable food alone; and to strike at the root of the matter at once—for the root is faith—I am accustomed to answer such, that I can live on board nails. If they cannot understand that, they cannot understand much that I have to say."
— *Thoreau, Walden*

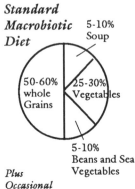

Standard Macrobiotic Diet

5-10% Soup

50-60% whole Grains

25-30% Vegetables

5-10% Beans and Sea Vegetables

Plus Occasional Foods
Fish and Seafood
Seasonal Fruits
Nuts and Seeds
Seasonings, Pickles, Condiments
Natural Desserts
Natural Beverages

Typical New England Meal

Pressure-cooked Brown Rice
Miso Soup
Aduki-Squash-Kombu
Boiled Vegetables
Dulse Salad
Pumpkin Pie

and Oceania).

Within temperate America, there are climatic and environmental differences, especially between the colder, more temperate North; the warmer, more humid South; the warmer, drier Southwest; the cooler, drier West; and the rainier Northwest. The same general way of eating may be observed in each of these areas—50-60 percent whole cereal grains, 5-10 percent soup, 25-30 percent vegetables, and 5-10 percent beans and seaweed, plus supplemental foods, as in the standard macrobiotic diet (*see chart*)—but the type of foods selected, the way of cooking, and the amount of seasoning will vary. In this book, we have included recipes for Southern, Southwestern, and Western-style macrobiotic cooking as well as the Northern style that predominates today. General guidelines for these regions follow.

Northern Macrobiotic Cooking

This region includes New England, the Mid-Atlantic, the Midwest, the Great Plains, southern and western border regions that experience the four regular changes of the seasons, and Ontario, Quebec, and the eastern half of Canada. Michio and Aveline Kushi pioneered this style of cooking after living for many years in New York and Massachusetts, and it has brought health and happiness to thousands of families, not only in the United States and Canada, but also around the world.

In this way, American macrobiotics is the last in a long line of revolutionary movements that began in New England—the Pilgrim landing, the American Revolution, Abolition and the anti-slavery movement, Women's Suffrage, and the Vietnam peace movement. The region's long, cold winter, variable climate, hilly, rocky soil, short-growing season, and rugged seacoast stimulate inventiveness and industry. Also according to traditional Far East directionology, the northeast is the direction in which the earth's natural electromagnetic energy, or *ki* flow, begins to change, spreading across a country or region from East to West.

Like earlier revolutions that began in New England, macrobiotics spread from Boston to New York, Philadelphia, and Baltimore and down the Atlantic Seaboard, to Minneapolis, Chicago, and Detroit, and other parts of the Midwest, and from there to every part of the continent. Traditional Yankee values of thrift, haste, prudence, and moral righteousness have also accompanied it—a legacy of the New England soil and sky.

In Northern or standard macrobiotic cooking, short-grain

brown rice is the principal daily grain, millet and barley are secondary grains, and all other grains and grain products are eaten on occasion. Miso soup is taken daily and other soups from time to time. Adukis are considered the chief of beans, with tofu, tempeh, and natto eaten regularly in one form or another. A wide variety of land and sea vegetables is consumed (including those harvested from Maine waters) with a slight emphasis on round and root vegetables which give added strength in the fall and winter and on kombu, wakame, hiziki, arame, dulse, and stronger seaweeds. Seasoning is moderate to strong, with miso, soy sauce, and umeboshi used regularly in addition to sea salt. Pickles vary with an emphasis on strong, long-time pickles. The same with condiments. For those in good health, fish or seafood is usually enjoyed once or twice a week (or more often in cold weather). Fresh fruit and juice (mostly apple cider) are taken in summer or fall. Favorite foods are short-grain rice and sweet rice, wild rice, noodles of all kinds, pumpkins and squashes, and apples and berries and other foods that are as traditional as the first Thanksgiving. Favorite cooking methods are pressure cooking, long-time boiling, baking (in moderation), and deep-frying.

Typical Midwest Meal

Brown Rice with
 Wild Rice
Split Pea Soup
Boiled Kale
Wakame-Cucumber
 Salad
Cherry Pie

In actual practice, sweet vegetables, cooked greens, and occasional fresh salad tend to be overlooked in Northern-style macrobiotic cooking. Also there is often too much salt and condiments, too much pressure cooking and baking, and lack of variety (because of a higher price for vegetables from California and other regions). As a result, people tend to eat too much bread and flour products, too many sweets, and too much beer and sake. The natural tendency in a cooler (more yin) environment is to become active (more yang) and to eat more yang foods. The challenge is to remain balanced and not become too yang—arrogant, rigid, brusque, domineering. A well balanced Northern macrobiotic home will radiate truth, harmony, concord, peace, and the other values we associate with the native peoples, pilgrims, and visionaries who settled this land.

Southern Macrobiotic Cooking

The South is a vast region, spanning the Tidewater of Virginia, the rolling piedmont and hills of the Carolinas, the lower Appalachians and Ozarks, the Gulf Coast, the Delta, and parts of Texas. The natural tendency in a hot (more yang) climate is to become more relaxed (more yin) and to eat more yin foods. Traditional Southern cuisine—combining elements of Native American, Afro-American, Hispanic, and Creole cookery—

Typical Southern Meal

Boiled Long-Grain Brown Rice
Miso Soup with Yellow Squash
Black-Eyed Peas
Cornbread
Collard Greens
Lemon Tofu Pie

centered around light, fluffy rice, light unsweetened cornbread, and a wide assortment of beans and garden vegetables, especially leafy greens, as well as delectable nuts and fruits, and juicy, succulent seafood. Cooking emphasized simmering, frying, roasting, and the use of mild to moderate seasoning.

When we lived in Dallas for several years, we found that by making traditional adjustments like these, we could stay healthy and balanced. We enjoyed pressure-cooked short-grain brown rice (from nearby Arkansas) from time to time. But in the hot, arid climate of north Texas, we found medium-grain rice more suitable for daily consumption most of the year. We also enjoyed long-grain rice frequently, and often enjoyed boiling our rice rather than pressure-cooking it. Barley, bulghur, couscous, and other lighter, more cooling grains were used more frequently than in the North, especially in grain and noodle salads served at room temperature.

In the bean category, we enjoyed more variety than in New England, using pintos, kidney, lima, and other larger beans slightly more frequently in addition to the usual chickpeas, lentils, and adukis and tofu, tempeh, and natto. Fresh organically grown vegetables are in much greater abundance in the South and are available almost all year round. We especially enjoyed turnip greens, mustard greens, kale, collards, and other greens that are emphasized slightly more than round or root vegetables for this type of warm climate. We felt more comfortable adjusting downward the amount of salt and other seasonings in our daily cooking, and occasionally we would use light herbs or spices in beans or stews. Spices are very cooling and used customarily in tropical and semi-tropical areas. In New England, on the other hand, we rarely cook with spices (except for an occasional dessert such as squash pie) and usually get a strong reaction when we order something with spice in it.

Sea vegetables were an important part of our daily menu in Dallas, supplying us with vitamins and minerals lost from perspiring in the sweltering heat. But like most other foods, we prepared them in lighter ways. For energy, we had fish at least once a week and good quality fruits, juices, and desserts. Favorite foods included traditional Southern cornbread and grits, rice pilaf and rice salads, garbanzo soup, lemon tofu pie and melon kanten. Favorite cooking styles were boiling (grains and beans), steaming (greens), and sautéing (root vegetables).

In our experience, Southern macrobiotic households tend to prepare too little grain and seaweed, too much seasoned food, and too much fruit, juice, and desserts. Often there is not enough salt and condiments, a tendency to avoid pressure-cooking altogether, and lack of order (because of too much variety and availability). As a result, people tend to overconsume fish and other animal food for strength and vitality. The challenge is to remain balanced and not become too yin—passive, slow, lazy, and unfocused. Properly prepared, Southern-style macrobiotic cooking will create a household with vitality, patience, charm, grace, sociability, and the other virtues which we associate with traditional Southern hospitality.

Southwestern Macrobiotic Cooking

Geographically, the Southwest is the complementary pole to the Northeast. While modern macrobiotics developed in cold, rugged New England and radiated out across the country, the continent's still, silent hub of traditional understanding and practice remains in the desert Southwest.

The region—including Old and New Mexico, Arizona, and parts of Texas, Colorado, Utah, Nevada, and California—is predominantly hot and dry. Site of the oldest continuously inhabited villages and towns in North America, the Southwest is home to the Tarahumara, Hopi, and other native people who lived for thousands of years farming corn, beans, and squash, supplemented with mesquite, prickly pear, pinon nuts, and other wild plants. Graceful dances, intricate sandpaintings, and other seasonal festivals and celebrations center around the divine gift of corn and other plants to the human race.

In recent times, this traditional way of eating has virtually disappeared. On reservations and trading posts, Indians have adopted a diet high in white flour, white sugar, and other simple sugars available to them from federal surplus. In Arizona, one of every two adult Pimas, for example, has diabetes—the highest incidence in the world. However, several hundred miles south in the Occidental Mountains of Mexico, the Tarahumara retain their traditional diet of corn and beans and are free not only of diabetes but also of high blood pressure, obesity, heart disease, cancer, and all other degenerative disease. Medical researchers consider them to be the healthiest people in North America. Interestingly, the only other community that compares with their ideal heart and blood values are people eating macrobiotically in New England (who were tested by Harvard Medical School).

Present-day macrobiotic communities in the Southwest are beginning to rediscover and incorporate traditional foods into their daily diet, especially *masa* (whole corn dough) which can be used to make tortillas, *arepas* (corn balls), and other dishes, as well as pinto, black, white, turtle, and other beans. Modern

Health Note
Desert plants protected Native Americans from diabetes before their exposure to modern foods. A study of ancestral diets among the Pima Indians of Arizona found that a return to a traditional strain of corn, tepary beans, acorns, mesquite pods, and other native foods lowered insulin production and blood sugar to normal levels. The Pima, who today eat mostly white bread, potatoes, and sugar, have the highest rate of diabetes in the world.

Typical Southwestern Meal

Corn Tortillas with Rice and Pinto Beans
Turnip Greens
Kombu Chips
Sweet Corn Pudding

Tex-Mex cooking, heavily spiced, bathed in tomato sauce, and often prepared frozen or microwaved, is a poor imitation.

Native peoples of North America traditionally preserved and seasoned their food with fire and smoke, while Europeans and Asians commonly used salt. The use of smoking for cooking and drying foods is gradually being rediscovered. Delicious macrobiotic barbecues using tempeh, seitan, or tofu with onions, carrots, and other vegetables are now enjoyed not only in the Southwest but from coast to coast.

The Southwest's dry heat is usually easier to adjust to than the South's more humid heat. However, macrobiotic friends in this region share some of the same tendencies, especially an inclination to use too many spices and seasonings and to cool off by taking too much yin. By introducing some traditional foods and cooking methods into the standard macrobiotic diet, they can remain balanced and develop deep strength, unshakable calm, spiritual insight, and other qualities associated with the Mesoamerican land and sky.

Western Macrobiotic Cooking

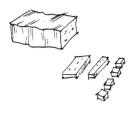

Typical Western Meal

Sushi Rolls
Stir-Fried Vegetables with Tofu
Sea Palm
Sprout and Filbert Salad
Apple Couscous Cake

The West—spanning the Rocky Mountains to the Pacific shore, as well as British Columbia, Alberta, the Yukon, Alaska and Hawaii—is an area of wild panoramic beauty threatened by expanding modern civilization. A region of colossal extremes—high mountains and deep valleys, parched deserts and rainy forests, isolated wilderness and sprawling metropolitan areas—the West holds a special place in the nation's heart as the last frontier, the direction one rides happily ever after into the sunset. Of course, Hollywood—one of the West's biggest industries—is the major retailer of this myth. However, to even the casual visitor there is something undeniably vast, spacious, and monumental to the region. The original vision of Washington, Jefferson, and the founders of the Republic—a nation of self-sufficient farmers, shopkeepers, artisans, and students of universal human culture—has been reborn in Boulder, Berkeley, and other countercultural communities, in the organic farms of the Central Valley and other regions in California, and the Ecotopian mythos of the Pacific Northwest.

Modern macrobiotics in this region is eclectic, spirited, innovative, nonjudgmental, and playful. Through the influence of Herman and Cornelia Aihara, Junsei and Kazuko Yamasaki, Noboru Muromoto, Jacques and Yvette DeLangre, Cecile Levin, Roy Steevenz, Meredith and Patrick McCarthy, and other pioneer macrobiotic teachers and food producers, thousands of families have begun to practice macrobiotics and recover their health and happiness. High quality food is available from Chico-San, Lundberg Brothers Farm, Granum, Grainaissance, Westbrae, Eden Foods, Ohsawa America, Goldmine, and other macrobiotic growers, manufacturers, and distributors. Sea palm, sweet kombu, and other sea vegetables are harvested in mild waters off the Pacific coastline.

The West is the melting pot of innumerable cultures. The descendants of Chinese railroad workers, Portuguese and Italian fishermen, Scandinavian lumberjacks, Hispanic and Japanese gardeners, Welsh and Yugoslavian miners, and others who settled the last frontier today still retain vestiges of their ancestral cuisine. Ethnic dishes, restaurants, and influences are ubiquitous. As a whole, the region is noted for its majestic rice and other grains, sun-kissed fruits and nuts, hearty trout and salmon, and fragrant teas and beverages. These flavorful foods, with a strong infusion of natively produced miso, tofu, umeboshi plums, mochi, and other naturally processed foods, form the core of contemporary Western-style macrobiotic cooking. Sautéing, stir-frying, steaming, and other lighter cooking methods are preferred. Seasoning is generally light in keeping with the pleasant climate. Naturally evaporated sea salt from the coastal waters of Baja California serves as a source of salt for many macrobiotic households across the continent.

Amid so much natural beauty and abundance, there is a danger of losing one's direction. The challenge in California and milder parts of the region is to avoid becoming too yin—too self-absorbed, unfocused, and weak to accomplish one's goals. There is also an inclination to the other extreme, which shows up in yang, doctrinaire quests for salvation in specific foods and ingredients. This is the legacy of the Conquistadors' quest for El Dorado, the Fountain of Youth, and the Seven Cities of Gold. The West is the abode of Coyote, don Juan Matus, and other Tricksters. To its earliest inhabitants, the continent as a whole was known as Turtle Island. Westerners need to achieve a balance among all the energies and tastes.

At its best, the East represents the visualization of the American Dream and the West represents its practical realization—a melting pot of different people and cultures living in health and harmony. Looking out across the Pacific Ocean (the Sea of Peace), the West also offers a window to the Far East and the promise of a planetary family of nations. The key to remaining balanced in both East and West is remembering the principles of natural order by which to navigate between the soil and stars.

Native Regional Foods and Cooking in America*				
Region	**North**	**South**	**Southwest**	**West**
Main Grain	Wheat	Rice	Corn	Wheat
Other Grains	Corn Oats Barley Wild Rice	Corn Wheat	Rice Amaranth Wheat	Rice Quinoa
Beans	Peas Navy Beans Aduki Beans Soybeans	Blackeyed Peas Chickpeas Kidney Beans Lima Beans	Pinto Anazaki Black Spotted Tepary	Lentils Tofu Tempeh
Vegetables	Squash Pumpkin Carrots Milkweed Burdock Daikon	Collard Greens Turnip Greens Mustard Greens Kale Purslane Wild Onion	Squash Mesquite Cactus Yucca	Lettuce Sprouts Broccoli Cauliflower Watercress Acorns
Sea Vegetables	Dulse Alaria Kelp Laver	Irish Moss	Spirulina	Sea Palm Ocean Ribbons Sweet Kombu Arame/Hiziki
Seafood	Scrod Cod Clams	Oysters Catfish	Trout Shrimp	Salmon Trout Crab
Fruit/Nuts	Apples Cherries Berries	Peaches Watermelon Pecans	Prickly Pear Pinon Seeds	Apples Grapes Filberts
Seasonings/ Sweeteners	Miso Soy Sauce Maple Syrup	Kuzu (Kudzu) Arrowroot Nut Milks	Salt Corn Silk	Umeboshi Barley/ Rice Malt Amasake
Cooking Styles	Boiling Pressure cooking Baking	Fried Deep-fried Raw	Baked Sun-Dried Smoked	Sautéed Stir-Fried Tempura
Culture Bearers	Ben Franklin The Kushis	Jefferson Lafcadio Hearn	Hopi/Zuni Pioneers	Chinese & Japan-ese Americans Aiharas

* Many other foods could be listed besides the examples here.

3
The Whole Graining of America

America's destiny is intertwined with its sunny fields, amber grains, and golden harvests. Legends and stories from earliest times recount the sagas of pilgrims arriving from distant homelands, bold adventurers questing for gold, and lost journeyers thrown up on strange shores. Wild and cultivated cereals not only saved their lives but also became the foundation of their prosperity.

From the West, the Hopi tell of their ancestors arriving by rafts after their Third World was destroyed by floods, settling in the desert Southwest, and receiving the life-giving gift of maize. From the North, Viking explorers landed on the rocky North Atlantic coast, lived on wild grains and grapes, and christened the bounteous new land Vineland. From the East, Christopher Columbus touched land in the Bahamas, and his hungry crew replenished themselves with maize, bread made of sweet potatoes and cassava, and other native produce. In Virginia, the colonists at Jamestown received bowls of nourishing porridge from the Powhatans.

On Cape Cod, the Pilgrims arrived in the middle of winter, also surviving on stores of Indian corn and other foods. The first Thanksgiving, celebrating the fruits of the earth and harmony between settled inhabitants and the new arrivals, featured a multitude of grains, beans, squash, pumpkins, and other pre-

"The Earth-Mother blew her soul into corn."
— Hopi Emergence Myth

"And sure it was God's good providence that we found this corne, for else we know not how we should have done."
— William Bradford, Governor of Plymouth Colony

43

dominantly vegetable-quality food. From across the Pacific Ocean, Michio Kushi set foot on American soil in San Francisco on Thursday, Nov. 24, 1949, the 328th anniversary of this harvest festival. The young Japanese educator, accompanied on the long journey by steamship with rice balls and other simple foods, went on to launch a peaceful revolution that would restore whole cereal grains as the staff of life in America and enable thousands of individuals and family to recover their health and happiness.

America—midway between East and West, Europe and Asia, Africa and the Pacific Islands—seemed destined to embrace all cultures and peoples, all grains and traditional ways of eating. While Columbus and later Conquistadors never found gold, they discovered something more precious—maize, amaranth, quinoa, wild rice, and other native grains. The true riches of the Orient—rice, millet, pearl barley, soybeans, and other health-giving foods—took several more generations to arrive. The new continent was named after Amerigo Vespucci, the Italian explorer who first recognized that the islands and coastline constituted a New World. Amerigo hailed from Florence, a region nourished on rice and millet since the Crusades and one in which Dante, Leonardo, and other native sons extolled the virtues of a simple grain and vegetable diet. Toscanelli, the grandfatherly Florentine cosmologist who sent Columbus a letter and map advising him that the shortest route to the East lay by way of the West, was a vegetarian.

Four distinct ways of eating developed in early America as new and old streams mingled. In the North, East, and West, bread—made of wheat, sometimes mixed with barley, cornmeal, or rye—was the staple. In the South, rice served as principal food. In the Southwest, maize continued to be the foundation of native cultures, also being eaten, until recent times, as a main or supplemental grain in the three other regions. Let's look briefly at each of the three major grains and their spread across the continent.

"The trees were so beautiful and so fragrant that we thought we were in a terrestrial paradise."
— Amerigo Vespucci 1500

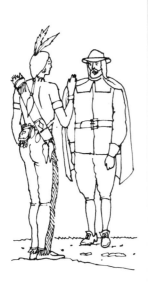

Corn

Known as maize, Indian corn, or simply corn, this prolific grain originated in South or Central America, reaching North America some five thousand or more years ago. Along with squash and beans, it constituted the staple food of native people from the desert Southwest to New England. Corn grew in six colors—yellow, white, red, black, blue, and spotted—corresponding in traditional myth and legend with heaven and earth and the four cardinal directions. Among mesa and cliff dwellers, maize was known as the Seed of Seeds, and blue corn was the most sacred since it reflected the color of water without which life would not be possible. In the Eastern Woodlands, maize was grown by girdling the trees to allow sunlight to penetrate the forest canopy and quicken the young stalks.

Corn was eaten primarily in the form of flatbread or other baked goods made from whole corn dough. This *masa*, as it was called, was made by grinding the kernels of corn between stones or rocks. The *metate*, made of hollowed out volcanic stone, and the *mano*, a hand-held stone, produced a malleable dough which, mixed with wood ash or lime and a little water, could be fashioned into thin round tortillas, corn balls, dumplings, and other shapes and cooked on hot stones or baked in an adobe oven. A variety of other corn dishes, including grilled corn on the cob, dried parched corn, *suppone* (porridge), popping corn, and fermented corn puddings and beverages could also be made from this versatile staff of life.

With their more advanced technology, the new Europeans could grind maize into finer meal than the Indians. In New England, cornmeal was used with barley, oats, wheat, or rye for making loaf bread. The children scraped the dried kernels from the corncobs while reciting their alphabets and numbers, and mothers ground *samp*, or meal, with pestles tied to saplings which did the lifting. Out at sea, fishermen followed the pounding rhythm of the mortars to a safe harbor in a storm. Later, grist mills were set up by streams and rivers which turned large stones for grinding. Johnnycakes, a type of journey-cake or pocket-bread, became popular up and down the Eastern Seaboard. Massachusetts, the Cradle of Liberty, featured Old Glory, a variety made of red, white, and blue speckled corn. Rhode Island, the first state to ratify the Constitution, became famous for its pure white cornmeal.

In the South, maize vied with rice as the main staple. Cornmeal was used daily for making *hoecake*, a thin fried bread fried in the fields on a hoe or other piece of metal by families of African descent; *ashcake*, a bread roasted in the ashes of the hearth; *pone*, a porridge; corn dodgers or fried corn balls; *hominy*, coarsely ground cereal; and *grits*, a finely ground meal. Cornbread, the accompaniment of almost every meal, was originally made without milk, eggs, or sugar—a practice still observed in many Southern households.

Today, most of the corn grown in America is a modern hybrid variety. It is larger, more uniform in color, taste, and shape, and more abundant than traditional Indian corn. Standard or open-pollinated varieties are available in some native communi-

"Pray let me, an American, inform the gentleman, who seems ignorant of the matter, that Indian corn, take it all in all, is one of the most agreeable and wholesome grains in the world; that its green leaves roasted are a delicacy beyond expression; that samp, hominy, succotash, and notehock [parched corn], made of it, are so many pleasing varieties; and that Johnny or hoecake, hot from the fire, is better than a Yorkshire muffin."
— Ben Franklin, defending American grain from English criticism 1765

Diet & Religion

"It was a common saying among the Puritans. 'Brown bread and the Gospel is good fare.'"
— **Matthew Henry, Commentaries on Isaiah**

"Sermons on diet ought to be preached in the churches at least once a week."
— **G.C. Lichtenberg Reflections 1799**

The Fall from grace began when people "put asunder what God joined together: the bran and the germ."
— **Rev. Sylvester Graham**

"I consider it a settled and unalterable truth, that until the physiological and dietetic habits of men are corrected, spiritual declensions and backslidings are inevitable. The laws of the physical system are the laws of God."
— **Rev. Charles Finney**

ties and in some natural foods stores. Most of the corn eaten today is sweet and tasty, but it bears little resemblance to the strong, colorful, diverse strains that once flourished across the continent. Also the highly processed form in which modern corn is enjoyed—cornflakes, corn syrup, and canned corn—is a decline from corn in whole form.

Wheat

Wheat came over with Columbus on the *Nina, Pinta,* and the *Santa Maria* and with the Pilgrims on the *Mayflower.* For millennia, its flour had been prized for making bread and baked goods. But until technical advances in the early nineteenth century, wheat was the aristocrat of grains, used sparingly and only on special occasions such as for the top layer of a pie—hence the expression "upper crust." The Puritans' principal food was a dark brown bread made of a coarse mixture of wheat flour and cornmeal or sometimes rye. In the Mass Bay Colony, every family was expected to donate a measure of this precious grain each year to Harvard. This was known as "College Corn."

The real impetus to wheat came from the Dutch, who settled in Manhattan, Long Island, Albany, and the Hudson River Valley. They brought with them a love of bread, dumplings, noodles, pancakes, waffles, doughnuts, pretzels, and other flour products. They built windmills for grinding wheat into flour and set up the first public bakeries in New Amsterdam (later to become New York) in 1656. The health-conscious Hollanders passed laws that bakeries could not sell sweetened pastries and cookies unless bread was also offered, nor could they sell white bread without making available dark brown. Wheat became the source of New Netherland's prosperity. The English, who later took political control over the region, continued to grow wheat, and during the late 1700s, New York was known as "the Granary of the Revolution."

With the opening of the Erie Canal in 1817, the cost of wheat fell sharply. Advances in milling from the 1840s through the 1880s made wheat flour readily available, though the vast majority of American families still made their own bread, pancake batter, and pies. Sleek clipper ships transported the cheap wheat abroad, undermining traditional agricultural products in Europe and spurring immigration to the Midwest, Great Plains, and other bountiful wheat-growing regions by newly unemployed farmers and their families. New, mechanized steel roller mills made available an almost 100 percent white flour. The invention of baking powder, baking soda, and commercial yeast made light muffins, biscuits, and other refined baked goods readily affordable.

Nineteenth century health reformers, led by Rev. Sylvester Graham, staunchly opposed this trend and encouraged people to return to "unbolted wheat" and other whole grains of their ancestors. But increasingly consumption of meat and other animal foods made unleavened breadstuffs unpopular. With whole grains no longer the center of the diet, the art of chewing declined. With the exception of the "sourdoughs"—the gold prospectors in California, the Yukon, and Alaska who lived on sourdough bread—most people preferred a light, easy-to-eat loaf. By the early twentieth century, the flour milling and baking industries had sold the American people on the superiority of their light, white products. Inexpensive, factory-made bread—enriched with the vitamins and minerals that had been stripped in the milling process—could be found in every household.

Following World War II, baking homemade bread became something of a lost art. Rediscovered in the 1960s by the counterculture, popularized by the macrobiotic community, and endorsed by the medical profession, whole wheat once again began to appear on the nation's table. Today a cornucopia of dishes and baked items is available made from whole wheat berries, cracked wheat, bulgur, couscous, whole wheat flour, and whole wheat gluten including many healthful and delicious breads and baked goods and entrées made from noodles and pasta and from seitan and fu.

Rice

For thousands of years, rice has been the staff of life in South Asia and the Far East. From China and India, rice traveled the ancient Silk Road to Europe and Africa. During the Renaissance, rice was a principal grain in Tuscany and other Mediterranean regions. Amerigo Vespucci, the Florentine astronomer and navigator after whom America is named, arranged for the first rice to be brought to the New World in 1512.

In the 1600s, rice was grown in Virginia, the Carolinas, and other English colonies, and it is likely that it arrived as part of the slave trade. West Africa had a sophisticated rice-growing technology extending back many centuries, and enslaved African farmers from the Rice Coast of present-day Ghana are believed to have developed and managed the first rice plantations in America. By the early eighteenth century, South Carolina was growing enough rice to send 60 tons to London. The new crop thrived in the marshy soil of the Piedmont and became the

"The destiny of nations depends on what they eat."
— Brillat-Savarin, The Physiology of Taste 1825

"Rice is life."

"Rice is Buddha's heart."

"Rice is more valuable than gold."

— Traditional Oriental Proverbs

"The [African] did not arrive in America naked. He brought with him a sense of sedentary life and of agriculture, while his wife brought a concept of domesticity. He brought as well culinary recipes, a sense of dietary balance . . . medical formulas and plants unknown in America."
— *Frederic Mauro, The European Expansion*

"Erewhon quickly grew from a small storefront to a chain of retail stores. In a few years, it became the largest distributor and manufacturer of natural foods on the East Coast with a fleet of delivery trucks criss-crossing New England and New York. There was also a West Coast Erewhon. The whole foods movement developed from this tiny seed."
— *Aveline Kushi*

colony's most important product.

In the nineteenth century, rice moved west with the rest of the country. From the Carolinas it traveled to New Orleans, and Southerners throughout the region celebrated the New Year with bowls of rice cooked with colorful red, black, or brown beans. Native Americans discovered that rice could be parched, salted, and eaten like popcorn. Rice-parching socials became as fashionable in the South as chestnut roasts in New England. Other popular dishes included rice croquettes, rice pudding, rice waffles, rice bread, rice jelly, and rice milk. Today, rice is grown throughout the continent, as far north as Ontario, and in Hawaii. However, Louisiana, Arkansas, Texas, California, and other warmer regions remain the center of commercial rice production. With improvements in technology, refined white rice became widely available. By the 1950s most of the rice eaten in the U.S. and Canada was 100 percent polished white rice.

The waves of Chinese immigrants to the West Coast, and the arrival of families from the Philippines, Japan, Vietnam, Cambodia, India, Pakistan, and other countries, popularized rice. But most of the rice eaten in Asia for the last several generations has been polished to some degree.

The reintroduction of whole-grain brown rice is due largely to Michio and Aveline Kushi and the modern macrobiotic community. In the 1960s, the Kushis and their associates arranged with farmers to begin growing organic brown rice. After several generations of chemical farming, there was widespread skepticism and resistance to growing traditional rice with traditional methods. However, after Erewhon—the Kushis' pioneer natural foods store—agreed to buy their entire crop, pioneer rice farmers in Arkansas and California began to experiment with organic methods.

Today, organically grown brown rice has spread around the world. The Lone Pine Farm in Arkansas and the Lundberg Brothers Farm in Richvale, California, supply much of the organic brown rice on this continent.

Rice—the most evolutionary developed and balanced of all the cereal grains—has become the principal food of the worldwide macrobiotic movement. Everywhere it is recognized as a healthy daily food and one that contributes to social harmony and spiritual development. Every civilization in which it has been cultivated—Far Eastern, South Asian, Southeast Asian, African, European, and now American—has contributed to the development of rice cookery. Rice will truly become a foundation of the planetary cuisine in the new era of humanity ahead.

The Political and Economic Revolution

There have been three major revolutions in modern American history: 1) the political and economic revolution which saw the original thirteen colonies declare their independence from Europe and consolidate their control over native peoples in the eastern half of the land; 2) the social and cultural revolution which saw the new American Republic nearly break up over slavery and then extend its domain west, absorbing wave after wave of immigrants from around the world; and 3) the health and environmental revolution which saw the country imperiled by industrial pollution, chemical agriculture, and the spread of heart disease, cancer, AIDS, and other degenerative diseases. The place of whole cereal grains in the life of the continent shaped and influenced each of these three eras. Let's look briefly at each.

When representatives of the New World and Old World first encountered each other, they shared common food and forged common bonds based on mutual respect. However, the early macrobiotic lifestyle and way of eating of the colonists and native peoples was challenged by the increased availability of meat, dairy, fish, and other animal food. On the European side, the abundance of wild game—spurred by the fur trade—and almost unlimited land to raise livestock influenced changing dietary patterns. On the Native American side, the introduction of the horse and rifle turned animals such as the bison from a rarity in the diet to a staple. Combined with strong yin in the form of rum, whiskey, and other alcohol, this made for an explosive combination, especially as white settlers moved westward infringing on hunting grounds used by native peoples.

Still, the amount of meat and dairy products consumed was modest by later standards. The manifest for one of Columbus' expeditions shows that the first of the conquistadors arrived in the New World with a cargo containing about 70 percent grains (in the form of wheat, wheat flour, and biscuit), about 10 percent beans (mostly garbanzos), about 10 percent assorted vegetable-quality foods (olive oil, vinegar, wine, and raisins); and the remaining 10 percent animal food (dried fish, cheese, and salt pork). Though small in volume, this strong salted, dried, and aged animal food, along with a lack of grain consumed in whole form and fresh vegetables and fruits, gave rise to a pattern of ruthless aggression and exploitation that characterized

"Your Highnesses may believe that this is the best and most fertile and temperate and level and good land that there is in the world."
— *Columbus*

"Their maize is a kernel-berry that was well tast'ed raw or cook'd. But could also be bak'd, dry'd and ground into a flour."
— *First description of corn by Columbus' crew 1492*

the early explorers.

By the end of the seventeenth century, the Europeans' overall rigid, excessively yang approach culminated in England's supremacy over the sea and domination of the other imperial powers. A small island nation, Britain was naturally more yang than its continental neighbors, by virtue of its more compact size and its more northerly location. With the agricultural revolution of the early 1600s, new methods of breeding sheep and cattle resulted in passage of enclosure laws that overturned traditional English ways of farming and eating that existed for centuries. Merry Old England—the land of John Barleycorn and pease porridge—became wedded to beef, mutton, rashers, and other animal food as leader of the emerging mercantile system.

To roughly balance this strong yang food, England—and other European empires—were attracted to spices, sugar, and other extreme yin from Asia, Africa, South America, and especially the Caribbean. Essentially a war between traditional farming and the new industrial way of life, the American Revolution cannot be understood apart from this sweeping agricultural and dietary revolution that saw meat and sugar replace grains and vegetables as the center of the modern diet.

The main events leading up to the conflict—the Sugar Act, the Stamp Act, and Boston Tea Party—are all intimately linked with articles of food. The Triangular Trade which developed saw Britain export finished goods to Africa, enslaved peoples from that continent being transported to the West Indies to work in the sugar plantations, and tropical commodities, especially sugar, returning to Britain and her far-flung colonies. The colonies on the North American mainland were drawn into this trade by another triangle. Molasses from Barbados, Jamaica, and other West Indian islands went to New England to make rum, rum from New England went to Africa, and human cargoes from Africa returned to the West Indies.

England sought to control the flow of this trade through a series of laws and tariffs and reaped the lion's share of the profits. This taxation without representation, especially to pay for the cost of Britian's war with Spain, France, and other imperial powers in the West Indies, put the American colonies on a collision course with Britain. Though minute in size, the West Indies were the most important source of England's wealth, as well as the source of a commodity that had become a necessity in the daily diet. "I know not why we should blush to confess that molasses was an essential ingredient in American independence," John Adams observed in 1775. It also owed its success to the outcome of the naval conflict among the rival powers in the Caribbean. "If we lose our Sugar Islands," King George III

"Around 1634, eight years after they bought the island of Manhattan from the Indians, the Dutch entered the Caribbean with the capture of St. Eustatius and St. Maarten and of Curacao and Surinam on the Spanish Main. Sugar was a treasure greater than the spices, attracting the eager predators of every nation. The sudden delight of sweetening on the tongue as a regular article of diet and sweetener of other foods raised high the real-estate value of the West Indies."
— *Barbara Tuchman, The First Salute*

wrote, "it will be impossible to continue the war [in the colonies]." Six years after the first shots were fired at Lexington and Concord, the Revolutionary War ended when France, engaged in competition with England for control of Dominica, Martinique, Granada, and St. Lucia, entered the war and provided the decisive margin of victory at Yorktown. "The loss of the Sugar Islands to the French and their [England's] determination to get them back," concludes Sidney Mintz in *Sweetness and Power: The Political, Social and Economic Effects of Sugar in the Modern World*, "explains the otherwise inexplicable willingness of the French government to enter the War of American Independence on the side of the Americans."

Among the first to perceive this economic and political collision course and take action was a young Virginia planter by the name of George Washington. At his Mount Vernon estate, the young surveyor and frontiersman grew primarily corn, wheat, and other cereal grains, raised vegetables and fruits, produced a small amount of animal food, including fish from the Potomac, and tobacco. Early in his career, he invented a plow which automatically dropped seeds into furrows and throughout his life tinkered with ways to improve the quality and yield of grain. Meanwhile, most neighboring plantations in the Virginia Tidewater had converted to growing tobacco exclusively which found a ready market in England.

Washington strongly opposed this trend. He felt that tobacco destroyed the land, required too much labor, left the planter vulnerable to starvation and bankruptcy if the crop failed, and made Virginians dependent on Britishers who supplied them with obsolete and inferior goods. Washington abhorred slavery, and the toll it took in the labor-intensive tobacco fields was another reason he declined to abandon grains. Taking his cue from farmers in the inland Piedmont who had no access to British markets, he decided to step up grain production and develop a local market.

By 1766, Washington had stopped growing tobacco to concentrate on corn and wheat. To process his crops, he built a new stonemill which could grind grain for the surrounding community. Later he invited a Philadelphia inventor to automate it. Thus an entire decade before the Revolution broke out, we find that Washington had broken psychologically with England over the central issue of whether the land should be used to grow grains which benefited everyone or luxurious cash crops which profited a few. That his allegiance to cereals was not economically motivated is further shown by Washington's own moderate way of eating. Throughout his life, friends, associates, and visitors remarked on his simple tastes and practice of often eat-

George Washington, Rule No. 55:

"Eat not in the streets, nor in ye house, out of season."

Traditional American Proverbs

"Hunger is the best sauce."

"Bad meals kill more than the best doctors ever cured."

*Proverbs from
Poor Richard's
Almanac*

*"A fat kitchen maketh
a lean will."*

*"To lengthen thy life,
lessen thy meals."*

*"Many dishes, many
diseases."*

*"What one relishes,
nourishes."*

— Ben Franklin

ing only a single dish. For breakfast, he customarily enjoyed "three small Indian hoecakes" and "as many dishes of tea (without cream)."

Throughout his administrations as president, Washington upheld the ideal of economic self-sufficiency for the new Republic, balancing Thomas Jefferson's even more radical vision of a nation of small farmers and shopkeepers with Alexander Hamilton's perception of the need for a strong central economy. A watermark of the Goddess of Agriculture sitting on a plow, holding a staff of liberty in one hand and a flowering branch in the other, adorned Washington's last will and testament.

At various stages in their lives, Benjamin Franklin and Thomas Jefferson also adopted a macrobiotic or semi-macrobiotic way of eating. Franklin became a vegetarian as a youth growing up in Boston, as he writes in his *Autobiography*, and dined mainly on rice. His arrival in Philadelphia with a loaf of whole-grain bread under each arm has entered American folklore. Franklin's peaceful, even-minded temper and creative spirit of inquiry led him to seek out and befriend the Huron. Franklin's Albany Plan for federal-style rule, later adopted by the Continental Congress, drew upon the model of Deganawida, "the Peacemaker," the sixteenth century founder of the Iroquois League of Five Nations and developer of the Great Law of Peace. (The Iroquois model went farther than the Philadelphia model, granting suffrage to women and infants, making provision for impeachment of officials, and prohibiting unlawful entry into private homes.)

Like Washington, Jefferson managed one of the South's largest plantations, growing a multitude of grains, vegetables, and other produce and lent his inventive mind to creating new farm implements. "The greatest service which can be rendered any country," he declared, "is to add a useful plant to its culture." During the Revolution, the British confiscated the entire harvest of rice in the South, including seed rice, threatening to destroy what had become a staple grain throughout the region. During a visit to France, Jefferson noticed that hardy unpolished rice was used by many people as a staple, especially during religious holidays such as Lent when meat was not eaten. Most of the rice consumed in France came from Italy, so Jefferson went to that country for the purpose of obtaining rice seed to send back to America and to see a newly developed rice-cleaning machine that Edward Rutledge had described to him in Congress in 1775. The Italian government, however, had strict laws prohibiting the export of rice seed. Determined to introduce this food item to North America, Jefferson risked a diplomatic scandal by hiring an Italian mule driver to illegally cross the border with several large sacks of seed from the best rice-growing district in Italy—the region between Turin and Milan, which had been growing rice since Dante's time. The shipment was stopped at the border and turned back. Undaunted, Jefferson filled the large pockets of his coat with seed and carried it across the border himself. Upon arriving back in France, he sent the seed to Charleston where it was divided among a select group of planters. Jefferson was so pleased with the outcome of this project that he later arranged for seeds of rice to be sent to the Carolinas from Egypt, China, and elsewhere. The main author of the Declaration of Independence also brought back noodles and a noodle-making machine from Italy and a waffle iron from Holland to make rice waffles.

For most of his presidency, Jefferson observed a cosmopolitan style of eating, experimenting with new foods and introducing French cuisine, delicate wines, and ice cream to the White House. Fellow Virginian Patrick Henry castigated him for his foreign tastes and neglect of American beef. Overseeing the purchase of food for the White House every day, "Jefferson would get out the wagon in the morning and [with his steward] go . . . to Georgetown to market"—a custom observed in the breech by his successors. Toward the end of his life, Jefferson gave up animal food almost altogether. *The Virginia Housewife*, a cookbook by his daughter, Martha Jefferson Randolph, includes a recipe in his own handwriting for "The Chinese Mode of Boiling Rice." Oriental thought also influenced Jefferson, and sentiments in his writings such as "the government of a family bears a Lilliputian resemblance to the government of a nation" may owe their origin to the philosophy of the *I Ching* and the *Yellow Emperor's Classic* as much as *Gulliver's Travels*.

Three other signers of the Declaration of Independence from the South were also rice farmers. Another signer, the famous medical doctor, Benjamin Rush, recommended a temperate way of eating to his patients, including rice and vegetables, and warned against highly spiced foods. Further north, John and Abigail Adams' wartime correspondence includes reminiscences of simple home-cooked food. Not since Renaissance Italy had the world witnessed such a creative flourishing of the arts and sciences as that which accompanied the movement for American political liberty. And like the Florentine painters, the small group of men and women who guided the American Revolution were eating primarily whole grains and were devoted to their cultivation as the foundation of a new order of the ages.

"I was determined therefore to sift the matter [of the superiority of Italian rice] to the bottom by crossing the Alps into the rice country. I found the machine exactly such a one as you had described to me in Congress in the year 1775. There was but one conclusion there to be drawn, to wit, that the rice was of a different species, and I determined to take enough to put you in seed: they informed me however that its exportation in the husk was prohibited; so I could only bring off as much as my coat and surtout pockets would hold."
— *Thomas Jefferson, letter to Edward Rutledge of Charleston 1787*

The Social and Cultural Revolution

The nineteenth century brought rapid expansion of the new Republic, but also deep division and bloody conflict. Washington, Jefferson, and other founders had hoped to end slavery and prohibit its expansion to new territories. But in order to hold together the fragile coalition, a compromise was reached, allowing the South to retain slavery for a limited time. Meanwhile, growing prosperity led to increased consumption of meat and sugar, especially in the border states where land had not yet been completely cleared for planting, hardening attitudes between Northerners and Southerners. Davy Crockett's youthful exploits killing bears and other wild game for his family further enshrined the virtues of animal food in frontier mythology. Andrew Jackson, Zachary Taylor, and other generals rode into the White House in the wake of popular military campaigns against Indians and Mexicans whose lands were needed for the nation's manifest destiny of growing sugar and cotton and raising cattle. Uncle Sam, the sinewy symbol of the emerging Republic, derived from Samuel Wilson, a Hudson River meatpacker.

Polarity between North and South increased as ways of eating between the two halves of the country continued to diverge. In the more industrial North, wheat supplanted corn as the main grain, beef became the meat of choice, and dairy food became a more regular item in the diet. In the mostly rural South, corn and rice continued as principal grains, with pork serving as the main source of animal food. Sugar and alcohol consumption increased in both regions, contributing to family and social tensions. Natural foods, vegetarianism, and anti-temperance sentiment were an integral part of many utopian communities during this era, and health food became inseparable from political and social change. Charles Finney, president of Oberlin College and a prominent Grahamite, assumed leadership of the Abolitionist movement. Other dietary reformers took part in the emerging women's suffrage movement. Quaker John Woolman refused to eat sugar because of its role in the slave trade, and many Abolitionists boycotted rice, sugar, molasses, cotton, and other articles produced by slave labor. The Amistad Affair—a *cause célèbre* growing out of a rebellion among thirty-six Africans who seized their slave ship—included many rice farmers who had been abducted from their fields and transported to America.

Following the election of Abraham Lincoln as president, war broke out in 1861. While a nation's destiny is rarely altered by a single individual, historians agree that without Lincoln's leadership the Union would not have been preserved. The attributes that carried him through—patience, perseverance, common sense, good humor, and magnanimity—are qualities of moderation and balance traditionally associated with whole cereal grains. Growing up in Kentucky and Indiana, young Lincoln helped his father in the fields planting wheat and corn. As a young man he ferried a boatload of produce down the Mississippi to New Orleans where he saw human beings bought and sold and developed a life-long abhorence of slavery. Relocating in Illinois, he took a job as a clerk to a man who owned a grain mill and became a partner in a general store in New Salem. In 1834, he ran for the state legislature and won the hearts—and votes—of many farmers by cradling more wheat than anyone else. In his speeches against the extension of slavery to new territories, Lincoln attacked human bondage as an institution that prevented black people from "eating the bread which his own hand earns" and invoked an image of America as a nation of self-made agrarians, merchants, and shopkeepers. In a poem written after a visit to his birthplace in 1844, he recounted walking "the very spot where grew the bread that formed my bones"—a remarkable consciousness of the transformative powers of food in general and whole grains in particular.

In his personal life, Lincoln followed a very simple way of eating, preferring mostly grains and vegetables and eating in small volume. His favorite food was fruit, especially apples, cherries, and oranges. Occasionally he ate animal food, especially fish and seafood, though as a politician and frequent public speaker he would be expected to partake at banquets and county fairs where all and everything was served. In the White House, he was legendary for his modest eating habits, often taking just bread or an apple for a meal. This plain, more centrally balanced way of eating contributed to his broad vision of a unified America, to a calm, peaceful mind in the most trying of circumstances, and to a firm, steady hand on the ship of state through the entire course of the war.

Many turning points have been advanced in the Civil War, such as the Battle of Gettysburg, the Emancipation Proclamation, and the victory at Vicksburg. It has also often been said that the North could not have prevailed if England had continued trading with the South. During the last several years of the war, the Confederacy made every effort to maintain commercial ties with Britain in order to secure scarce goods as well as hard currency needed to continue the war effort. The British were particularly dependent on Southern cotton for textile factories— the foundation of the new industrial revolution—in Manchester, Liverpool, and other cities. Had Britain challenged the North's blockade of Southern shipping, the South would probably have

"[Young Abe's] earliest recollection—a memory swimming out of some secret river of time—was a scene at their subsequent homestead on Knob Creek, several miles to the north. The scene floated in his memory like a photograph: Thomas Lincoln, his stout, barrel-chested father, hoeing down in the creek bottom while little Abraham followed along dropping pumpkin seeds between hills of corn."
— Stephen Oates, With Malice Toward None: The Life of Abraham Lincoln

remained strong enough to successfully sue for peace. Southern commanders and troops are generally conceded by observers on both sides to have been more imaginative and flexible. But few have attributed this to their simpler food, mostly corn and rice, in comparison to the Northerners' tins of beef and mutton. As it was, Lincoln narrowly won reelection in 1864 amid widespread Northern sentiment to end the war on terms favorable to Richmond. Ultimately, England decided not to make an alliance with the South. While moral reasons played some role in this decision, the underlying reason was economic. Britain had become dependent upon American grain and flour following massive crop failures in Europe. The wheat she required came from the Midwest, Great Plains, and other Northern areas. As a proverb at the time put it, "King Corn proved more powerful than King Cotton." England's decision not to intervene in the Civil War was as crucial to the outcome as France's decision to intervene in the Revolutionary War. In both cases, food commodity exchange, agriculture, and way of eating determined the result.

Spurred by changing agriculture and patterns of food consumption, millions of immigrants came to America from Northern and Central Europe. In addition to crop failures, land that had been used for millennia to grow grains was now given over to pasture and livestock grazing, as well as new crops from the tropics such as the potato. In Ireland, Germany, and other countries, the failure of these crops led to widespread famine, giving further impetus to the exodus. Meanwhile, technical innovation in America, encouraged by the war effort, resulted in a host of new inventions and improvements in farm equipment, storage facilities, food preservation and processing, and transportation. In the wheat belt, as we saw, this led to cheap American wheat being exported to Europe, further undermining local economies.

The influx of families from many lands had overall an enriching effect on North American life and culture. However, in the short run, it served to aggravate tensions with native peoples. As president, Lincoln had signed the Homestead Act, granting 140 acres of land to any family who would cultivate it for five years. While this was a logical extention of his vision to transform the continent into "a garden" of farms and orchards producing grains and plenty for all, the act unwittingly accelerated the destruction of native cultures. By the end of the nineteenth century, the new nation reached from coast to coast, unified by golden grains but also by a legacy of unchecked expansion that would lead to more unfortunate consequences in the future.

The 19th Century Health Reformers

"A vegetable diet lies at the basis of all reform."
— *Dr. William A. Alcott*

"The health food business is one of the Lord's own instrumentalities."
— *Ellen G. White, founder of the Adventist movement*

"The decline of a nation commences when gourmandizing begins."
— *Dr. John Kellogg*

The Health and Environmental Revolution

Toward the end of the nineteenth century, millions of East Indians, Chinese, Javanese, and other Asian immigrants flocked to the Caribbean to handle sugarcane and other commodity crops following the cessation of slavery by the European powers. In the United States, millions of Chinese were imported to work on the railroads and in the fields. Friction between different racial and ethnic groups often resulted. Meanwhile, at gunpoint, the Western nations compelled China, Japan, and other traditional societies to open their doors to disadvantageous trade and market agreements. An anticolonial reaction beginning in the 1880s set off a wave of bloodshed in Asia and Africa, culminating in the political freedom movements and social revolutions of the twentieth century.

Although the Industrial Revolution increased material prosperity, it also increased the pace of life, and infectious diseases, including tuberculosis, typhus fever, smallpox, and measles, assumed epidemic proportions. Prior to this time, degenerative diseases were virtually unknown. In the late eighteenth century, individual cases of cancer, heart disease, and other chronic disorders began to emerge in the upper classes which were most prone to dietary excess. Further, as in past eras, disease and pestilence followed waves of international food exchange. During the nineteenth century, typhoid, dysentery, cholera, and other water-borne diseases and malaria, yellow fever, and other fly-borne diseases became epidemic in the manufacturing countries and their foreign colonies. Continued quantification and specialization in science led to the rise of metabolic theory and advances in surgery and drug use. Liebig, the founder of modern nutrition, classified nourishment into categories and subcategories and devised an infant formula to replace mother's milk. The superiority of meat, eggs, and dairy food gained widespread acceptance following the Darwinian biological and social revolutions which ranked civilizations, like species, according to the amount of animal protein they consumed on the evolutionary ladder. Simple carbohydrates that gave quick energy such as white flour, refined sugar, and potatoes were touted as productive foods for workers and miners and became even more desirable.

"It is the exhaustion of the cereal seeds that causes the weakening of the seed of humanity," Emile Zola warned at the end of the nineteenth century as modern civilization reaped the first

"White bread, red meat, and blue blood make the tricolor flag of conquest."
— A New York doctor, ca. 1900

fruits of mechanized agriculture. Industrial society, however, remained blind to the admonitions of the French novelist, as well as other early health reformers such as Ellen Harmon White and John Harvey Kellogg, the Adventist leaders who opened a vegetarian healing center in Battle Creek, Michigan, and Horace Fletcher, a Yale researcher who popularized the art of chewing and attracted such celebrated disciples as William and Henry James, John D. Rockefeller, and the cadets at West Point.

By the start of the new century, Europe and North America's desire for excessive yang food increased, and livestock producers (such as the ranchers in the western U.S., Argentina, and Australia) could not fill society's demand for beef. A further round of yin stimulants, pacifiers, and narcotics brought back by Western military expeditions in Cuba, the Philippines, the Congo, and elsewhere began to have devastating social consequences. Even alcohol, a longstanding yin balance to yang meat and animal food, grew out of control, and a movement to prohibit it spread in the industrial countries because of its effects on family life. Pasteurized milk became available, and the invention of the cream separator, the milking machine, and advances in commercial refrigeration launched the modern dairy industry. Between 1875 and 1915, sugar consumption doubled to 80 pounds per capita, and Coca-Cola and other soft drinks became widely available, with their popularity increasing with each new decade.

In 1914 the assassination of an Austrian archduke lit the fuse that set off fighting among the European powers locked in a bitter competition to colonize Africa and Asia and control the Suez sea routes to the East. In 1917 the United States joined the war when German U-boats threatened to starve England into submission by sinking food vessels off the south and west coasts. On the other side of the Atlantic, U.S. Food Administrator Herbert Hoover purchased the entire U.S. sugar and hog crops to save Britain.

From a biological perspective, World War I represented an explosive discharge of stagnant metabolic energy that had been accumulating in Europe for many decades as a result of dietary and environmental excess. The increasing mechanization of modern life at this period reflected the increasing mechanization of the modern food and agricultural system. The advent of skyscrapers, the use of glass as a primary building material, and the development of the automobile, luxury liner, and airplane coincided with the increasing use of metal and glass in canning, bottling, and other packaging. When war came, these vehicles were transformed into tanks, battleships, and fighter planes. Developments in long-range striking power (rifles, machine guns,

*I choose to chew because I wish to do
The sort of thing that nature had in view.
— Horace Fletcher's
Chewing Song*

*"Health and Freshness Comes in Cans."
— Continental Can slogan, early 1900s*

artillery) also paralleled the rise in meat and sugar consumption, and the introduction of poison gas followed the chemical adulteration of commercial food.

The myth of Western progress and European superiority was shattered by the war. By the time global fighting ended, nearly 40 million people had died, about half from direct fighting and about half from an epidemic of influenza that swept the world. Few lessons were learned from this war as the trend toward greater mechanization in all aspects of life continued. But the fundamental role of diet as the hidden mechanism of history was not lost on a few prophetic voices. Sir William Osler, the father of modern medical education, observed, "More people are killed by over-eating and drinking than by the sword." Cancer researcher William Howard Hay, M.D., concurred, "White flour and white sugar have cost more lives than all the wars of all time."

After World War I, the efforts to balance extreme foods reached a new plateau. The creation of mammoth incubators led to the mass producton of poultry. In the 1920s home refrigeration come into vogue, and prepackaged frozen foods reduced the consumption of fresh garden produce. Refined, canned, and dehydrated foods also took an increasing share of the market. In the 1930s the vitamin industry developed, selling back to the consumer the nutrients removed in processing grain. Artificial colors, chemical preservatives, and other additives found their way into daily food as new synthetic flavors, cosmetic appearance, and extended shelf life replaced wholesomeness and nutriton as primary concerns. Monoculture, itself a departure from traditional farming techniques, failed to meet the rising demand for unseasonal fare, and modern society began to turn to chemical agriculture to increase production, stretch quantity, and meet demand. These changes, along with increased consumption of beef and other animal foods high in saturated fat and cholesterol, laid the foundation for the modern epidemics of heart disease, cancer, and other degenerative diseases that developed in the middle of the century. The rise in cigarette smoking, increased industrial pollution, and a more sedentary way of life resulting from the spread of the automobile and other modern conveniences contributed to the increased incidence of these diseases.

As chaotic dietary habits spread around the world, intuition and native common sense declined. Populations in the industrialized countries became subject to delusional ideologies and the manipulation of rigid or unstable political and military leaders. The end result was another devastating world war among Germany, France, Britain, the U.S., the U.S.S.R., Japan, and other

"Much fat had been diverted to use as glycerine in the manufacture of explosives, and much sugar consigned to military rations as quick energy for going over the top."
— *Hillel Schwartz, Never Satisfied*

"The supermarket was born in the 1930s. Before that, people shopped at meat markets, fruit stands, greengrocers, and dairies . . . Everyone knew the grocers and asked after their health and family, and the grocers knew everyone else's business as well. Food shopping was part of belonging to a community . . . The birth of the supermarket changed all that . . . Food was checked out by someone from a different neighborhood. You had to have the money to pay for the food, whether you were working that month or not. Nobody asked after your health, either."
— *Amanda Spake, article in Mother Jones*

"The divine chemistry works in the subsoil."
— *Nathaniel Hawthorne*

"And this was easy and efficient [the tractor] so easy that the wonder goes out of work. So efficient that the wonder goes out of the land and the working of it, and with the wonder the deep understanding and the relations. And in the tractor man there grows contempt that only comes to a stranger who has little understanding and no relation. For nitrates are not the land, nor phosphates. And the length of fiber in the cotton is not the land. Carbon is not a man, nor salt, nor water, nor calcium. He is all these, but he is much more. And the land is so much more than its analyses. But the machine man driving a dead tractor on land he does not know and love, understands only chemistry. And he is contemptuous of the land of himself."
— *John Steinbeck, Grapes of Wrath*

nations eating the modern diet and a new rise in the level of inhumanity toward the Jews, the Chinese, the Vietnamese, and other people eating more traditionally. Following World War II, the final artificialization of modern agriculture, food production, and medicine took place. Chemical farming became nearly universal as inexpensive petroleum-based fertilizers, herbicides, and pesticides became available. DDT, a powerful insecticide that proved successful in reducing malaria during the war, was introduced as a common pesticide. Synthetic antibiotics, hormones, and preservatives further weakened the quality of meat and poultry, and more animal products had to be consumed to maintain the same level of energy and sensory satisfaction. The consumption of soft drinks and citrus juices, which are very yin, skyrocketed and helped to balance this overly yang intake.

Beginning in the 1950s, mass television advertising campaigns began to sell the appearance of food, including its packaging and social status, rather than the quality of the food itself. Beef, milk, cheese, ice cream, and other products of the cow completely replaced whole grains, bread, noodles, and pasta as the staple in the American diet. With the introduction of fast food and TV dinners and the growth of neighborhood drive-ins, pizza parlors, and hamburger chains, the home-cooked family meal became the exception rather than the rule. From eating so much animal food, American women became too yang and often left the home, and a majority gave up breastfeeding for infant formula. The medical profession and the dietetic associations lent their seal of approval to the new way of eating, promoting imbalanced nutritional theories such as the Basic Four Food Groups and endorsing the superiority of enriched, processed foods over whole, natural foods, including mother's milk.

For the first time in human history, daily cooking left the home and became largely the responsibility of people outside the family. Automats, vending machines, and other mechanical, assembly-line techniques insulated much of the food that was served from any human contact. Electricity and the microwave replaced wood and gas as main methods of cooking, subjecting food to further artificial electromagnetic vibrations, loss of natural energy, and even changes in molecular structure. Grace, or giving thanks for the bounty of the earth—a custom that had sustained generations from the earliest settling of the continent—largely disappeared from the family dining table along with real food. If modern people thought about their way of eating at all, they recognized a vague allegiance to a godhead of fat, protein, and carbohydrates; a devil called calories; and a minor pantheon of vitamins and minerals.

Television replaced the hearth as the center of the modern household. The nightly news—featuring the nuclear arms build-up, hostilities between the superpowers, and regional wars around the globe—supplanted ordinary dinnertime conversation. An atmosphere of international fear and crisis surrounded the meal, further contributing to feelings of isolation and despair. Everyone knew that the world could be blown up in the time it took to microwave dinner. During the postwar period, the latest turn in the international food exchange spiral witnessed Western soldiers (the most physical or yang element of society) returning from Vietnam, Afghanistan, Lebanon, El Salvador, and other tropical and semitropical regions with marijuana, cocaine, heroin, and opium. Once again, the influx of extreme yin from the tropics began to seriously undermine family life and social order in the United States and other industrial nations. Legislative efforts to prohibit illicit drugs proved as futile as the efforts of previous generations to control sugar and alcohol.

Black and native peoples experienced an especially heavy burden of sickness and suffering as a result of the modern diet. Modern soul food includes large quantities of meat (usually pork parts); collards, mustard, and turnip greens; butter beans; black-eyed peas; sweet potatoes; and cornbread—all cooked in or laced with pork fat, lard, milk, eggs, butter, salt, spices, and sugar. This way of eating and cooking derived from slavery under which black people were given the cheapest, most indigestible foods and learned to make them edible by marinating and smothering them with seasonings and spices. The Civil Rights movement targeted the serving of food at segregated lunch counters and other eating establishments. However, the influence of diet on consciousness and behavior during this period is largely unexplored. From the macrobiotic view, the essentially vegetable quality diet of Southern blacks enabled them to remain more flexible, peaceful, and nonviolent than whites, who were eating higher up on the food chain.

Similarly, American Indian communities, uprooted from their homelands and often forced to convert to a new religion and learn a new language, forgot their ancestral traditions and adopted a modern diet. Dispensed freely as part of government surplus programs, white flour, sugar, and dairy food led to epidemic rates of diabetes, high blood pressure, and lung disorders on many reservations.

As a result of tampering with the elements and refusing to abide by the limits of the four seasons, cancer, heart disease, AIDS, and other denegerative disorders proliferated through the modern and traditional world, reaching epidemic proportions by

"Americans, and colored people in particular, eat too much."
— *W.E.B. DuBois*

"There was white meat, white gravy, white bread, and white shortening on the table, white supremacy at the polls, and white gloves for pall bearers at the graveside."
— *John Egerton, Southern Food*

"When he returned from his speaking trip, the students caught up with him again at his parents' home, where Mother King nearly always had some turnip greens on the stove. [Martin Luther King, Jr.] was munching the greens, dipping bread into the juice, as the students pressed him toward consent, saying they were ready to move within 48 hours, their plans couldn't wait."
— *Taylor Branch, Parting the Waters: America in the King Years 1954-63*

"During this century, the composition of the average diet in the U.S. has changed radically. Complex carbohydrates—fruit, vegetables and grain products—which were the mainstay of the diet, now play a minority role. At the same time, fat and sugar consumption have risen to the point where these two dietary elements alone now comprise at least 60 percent of total caloric intake, an increase of 20 percent since the early 1900s. In the view of doctors and nutritionalists consulted by the Select Committee, these and other changes in the diet amount to a wave of malnutrition—of both over- and underconsumption—that may be as profoundly damaging to the nation's health as the widespread contagious diseases of the early part of the century.
— *Dietary Goals for the United States*

the end of the century. In the face of the collapse of natural human beings, scientists and genetic engineers began to tamper with the basic quality of human life itself.

During the second half of the century, spearheaded by Michio and Aveline Kushi and the modern macrobiotic community, the continent's direction began to reverse course. Though initially ignored and ridiculed by the scientific and medical profession, macrobiotics began to be taken seriously after researchers associated the standard American diet with the nation's epidemic levels of degenerative disease. One of the first steps in this direction followed President Eisenhower's heart attack in 1955. The White House physician, Paul Dudley White, who had an interest in vegetarian and traditional societies such as the Hunzas, put Eisenhower on a modified low-fat diet. The change in way of eating not only enabled him to run for reelection, but also may have relaxed his thinking and vision. His famous speech warning of a "military-industrial complex" in the body politic appears to have followed naturally the reduction of fat and cholesterol in his own system.

The turning point in the nation's declining health came in 1977 with the publication of *Dietary Goals for the United States*, the landmark report of the Senate Select Committee on Nutrition and Human Needs chaired by Senator George McGovern which connected the modern diet with six of the ten leading causes of death. The concerns and values of the macrobiotic community, the natural foods movement, and the organic farming movement echoed in schools and classrooms, hospitals and clinics. The medical profession began issuing dietary guidelines for the first time recommending substantial reduction in animal foods and simple sugars and corresponding increases in whole grains and vegetables. Though George McGovern lost the presidency, the *McGovern Report* may be regarded by future generations of Americans as the Emancipation Proclamation of the health revolution of the late twentieth and early twenty-first centuries.

Like the dietary threat, pollution and the destruction of the environment took decades to be recognized as dangers to the health and safety of modern society. By the last decade of the century, it was widely acknowledged that destruction of the tropical rain forests was primarily due to raising livestock for beef consumption and that on this continent water pollution (from pesticide runoff), soil erosion, and wildlife destruction were largely caused by modern agriculture and food processing, especially production of animal food. In addition, a significant proportion of the nation's energy and natural resources were used to produce, process, and prepare animal foods—a total of twice that supplied by all nuclear power plants and equal to total oil imports.

In 1981 a panel of the American Association for the Advancement of Science met to evaluate the national impact of implementing *Dietary Goals for the United States.* Beyond an improvement in public health, the AAAS symposium found that dietary changes would have far-reaching social and economic benefits. The scientists concluded that adoption of a diet centered on whole cereal grains rather than meat, poultry, dairy, and other animal foods would have significant effects on everything from land, water, fuel, and mineral use to the cost of living, employment rates, and the balance of international trade.

Today, these trends have reached a peak. Whole-grain fiber and bran have become national icons. Americans and Canadians of European descent are rediscovering whole grain porridge, bread, and pasta. Those of African heritage are beginning to recover their traditional culture and way of eating—based on millet, sorghum, rice, and other whole cereal grains—and native peoples are restoring open-pollinated blue corn and other strains of hardy maize. The health and environmental revolution has a long way to go. But a tremendous change in the continental eating habits and lifestyle has already begun to translate into healthier families, greener fields, and cleaner air. Heart disease dropped 40 percent since the dietary guidelines were issued, and by the new century we can expect some cancer rates to begin leveling off for the first time.

The end of the Cold War came during this period. After decades of hostility and competition, the United States and Soviet Union began to cooperate and embark on friendly relations. Mirroring these social changes, which saw animal food begin to be replaced with grains and more vegetable-quality fare in both countries, was a change in the personal diets and lifestyles of world leaders. In the early 1980s, when President Reagan was diagnosed with colon cancer, his physician chose to put him on a whole-grain based diet rather than treat him with harmful radiation or chemotherapy. Red-meat was limited to only once a week, and whole-grain bread, muffins, cereals, and other products were prepared by the White House chef daily. Other influences included his daughter, Patty, who was a vegetarian; his United Nations ambassador, a bachelor, whose sister was macrobiotic and as his hostess introduced macrobiotic foods at U.N. functions; and other political figures in Washington who had also been influenced by macrobiotics. President Reagan's view of life changed from this time. He became more conciliatory toward the Soviet Union, which he had previously denounced as "the evil empire." Diet also played a key role in the life of So-

"Sunday dinner: the turkey is from Greyhound, and the ham is from IT&T; the fresh vegetable salad is from Tenneco, with lettuce from Dow Chemical; potatoes by Boeing are placed alongside a roast from John Hancock Mutual Life; the strawberries are by Purex, and there are after-dinner almonds from Getty Oil."
— *James Hightower, Hard Tomatoes, Hard Times*

"What you seek in vain for, half your life, one day you come full upon, all the family at dinner."
— *Thoreau*

viet Premier Gorbachev, the architect of *glasnost* and *perestroika*. As a child in famine-stricken Russia, he grew up on whole millet—a grain associated with creativity, clarity, and balance—and sunflower seeds.

The Way to Peace

The traditional word for peace in the Far East—*wa*—is made up of the ideograms for "grain" and "mouth." In the East, traditional societies knew that by eating whole grains, human beings naturally became peaceful. In the West, the symbol of the Iroquois Confederacy was a common eating bowl from which knives and blood (symbolic of animal food and war) were prohibited. This suggests that native peoples on this continent also recognized eating together created a common mind and spirit. As the foundation of the Great Law of Peace, a respect for nature and a balanced way of eating enabled the Six Nations to maintain the longest-enduring union of states in North America.

From the arrival of Columbus to Michio Kushi, from Deganawida and Hiawatha to Ben Franklin and Thomas Jefferson, from George Washington to Dwight D. Eisenhower, from the Emancipation Proclamation to *Dietary Goals for the United States*, from Squanto and William Bradford to Mikhail Gorbachev and Ronald Reagan, amber waves of grains have played a pivotal role in shaping the life and destiny of the continent. In the century ahead, America will continue to serve as a fount of new ideas, practical inventions, and a universal spirit of brother- and sisterhood as the world develops into a planetary family.

Part II

Recipes –
Gifts of Peace

"O Beautiful, For Spacious Skies"

1
Soups

The word *soup* comes from the word *sup*—to take supper—and was originally associated with sopping a piece of bread in broth. Soups are a mirror, reflecting the balance of the meal. If we are preparing an elaborate repast, the soup may be clear and simple. If the rest of the meal is plain, the soup may be thick and hardy. The color, shape, size, and manner of cutting of the ingredients in soup should also complement the other dishes to be served.

Almost all foods—including grains, beans, vegetables, seaweed, seeds, and others—can go into soups. But most important is the seasoning or saline quality of the broth itself. Soups replicate the salty ocean in which life began. They stimulate the appetite, prepare the stomach for digestion, and provide warmth and energy. The human body needs salt and digestive enzymes to survive, and soup is a principal way we take in essential minerals and compounds. For this reason, miso, soy sauce, or some other fermented seasoning is frequently used in macrobiotic cooking. These traditional soybean products are especially beneficial to the intestines. And Freud notwithstanding, good intestines produce strong, healthy blood which in turn produces clear, balanced thinking. A calm, peaceful mind naturally follows from a balanced meal. Whether we experience spacious

*"Now good digestion
waits on appetite,
And health on both."
— Shakespeare*

"Whole grains evolved parallel with human beings and therefore should form the major portion of our diet, just as nuts and fruits developed with chimpanzees and apes and formed the staple of their diet and as giant ferns and other primitive plant life evolved in an earlier epoch in conjunction with the dinosaurs.

"The remainder of our food as human beings may be selected from earlier evolutionary varieties of plants and animals, including land and sea vegetables, fresh fruit, seeds and nuts, fish and seafood, and soup containing fermented enzymes and bacteria representing the most primordial form of life in the ancient sea."
— *Michio Kushi, The Book of Macrobiotics*

skies or cloudy ones is often a direct result of the soup of the day.

In our home, we serve soup once or twice a day. Soup helps us to keep from overeating, but we are careful not to take too much soup. A cup or small bowl is sufficient. Variety is important, so that even if we prepare miso soup daily we frequently change the ingredients. In the spring and summer, we will use lighter vegetables such as Chinese cabbage, celery, and scallions, occasionally add tofu or other lighter bean products, and use slightly less or lighter miso in seasoning. In the fall and winter, we will use stronger vegetables such as onions, carrots, and other root vegetables, occasionally add tempeh, seitan, or heavier products, and use slightly more or stronger miso in seasoning.

The long white radish, known as daikon, goes well in miso soup. It helps remove old animal fat from the body and is used often when people are beginning macrobiotics. However, daikon also can have a diuretic effect on the kidneys, so that over time as your health is restored, you may wish to use less of it less often.

Miso, soy sauce, or sea salt in soup helps to balance the natural sweetness of many vegetables such as squash, onions, and cabbage. The soup, however, need not have a salty taste. Overall, a slightly sweet flavor can predominate. If you can taste the salt in the soup, it is too salty.

Soups are an excellent way to use leftover grains and beans.. But we do not use leftover vegetables for soups because they will have cooked too long, losing their appearance, taste, and energy. In our experience, we've found many people cook fresh vegetables in soup too long. Vegetables should be crisp and in most cases need to boil only 2 or 3 minutes.

It is also important to make soup fresh every day. Some people reheat it every time or make a big pot and use it over several days. This can produce both weakening yin effects—lack of energy and vitality—and tightening yang effects—contraction from cooking down the liquid and ingredients over and over again. Once a man from Colorado came to us for advice. He was restless and couldn't sit still or relax. He assured us he was not deviating from the standard diet. He was clearly too yang and so we immediately focused in on salt quality and volume. In answer to our questions, it appeared that the sea salt, miso, and soy sauce he was using were all good quality, and he was not using excessive volume. We then asked him how he was making his soup, and he said that he made a a big pot of miso to last for the entire week and reheated it every time. That turned out to be the cause of his problem. When he started making it fresh each day, his overly yang symptoms disappeared and he felt more comfortable.

Sometimes a very yangizing soup is called for, such as Pepperpot Soup, one of the most famous soups in American history. At Valley Forge, George Washington's army had virtually nothing to eat and he was afraid that they would go home and the campaign for liberty against England would be lost. In exasperation, the General told the cooks who were in charge of feeding his men that they must rise to the occasion. From local merchants, the cooks were only able to obtain some tripe—a fish considered of the lowest quality—and peppercorns—the hot spice imported from the East Indies to Philadelphia. They made a strong soup from the fish and spices, and the fiery result filled up the men's stomachs and reignited their courage, leading to Washington's most celebrated victory. While we don't particularly recommend this combination of strong yin and yang, many other soups, stews, chowders, and gumbos in American history are thoroughly macrobiotic, and most others can be modified or adjusted using better quality ingredients.

Below are a couple dozen of our favorite soups.

Miso Soup

In the Far East, miso is known as the "Gift of the Gods" and has long been respected as one of the healthiest foods. From China, Japan, and other Oriental lands, knowledge of miso came West. Francesco Carletti, a Florentine traveler to Japan, referred to it in 1597, and Englebert Kaempfer, a German scientist, descibed the process of making miso and shoyu (soy sauce) a century later. It is believed that the earliest Chinese immigrants who worked on the railroads in the West brought the first homemade miso (known in Chinese as *chiang*) to America. The first miso shop in America opened in San Francisco in 1917. During World War II, all the miso companies on the West Coast were closed down when Japanese-Americans were rounded up and put in concentration camps.

In the 1950s and 1960s, miso was introduced by the Ohsawas, Kushis, Aiharas, and other macrobiotic teachers, and the U.S. Department of Agriculture began studies of miso and other fermented foods at a research center in Peoria, Illinois. In 1967, Bill Shurtleff, an ex-Peace Corps teacher and student of Zen, was introduced to miso by poets Allen Ginsberg and Gary Snyder. In Japan, Shurtleff and his wife and partner, Aikiko Aoyagi, studied traditional miso-making, published *The Book of Miso* in 1976, and like modern day Johnny Appleseeds promot-

"From nothing, you must create a great dish."
— *George Washington at Valley Forge*

Health Note
The National Cancer Center in Japan reported that people who ate miso soup every day had 33% less stomach cancer, 43% less deaths from coronary heart disease, 29% less lethal strokes, and 3 1/2 times less deaths from high blood pressure and all other causes than those not eating miso.

"In much the same way that the Japanese, over a period of 1,000 years, gradually transformed Chinese soybean chiang into unique and truly Japanese-style misos, so may we also expect that Westerners will continue the creative process, adapting miso to their own tastes, technology, and cuisine. There are many reasons to believe that miso will play an increasing role in America's evolving cuisine and become a standard household seasoning, just as soy sauce now is, as people discover the great variety of delicious flavors and aromas found in the many and varied types of fine miso."
— Bill Shurtleff and Akiko Aoyagi, The Book of Miso

ed and distributed miso across the country. The first non-Oriental miso companies were founded by macrobiotic students in the 1970s, including Ohio Miso by Thom Leonard, American Miso in North Carolina by John and Jan Belleme, South River Miso in Massachusetts by Christian and Gaella Elwell, and Imagine Foods/Montaeu Farm in Missouri by Dale Deraps. Made from the highest quality organic soybeans, grains, and *koji* (an inoculated grain-based starter) and processed using traditional methods, native American miso is a wonderful addition to our culture and cuisine. Its healthful properties have been experienced now by a new generation of daily miso soup lovers. Miso is especially helpful in detoxifying the body from excessive fat and sugar, as well as chemicals, pollutants in the water and atmosphere, and nuclear contamination. It is a truly a food encompassing the ancient and future destinies of our species and one which will spread across the continent and around the world.

There are many varieties and strengths of miso. For everyday miso soup, we prefer *barley miso* that has aged at least two years. *Rice miso* is lighter and we enjoy it on warmer days and in warmer seasons. *Hatcho* (all soybean) miso is dark, strong, and energizing. It is nice in fall and winter and for medicinal purposes. *White, yellow,* and other light misos that have aged several months are sweet and delicious and used mainly in sauces and dips rather than soup, though they can be mixed in small amounts with barley, rice, or hatcho miso to give a distinctive flavor and taste. American ingenuity has led to the development of new misos using beans other than soybean and grains other than barley and rice. We especially like chickpea miso, corn miso, and millet miso.

Just Right Miso Soup

1 small onion, thinly sliced
1 carrot, thinly sliced
2-inch strip of wakame
2 cups spring water
barley miso (1/2 teaspoon per person)

Soak wakame for a few minutes and cut into smaller pieces. Add water and bring to a boil. Boil for 5 minutes while cutting the onion and carrot.

Add the vegetables to the wakame broth and boil together for 3 to 4 minutes until vegetables are cooked but not mushy. Purée the miso in a little water and return to the pot. Simmer for

3 to 4 minutes over low flame. Garnish with scallions and serve warm.

• Many different types of vegetables may be used in miso soup, but it's important to include upward growing vegetables often such as bok choy, collard greens, kale, Chinese cabbage, and chives. We also enjoy miso with yellow squash and thinly sliced mushrooms.

Lentil Soup with Barley

A hint of barley makes for a chewy, sweet, and delicious soup.

2-inch piece of kombu, soaked and cut into strips
1/2 cup lentils
1/4 cup barley
1/2 cup celery, thinly sliced
1/2 cup carrots, thinly sliced
2 teaspoons miso
4 cups spring water
1/8 teaspoon sea salt

Layer the kombu, onions, barley, and lentils in a saucepan. Slowly add water. Bring to a boil, lower the heat, and simmer for about 30 minutes until the barley is almost done. Add celery and carrots and cook 10 to 15 minutes more. Add the miso puréed in a little water and simmer for 3 to 4 minutes.

Smooth Red Lentil Soup

This is a Texas-style favorite.

1 small onion, diced
1 cup hard butternut squash, cut in chunks
1 cup red lentils
celery, small piece
1 1/2 cups cabbage
1 cup barley, cooked
2 teaspoons miso
4 cups spring water

Sauté onions in oil until transparent and add to lentils and spring water. Bring to a boil and simmer for 20 minutes. Then add cabbage, squash, celery, and barley. At end add a combination of dark barley and chickpea miso for seasoning.

Health Note
In Nagasaki, after the atomic bombing, Dr. Akizuki saved all of his patients from radiation sickness by giving them a strict macrobiotic diet including strong miso soup with each meal.

To test miso's effectiveness, scientists in Hiroshima later found that mice fed miso are five times more resistant to radiation than usual.

"If a man bakes bread with indifference, he bakes a bitter loaf that feeds but half his hunger."
— Kahlil Gibran

Cooking Tip
Don't use miso with
more yang foods like
aduki beans, tempeh,
and seitan. Miso is
better with more yin
foods like lentils and
chickpeas.

"[Douglas' principles
are like] the homeo-
pathic soup that was
made by boiling the
shadow of a pigeon
that had starved to
death."
— Abraham Lincoln
in the Lincoln-
Douglas Debates

Chickpea Soup with Couscous

Chickpeas, or garbanzos as they are known in Spanish, came to the New World with the Spanish. Garbanzo soup was a favorite dish in Old St. Augustine and other early Spanish communities. Chickpeas go well with many vegetables. We are fond of adding a little couscous to this soup for texture and lightness. It is especially cooling in summer or warmer regions of the country.

1 cup chickpeas
2-inch piece of kombu
1/2 carrot, diced
1/2 cup onions
1/2 cup cabbage (optional)
1/2 cup tiny broccoli flowerettes
barley miso
scallions
1/2 cup couscous, pre-cooked
4 cups spring water

Soak chickpeas and pressure cook with kombu for 40 minutes. When nearly done, add diced onions, carrots, cabbage, and broccoli. Cook for 5 to 10 minutes. Purée miso and add to ingredients, simmering 2 to 3 minutes longer.

Spoon 2 to 3 tablespoons of couscous into a cup and spoon soup over. Garnish with sliced scallions and serve.

• This soup can also be served over leftover millet, rice, or barley.

Split Pea Soup with Cabbage

Split pea soup is good with cabbage, which sweetens it.

1 cup split peas
3-inch piece of wakame
1 leek, sliced
1 carrot, sliced
1 cup cabbage, chopped
1/8 to 1/4 teaspoon sea salt
4 cups spring water

Add split peas to water and cook with wakame. After 20 minutes add remaining vegetables and sea salt. Continue cooking for another 10 minutes.

Navy Bean Soup

One of the most famous soups in America, Senate Bean Soup, is made with white navy beans from Michigan and is served in the restaurant of the U.S. Senate in Washington. It is also made with a ham base. The following recipe is both healthier and productive of a calmer, more peaceful mind—something which the Senate and our leaders as a whole need to cultivate more.

2/3 cup navy beans
2-inch piece of kombu
1 cup Brussels sprouts, cut into quarters lengthwise
1 cup carrots
1/2 cup celery
pinch of sea salt
1 teaspoon puréed barley miso
4 cups spring water

Soak beans for 6 to 8 hours. Soak kombu for 20 minutes and cut into 1-inch squares. Cook beans with kombu underneath until almost done (about 1 1/2 hours). Add the Brussels sprouts, carrots, celery, and sea salt. Cook 10 to 15 minutes until vegetables and beans are tender. Add miso and simmer 4 to 5 minutes. Serve warm.

Black Bean Soup

Black soy beans, turtle beans, and other dark beans make rich, thick, delicious soups.

2 cups black soybeans
2-3 cups spring water
2 teaspoons red miso

Soak beans and boil until done. Then purée the black soybeans with water in food mill or a blender. Pour into saucepan and heat. Add water if you like a thinner soup. Purée red miso and add to liquid. Simmer 3 to 4 minutes. Garnish with chopped parsley, carrot flowers, or scallions and serve.

"If a man will be sensible and one fine morning, while he is lying in bed, count at the tips of his fingers how many things in this life truly give him enjoyment, invariably he will find food is the first one."
— Lin Yutang

Menu Planning

If the soup is full and thick, the rest of the meal should be small and modest. If the meal is large, the soup can be thin, for example, a clear soup served at a banquet.

If the soup is sweet, other tastes should be emphasized in the meal and vice versa.

Creamy soups complement crisp, baked textures or chunky vegetables in the meal. Chunky soups balance simple meals.

"I would rather stuff myself with gazpachos than be subject to the misery of an impertinent physician who kills me with hunger."
— *Cervantes, Don Quixote*

Creamy Squash Soup

Squash soup is very sweet and delicious and can be made with any fall- or winter-season squashes. It is a favorite at our home and at the Kushi Institute.

1 large butternut squash
soy sauce to taste
spring water

Wash and peel squash. Cut into 1-inch chunks and put in a saucepan. Add water to partially cover the squash. Bring to a boil, reduce heat, and simmer until tender.

Remove from heat and purée in a food mill. Add additional water to desired thickness. Return to the pan, add a small volume of soy sauce (1 to 2 teaspoons) and simmer for a few minutes. Garnish with chopped parsley or scallions and serve.

• Cauliflower soup may be prepared in the same way, except it isn't necessary to purée the cauliflower.

Onion Soup

Gazpacho, the Spanish-style vegetable soup that is served cool or at room temperature, originally was made with onions and other sweet vegetables. Tomatoes, the main modern ingredient, were a late addition. This onion soup is a very sweet, tender, soft, and delicious broth we often enjoy in the Berkshires.

1 onion, diced
pinch of sea salt
soy sauce to taste
spring water

Water-sauté the onion with a pinch of salt for sweetness, add more water, cook until very soft, about 30 minutes. Season at the end with soy sauce. Garnish with scallions and serve.

• For an even sweeter soup, and one with a beautiful yellow and green color, combine leeks with yellow summer squash (sliced) and onion (cut in half-moons).

Creamy Leek Soup with Barley

Leeks are very sweet and go well in many soups. This makes a creamy, light, and colorful dish.

2-inch piece of kombu
1 leek, sliced
1 medium carrot, sliced
1/3 cup uncooked barley
1/2 cup mushrooms, sliced
5 cups spring water
1 tablespoon miso

Soak kombu and cut into small pieces. Wash leeks well (slit in half lengthwise and wash each half separately) and slice. Wash and cut carrot and mushrooms. Layer mushrooms, leek, carrot, and barley in a saucepan. Slowly add water and bring to a boil and simmer for 45 to 50 minutes. Purée miso in soup broth and return to soup. Simmer for 5 minutes. Garnish with chopped parsley.
   • Leftover oats may be substituted for barley.

Harvest Parsnip Soup

This is a nice thick, warming soup for early fall or winter.

3 parsnips, cut into chunks
2 cups spring water
pinch of sea salt
soy sauce to taste

Cut parsnips into chunks, add water and sea salt, and cook until tender. Put through food mill. Then return to stove, add another 1/2 cup of spring water and soy sauce to taste. Simmer lightly, garnish with chopped parsley or scallions, and serve.

Cooking Tip
While president, Dwight D. Eisenhower enjoyed cooking, particularly soups. His favorite garnish was nasturtiam stems (traditional Indian cress), picked when green and tender in the spring, cut in small pieces, boiled separately, and added to the soup at the end of cooking.

Rice Soup with Corn and Vegetables

Leftover rice goes well in soups and stews. It is not necessary to season this dish as it is deliciously sweet from the vegetables, but it may be seasoned with miso, soy sauce, or sea salt if desired. We served it one cold winter evening with unleavened sourdough bread and a sea vegetable dish, and it was very satisfying.

2 cups pre-cooked rice
1 carrot, diced
1 onion, diced
2 cups cabbage, cut in small chunks
2 ears of fresh corn with the kernels removed

Layer the vegetables in a pan and cover with water. Cook for about 15 minutes. Add the rice, stirring gently to mix it in with the vegetables. Cook for 10 more minutes.

Colorful Barley Stew

1 small onion or leek, sliced
1/2 cup barley
1/4 cup kidney beans, pre-cooked
1/2 cup corn kernels
5-6 cups spring water
soy sauce to taste

Layer ingredients and cook gently until barley is done, about 45 minutes. Add soy sauce toward the end of cooking.

Corn Chowder

Native peoples enjoyed corn chowder, and it was a favorite at the first Thanksgiving. In the South, it was made with parched grain which had been crushed and mixed with dried eels and other fish. Here is an all-vegetarian variety we like.

1 ear of fresh corn with the kernels removed
1 onion, diced
1 red radish, cut into flowers
1/2 bunch of watercress, chopped
umeboshi vinegar to taste

3 cups spring water

Cook fresh corn kernels with the vegetables for about 10 minutes. At the end, add chopped watercress, and cook for another minute. Season with umeboshi vinegar, let cool, and serve.

• Another type of corn soup can be made by sautéing onions, carrots, and burdock slivers, combining with leftover beans or grain, adding 1 cup of cornmeal, and cooking in 6 cups of spring water or soup stock for 25 minutes. At the end, add chopped celery and miso or soy sauce to taste, simmer for 3 to 4 minutes, and serve.

Sunny Millet Stew

This is another very sweet, delicious stew.

3/4 cup millet
3 cups spring water
1 small onion, diced
1 small carrot, diced
1/4 rutabaga, cut in small cubes
1 ear of fresh corn with the kernels removed
scallions for garnish
miso or sea salt to taste

Wash vegetables and millet and drain the millet. Cut vegetables and layer them. Place millet on top, add water, and bring to a boil. Cover and simmer for 40 minutes. Add puréed miso at the end of cooking and simmer for a few minutes longer and serve. (If salt is used for seasoning, add it at the beginning with the vegetables and millet.)

Vegetable Noodle Soup

We enjoyed this thick delicious soup in the wintertime in Texas.

1 onion, diced
1 carrot, diced
1 cup green beans, sliced
1/2 cup celery, diced
3/4 cup elbow noodles
3-inch piece of burdock
1 cup navy beans
3-inch piece of kombu

2 teaspoons barley miso
4-5 cups spring water

Cook beans with kombu and onion until 80 percent done. Add vegetables and cook until beans and vegetables are almost done. Add puréed miso and simmer 3 to 4 minutes more. Garnish with chopped scallions and serve.

Chowders and Gumbos

There are many delicious fish soups, chowders, and gumbos. We eat very little animal food and almost never prepare it at home. When we do feel a need for more energy and strength, we will go out and have fish soup or other fish dish. Of course, except in macrobiotic or natural foods restaurants, it is difficult to find a chowder that is not made with milk, butter, and strong spices.

The quality of the fish is also important. Like most macrobiotic families, we prefer white-meat fish which are less oily and fatty than red-meat or blue-skinned varieties. We also tend to prefer ocean varieties such as cod, haddock, and sole that are less polluted from chemicals in the environment than freshwater and inland varieties. In the Berkshire mountains where we live, however, we have found that it is harder to adjust to seafood than it is in Boston which is situated on the sea coast or other maritime regions.

Generally, the fish available here is fresh and clean. But even living so close to a good source is no guarantee. Once a few years ago, we were all enjoying a fish dinner in the staff dining room at the Kushi Institute. Michio came in late and joined us for dinner. Someone passed him the platter with fish, which he ordinarily likes in small volume, but this time he didn't take any. We wondered if maybe he was doing some spiritual practices, when eating animal food, including fish and seafood, is avoided. But he just smiled and pointed to Marble, the calico cat which the K.I. inherited from the Franciscan monks when it assumed the property, and which was sleeping in the windowsill. Michio picked up some fish with his chopsticks and held it up to Marble. The old cat, usually ravenous, took one sniff of the fish and walked away. Without saying a word, Michio went on to a bowl of rice, while the rest of us (full of this dubious fish) marveled at his intuition which was as strong and powerful as a cat's.

"[A] warm savory steam from the kitchen served to belie the apparently cheerless prospect before us. But when that smoking chowder came in, the mystery was delightfully explained."
— *Herman Melville, Moby Dick*

Fish Chowder

Most commercial fish soup or chowder is made with milk, potatoes, and salted pork for flavor. This recipe is more traditional, using just fish, vegetables, and mild seasonings.

1/2 cup onions, diced
1/2 cup carrots, diced
1/2 cup nappa cabbage, shredded
3 cups spring water
6 ounces fresh white meat fish (cod, haddock, sole, etc.)
miso or soy sauce to taste
grated ginger

Layer vegetables in a saucepan and add the water. Bring to a boil, lower heat, and cook for 10 minutes. Add fish, cut into small pieces, and cook 5 minutes longer. Add miso or soy sauce to taste. Garnish with grated ginger.

Oyster Soup

Oysters were the fast food of the nineteenth century—a national craze. Oyster bars, parlors, and saloons proliferated across the country. Everyone, from ordinary farmers and shopkeepers to presidents (Lincoln) and tycoons (Rockefeller after whom a fancy oyster dish was named) were infatuated with oysters. This macrobiotic variation is very creamy and delicious.

1/2 pint fresh oysters
1 small carrot, cut in thin rounds or flowers
1 small onion, diced
2 scallions, sliced
2 pinches of sea salt
3 rounded tablespoons oat flour
1 tablespoon soy sauce

Put onion, carrot, scallions, and water in a saucepan and boil for 5 minutes. Add oysters. Mix flour with a little water and stir into the mixture. Add the salt and simmer for 10 minutes. Add soy sauce and simmer 3 to 4 minutes more.

• Add a tablespoon of sesame seeds to the soup for garnishing if desired. In the Carolinas, sesame seeds (or *bennes* as they were known in Africa) were traditionally added to oyster soup.

Creole Proverbs

"It's the old pot that makes the good soup."

"Spoon goes to bowl's house; bowl never goes to spoon's house."

"When the garden is fair, the gumbo is spoiled."

"What you lose in the fire, you will find in the ashes."

— Lafcadio Hearn, La Cuisine Creole

New Orleans Seafood Gumbo

Gumbo *is another African term meaning "okra." This pungent small green vegetable came to the New World with enslaved peoples and became a staple in soups and stews. By the time it reached New Orleans, gumbo had come to signify a thick soup or stew combining fish and vegetables and served in large shallow bowls with boiled rice.*

1/4 to 1/2 cup fish, cut into small pieces
1 medium onion, diced
1 cup okra
1-2 cloves of garlic, minced
1/4 cup celery or green pepper
1 cup hot cooked rice, preferably long-grain
1/2 cup mushrooms, sliced
1 teaspoon sesame oil
pinch of sea salt
2 cups spring water
1 teaspoon arrowroot powder

Sauté onion, garlic, okra, and celery in sesame oil with a pinch of sea salt. Add water to cover and simmer until vegetables are tender, about 15 minutes.

Steam fish on top of this mixture. Add the rice, stir into mixture, and thicken with arrowroot powder dissolved in a little cold water. Serve in individual bowls.

• You can thicken the mixture after steaming the fish, adjust seasoning (adding soy sauce or red pepper if desired), and serve over rice in individual serving dishes.

Bouillabaisse

Bouillabaisse is another Louisiana speciality. Its name comes from the French for "boil" and "stop." Made with a colorful fish, usually red snapper and red fish, it is lightly boiled and served in individual tureens over slices of toasted French bread.

"For Amber Waves of Grain"

2
Whole Grains

Rice

America is blessed with wonderful, wholesome rice. There is more brown rice eaten in this country today than in any other part of the world, and the rice here is strong, balanced, and nourishing. Arkansas and California grow most of the organic rice crop for the natural foods market, though rice is grown in small farms and gardens in practically all states and provinces. At Kendall Foods near us in western Massachusetts, Charles and Yoko Kendall have successfully grown dry land rice, and we have heard of rice being produced as far north as Canada.

Short-grain is the most suitable type for daily use in most temperate regions, with *medium-* and *long-grain* used occasionally, especially in warmer seasons and on hotter days. In the South and other warmer regions of the country, medium- and long-grain rice can be used more frequently. *Sweet rice* is more glutinous than ordinary rice and is used in making *mochi*, *amasake*, and special dishes. *Basmati* is a long-grain variety, originally from India and Persia, and comes in different colors and is sometimes scented. It is suitable for occasional summer salads and light party dishes.

At home we use unhulled paddy rice and hull it ourselves in a

"The simplest dishes are the hardest to make. The highest art in cooking is the preparation of a bowl of rice."
— *Michio Kushi*

hulling machine. This preserves the natural energy of the rice right up until cooking and gives stronger, chewier, and more delicious rice. At the Kushi Institute in Becket, the rice is prepared freshly hulled this way, and almost everyone who visits notices the difference in taste and energy level.

Our usual pattern of eating is to have freshly cooked brown rice at least once a day. We enjoy it plain, then cooked together with about 20 percent millet, then with 20 percent barley, then with 10 percent aduki beans or other beans, then plain again, and so on. This way makes for endless variety and satisfaction.

Perfect Pressure-Cooked Brown Rice

Pressure-cooked brown rice is the principal staple in macrobiotic homes across North America. Pressure-cooking is the modern successor to cooking rice in cast-iron pots with heavy lids weighted with stones. The pressure contributes added energy and vitality to the rice, producing grains which are individually distinct.

2 cups short-grain brown rice
3 cups spring water
pinch of sea salt or 1-inch piece of kombu

Cooking Times for Grains
Pressure-Cooked Brown Rice 50"
Other Pressure-Cooked Grains 50-60"
Boiled Rice 50-60"
Boiled Barley 50-60"
Boiled Millet 30"
Oatmeal 15-20"
Whole Oats 1-3 hr.
Buckwheat 10-20"
Rye 50-60"
Corn on the Cob 10-15"
Couscous 5-10"
Bulgur 10-15"
Quinoa 25-30"
Amaranth 30"
Teff 20-30"

Sort through rice for hulls and stones. Then wash gently using cool water. Place rice and water in a pressure cooker. Place pressure cooker on a low flame for about 15 minutes without adding salt or the cover. After 15 minutes, place the salt in the pressure cooker and attach the cover. Turn the flame to high and bring to pressure. When the pressure is up, reduce the flame to low, and cook for 45 to 50 minutes. When the rice is done, bring the pressure down by placing a chopstick under the pressure gauge. Once pressure has been released, remove cover and let the rice set for 4 to 5 minutes to loosen it from the bottom of the pot. Releasing the pressure quickly seems to result in a lighter, fluffier rice.

• Alternatively, you can soak the rice for 3 to 5 hours or overnight, place in a pressure cooker with salt or kombu, cover and bring up to pressure over a medium high flame. Reduce flame and cook for 45 to 50 minutes. Turn off the flame and release the pressure with a chopstick. Remove gently from the pressure cooker, making sure that top and bottom rice are mixed.

• When done, rice may be left in the pressure cooker with the lid on until pressure naturally reduces. This takes about 10 or 15 minutes and results in rice that has strong, calming energy.

Boiled Rice a la Ben Franklin and Thomas Jefferson

Boiled brown rice is as American as Benjamin Franklin and Thomas Jefferson, who both enjoyed this light, fluffy lighter dish. In the Berkshires, we enjoy it occasionally instead of pressure-cooked rice, especially in the spring and summer.

2 cups brown rice
4 cups spring water
2 pinches of sea salt

Wash the rice and place in a saucepan. Add the water by pouring it gently into the side of the pan. Add the sea salt and cover. Bring to a boil, lower the heat, and simmer for about one hour. (Try not to remove the cover and check on it too frequently as this will release steam and leave the rice too dry.)

Sunrise Cereal

Soft rice is the main breakfast food in many homes from New England to Southern California. In fact, softly prepared cereal grains have traditionally been eaten in the morning all over the world. Oatmeal, rye flake cereal, and other porridges are popular across America, and we eat them on occasion. For strong morning energy, we prefer whole-grain porridges including soft rice, soft millet, and soft barley, which are all made in the same basic way.

l cup brown rice
4 cups spring water
pinch of sea salt or 1-inch piece of kombu
sliced scallions or nori strips

Wash the rice and pressure cook or boil as in the basic recipes. This is the best way to eat rice for breakfast because the water balances the contractive quality of the rice, making it more suitable in the early morning when we get up with the energy of the sun. If you eat left-over rice from dinner without adding additional water, your condition may become too tight. You may use the grain left over from the night before and add 2 to 3 cups of water to 1 cup of rice, letting it simmer for 15 minutes. Occasionally you can add squash, cabbage, onions, or other round or

"When about sixteen years of age I happened to meet with a book, written by one Tryon, recommending a vegetable diet. I determined to go into it. My brother, being yet unmarried, did not keep house, but boarded himself and his apprentices in another family. My refusing to eat flesh occasioned an inconveniency, and I was frequently chid for my singularity. I made myself acquainted with Tryon's manner of preparing some of his dishes, such as boiling . . . rice, making hasty pudding, and a few others . . . I made the greater progress, from that greater clearness of head and quicker apprehension which usually attends temperance in eating and drinking."
— Ben Franklin, Autobiography

root vegetables for variation. From time to time, you may also add a little puréed miso which is then simmered a few minutes before serving.

• Children enjoy raisins in their porridge (though they are best used only occasionally). Roasted sunflower or pumpkin seeds are also a nice addition.

Rice Porridge with Millet and Pearl Barley

*When we were living in Dallas, we enjoyed combining several grains in our morning cereal. The addition of pearl barley (*hato mugi) *is particularly cooling. This porridge is very soft, deli- cious, and chewy.*

1 cup short-grain brown rice
1 cup long-grain brown rice
1/2 cup millet
1/3 cup pearl barley (hato mugi)
6 cups spring water
2 pinches of sea salt

Combine ingredients and pressure cook for 50 minutes in the usual way.

Rice with Barley

A little barley cooked together with rice gives the grain a light- er, more expansive effect. We enjoy preparing barley rice at least once or twice a week.

2 cups brown rice
1/2 cup barley
4 cups spring water
2-inch piece of kombu or pinch of sea salt

Wash the grains and place in pressure cooker with kombu, or place over fire, and when the water is warm, add a pinch of sea salt. Put on the cover and bring up to pressure. Cook for about 45 minutes. Let set for five minutes. Bring down the pressure and gently remove from the pot.

Rice with Millet

Millet added to rice makes it a little more energizing and sweeter. We enjoy this dish frequently, especially in the autumn and winter.

2 cups medium-grain brown rice
1/2 cup millet
4 1/2 cups spring water
pinch of sea salt

Add millet to rice and pressure cook or boil in the usual way.

Rice with Corn

This gives a sweet, delicious flavor that's cooling for summer.

2 cups brown rice
1/2 cup of fresh corn
4 cups spring water
pinch of sea salt

Cut the corn from the cob with a knife and add it to the rice before pressure cooking or boiling in the usual way.

Rice with Bulgur

This is a tasty, fluffy combination which is especially nice in the spring.

1 cup brown rice
1/4 to 1/2 cup bulgur
3 cups spring water
pinch of sea salt

Add the bulgur to the rice and cook in the usual way.

"Seeds improve with age."
— Thoreau

"Good rice, stored well, can last for thousands of years, maintaining its ability to sprout when planted."
— Michio Kushi

Ecology Note
In its landmark report Alternative Agriculture, *the National Academy of Sciences found that "alternative farming methods are practical and economical ways to maintain yields, conserve soil, maintain water quality, and lower operating costs through improved farm management and reduced use of fertilizers and pesticides." Among the case histories in the report is the Lundberg Brothers farm in Richvale, California, which grows much of the nation's organic brown rice.*

Vegetable Fried Rice

Fried rice is warming and delicious. It is an especially good way to use leftover rice. Here is just one style.

2 cups brown rice, cooked
1 stalk celery, diced
1 medium carrot, diced
1 onion, diced
3-4 fresh mushrooms, thinly sliced
sesame oil
spring water
soy sauce to taste

Dice the celery, carrot, and onion and slice the mushrooms thinly. Brush the skillet with a small amount of sesame oil and sauté the vegetables until crisp but not overly cooked. Add several cups of brown rice on top of the vegetables and a few teaspoons of water. Cover and let the steam heat the rice thoroughly. Then season with a little soy sauce to taste and mix. Serve warm.

• Vegetables may be varied from time to time. Other combinations that are nice are sweet corn cut from the cob and diced nori; cabbage, carrots, and onions; and fresh English peas, carrots, and onions.

Rice with Aduki Beans

Aduki, the small red bean, has a very balanced energy. In Japan, rice cooked with adukis is known as Red Rice and is eaten on New Year's and other special occasions. The Kushi Institute in Becket often serves rice with aduki beans on holidays, and it is one of the basic dishes in K.I. cooking classes.

2 cups brown rice
1/2 cup sweet rice
1/4 cup aduki beans
4 1/2 cups spring water
pinch of sea salt

Soak the aduki beans for 5 to 6 hours. Wash the rice. Add the rice and beans together in the pressure cooker and place over a flame. When the water is warm, add a pinch of sea salt. Bring to pressure and cook for 45 to 50 minutes.

• The proportions may be varied to suit your taste. Some peo-

"No civilization worthy of the name has ever been founded on any agricultural basis other than the cereals. The ancient cultures of Babylonia and Egypt, of Rome and Greece, and later those of northern and western Europe, were all based on the growing of wheat, barley, rye, and oats. Those of India, China and Japan had rice for their basic crop. The pre-Columbia peoples of America—Inca, Maya, and Aztec—looked to corn for their daily bread."
— Paul C. Mangelsdorf, article in Scientific-American 1953

ple like 50 percent sweet rice and 50 percent short grain brown rice. But generally you do not need more than 50 percent sweet rice.

Rice with Lentils

2 1/4 cups brown rice
1/4 cup lentils
4 cups spring water
pinch of sea salt or 2-inch piece of kombu

Wash the rice and beans separately, then put in pressure cooker with kombu, or add a pinch of sea salt when the water is warm. Bring up to pressure and cook for 45 to 50 minutes. Transfer to bowl by lifting gently from the pressure cooker with a rice paddle.
    • Rice may also be cooked with 10 percent chickpeas, kidney beans, or black beans.

Limpin' Susan

Rice cooked with kidney or other colorful red beans is a delicacy in Louisana and other parts of the South. It is traditionally known as Limpin' Susan.

2 1/4 cups short-grain brown rice
1/4 cup kidney or pinto beans
4 cups spring water
pinch of sea salt

Combine rice and beans and pressure-cook or boil in the usual way.

Moors and Christians

Rice cooked with black beans is another Southern favorite. Its origin goes back to the Spanish heritage in Florida. But its nickname of Moors and Christians suggests that it goes back even further to the kingdoms of Castille and Aragon in which Christians, Muslims, and Jews lived in peace and harmony for many centuries.

2 1/4 cups short-grain brown rice

"[The Africans] affirm, which in their country is most of their food, [rice] is very healthful for our bodies."
— Gov. Berkeley of Virginia, A Description of the Province of New Albion 1648

1/4 cup black beans
4 cups spring water
pinch of sea salt

Combine rice and beans and pressure cook or boil in the usual way.

Hoppin' John

Rice with black-eyed peas is a traditional Carolina specialty known as Hoppin' John. It was customarily served on New Year's. The children hopped around the table in anticipation of receiving a good luck coin hidden in the pot—hence its name.

2 1/4 cups short-grain brown rice
1/4 cup black-eyed peas
1/4 cup seitan, diced
1/4 cup onions, diced
4 1/2 cups spring water
pinch of sea sea salt

Combine ingredients and pressure cook or boil in the usual way.

Rice with Chestnuts

Chestnuts make the rice taste very sweet. Women and children are especially fond of this dish.

2 cups brown rice
1/4 cup chestnuts, soaked for several hours
3 1/2 cups spring water
pinch of sea salt

Health Note
People with tight livers are not attracted to dry, pressure-cooked rice. Instead, give them soft rice or add rice to soup for a few days until their liver relaxes.

Soak the chestnuts and remove as much of the brown outer husk as possible. Wash the rice, layer the rice and chestnuts in the pressure cooker, and place over the flame. When the water is warm, add a pinch of sea salt. Put on the cover and bring up to pressure. Cook for 45 to 50 minutes. Remove from fire and let set for five minutes. Then lower the pressure and remove gently from the pressure cooker.

• The amount of chestnuts may be adjusted for your family's taste, but generally should be about 10 percent of the amount of rice.

Sweet Rice with Aduki Beans and Chestnuts

This is a rich tasting dish and very satisfying. It often eliminates the craving for desserts and other sweets.

1 cup sweet rice
1/4 cup aduki beans
1/4 cup chestnuts, soaked for several hours
3 cups spring water

Pleace rice, beans, and chestnuts in a pressure cooker, add water, and a pinch of sea salt before closing the cover. Pressure cook for 50 minutes. Bring the pressure down and serve warm.

Sweet Rice Mochi

Mochi is the Japanese name for pounded sweet rice. It is customarily prepared in small cubes or squares and pan-fried, sautéed, or fried. It is very strengthening and delicious. It is traditionally eaten on New Year's and other special occasions. Because of its sticky quality, it is said to help couples stay together, and we had mochi at our wedding in Dallas.

We usually purchase mochi from Kendall Foods or The Bridge in 12-ounce packages and keep it on hand to use as a snack or dessert. If you are unable to purchase good quality mochi in your area (Grainaissance makes mochi on the West Coast), you can make your own. It's a wonderful activity for the entire family.

2 cups sweet rice
2 1/2 cups spring water
pinch of sea salt per cup of rice

Pressure cook as per regular rice. Release the pressure and place rice in a large wooden bowl. Using a large wooden pestle, pound the rice vigorously until all the grains are broken and the rice becomes quite sticky. This will take some time. Occasionally, wet your pestle with water and sprinkle a few drops on the rice to keep it from sticking.

When the rice has been pounded, wet your hands and form the mochi dough into small pieces (what you can hold in one hand), and place them on a cookie sheet that has been oiled or

"Ordinary fruits have a very clear separation between the seeds and fruits. The uniqueness of grains is this compact combination of both into one edible form.

"In other words, the beginning (seed) and the end (fruit) have been made into one unity.

"When we eat grains, we eat the entire world of vegetables, and we can see the wholesomeness of this entire infinite universe."
— Michio Kushi

dusted with *kinako* or rice flour. Let it sit for awhile until it becomes firm.

Mochi Puffs

Brush the skillet with sesame oil (we prefer an iron skillet). Use several pieces from the cookie sheet or cut the purchased mochi into 2-inch squares. Place in the skillet and cover. Cook over low to medium flame until it expands and puffs up. (You'll have to check it frequently). You may turn it over and brown the other side or eat it as is. Drizzle barley malt over it for a rich dessert or add a few drops of soy sauce and wrap in toasted nori for a different taste.

Mochi Waffles with Apricots

These light, fluffy waffles are best made in a Belgian waffle iron. Children love them, and parents will too.

16 ounces of mochi
sesame oil

Sauce
1 cup apricots (fresh or dried)
1/4 cup barley malt or rice syrup
1 1/2 cups spring water
pinch of sea salt
2 teaspoons kuzu

Heat waffle iron and brush with sesame or corn oil. Cut mochi into small squares or strips (1/4-inch to 1-inch to a side) and place on waffle iron with a little space between them. Close lid and wait 3 to 4 minutes. Waffles are done when mochi puffs up and comes away from the waffle iron easily.

To prepare sauce, cook fruit until soft, thicken with kuzu dissolved in a small amount of cold water, and simmer for a few more minutes.

• For variety, serve waffles with strawberries, blueberries, or other fruit or with barley malt syrup (consisting of 1 part barley malt and 1 part water heated together), apple butter, or other naturally sweet topping.

Sushi Rolls

These delicious, small spirals of seasoned rice are made with vegetables, fish and seafood, or other ingredients and enclosed with paper-thin strips of nori seaweed. Properly made, sushi is very delicious and is customarily served with soy sauce, grated ginger and wasabi, Japanese horseradish.

1 sheet nori
1 cup cooked brown rice (approximately)
1 carrot
2 scallions
umeboshi paste (optional)

Toast the nori by moving it over a medium flame for a few seconds until it turns green. Place the nori on a flat bamboo sushi mat. Rinse your hands with water to prevent the rice from sticking and spread the rice evenly over the nori leaving about 1/2 to 1 inch along the top end of the nori and 1/4 inch at the bottom.

With your fingers, make a lengthwise groove in the center of the rice. Slice a carrot into long strips about 1/4-inch thick. Blanch the carrot strips in boiling water for 1 to 2 minutes. Remove and let them cool. Cut the scallion greens into 8-inch strips and blanch them in the boiling water. Place the carrot and scallion greens into the groove you have made in the rice. Spread the ume paste along the entire length of the vegetables.

Roll the sushi mat up, pressing firmly against the rice. Make sure the vegetables are in the center of the roll.

To cut, moisten a sharp knife and cut the sushi roll in half and then each half into 2 or 3 pieces. The nori may tear or the rice stick to the knife if the blade is not sharp and wet.

After slicing, arrange the rounds on a platter or serving bowl. The cut side with rice and vegetables should be facing up.

Serve with soy sauce as a dipping sauce and fresh grated ginger and a dab of *wasabi.*

• **Japanese-Style Sushi Rolls:** Traditional favorites from Japan include rice combined separately with cucumber (*kappa-maki*), *kanpyo* (dried gourd), umeboshi plums, natto, chyrsanthemum leaves, or tofu skin (*yuba*).

• **California-Style Sushi Rolls:** On the West Coast sushi made with avocado and seafood, including crab, shrimp, and lobster, is very popular. We prefer sushi with tempeh or seitan to these high-cholesterol favorites.

Health Note
People who eat a lot of animal food, including fish and seafood, are attracted to white rice, white bread, and other polished grains. If you are eating mostly vegetable quality foods, you appreciate the taste, texture, and chewiness of whole grains.

Sweet Rice Ohagis

Ohagis are made from sweet rice that has been pounded until the grains are partially broken. They are traditionally rolled into balls and coated with nut meal (from ground nuts), puréed aduki beans sweetened with barley malt, thick puréed squash, or chestnut purée.

2 cups sweet rice
2 1/2 cups spring water
pinch of sea salt

Pressure cook rice according to basic recipe. Place in a large, heavy wooden bowl and pound with a wooden pestle until the grains are about half broken and the rice is sticky. Form the dough into balls and coat with your preferred topping or variety of toppings.

Rice Pilaf

In Charleston, the lowlands, and tidewater regions of Virginia and the Carolinas, rice cooked with vegetables was called "perlew." In the central plains of the piedmont it was known as "pielow." Early American cookbooks spelled it "pilau." Originally, rice pilaf takes its name from the Middle East. By whatever name or spelling, it is a popular dish and can be made with many ingredients. This recipe, from our home kitchen, is light, chewy, and a nice alternative to regular rice.

3/4 cup short-grain brown rice
1/4 cup long-grain brown rice
2 tablespoons lentils
1 onion, diced
1 carrot, diced
pinch of sea salt

Roast grain very lightly while heating water. Pour grain into boiling water. Put vegetables on top with a pinch of sea salt. Cook 50 minutes.

Come, Ye Thankful People, Come

All the world is God's own field
Fruit unto his praise to yield;
Wheat and tares together sown,
Unto joy or sorrow grown:
First the blade, and then the ear,
Then the full corn shall appear:
Grant, O harvest Lord, that we
Wholesome grain and pure may be.
— Traditional American Hymn

Roasted Rice with Mushrooms and a Rice Flour Sauce

Roasting produces a fluffy, chewy rice. Roasted rice is also a traditional travel food. It will keep indefinitely and does not need to be recooked or heated. In Texas, we often enjoyed roasted rice. The mushrooms and sauce make this a cooling, moist dish.

2 cups of short-grain brown rice
4 cups spring water
pinch of sea salt
1/4 to 1/2 cup mushrooms

Rice Flour Sauce
1 tablespoon rice flour
1 tablespoon sesame oil
1 cup spring water
sea salt or soy sauce to taste

Dry-roast rice in a skillet until golden, about 5 to 10 minutes. Boil the water in a saucepan, add the rice, the salt, and the mushrooms. Cover and let simmer for 50 minutes.

For sauce, oil skillet. Mix flour with cold water (1 tablespoon of flour to 1/4 cup of water), add to oil, stir until thick, add 3/4 cup water and a pinch of sea salt or soy sauce to taste, and cook a little longer. Serve over the rice.

Leftover Rice

In a temperate area or cooler season, rice will keep for about two days after being cooked. We don't like to refrigerate it as that diminishes its energy and taste. We simply put it in a ceramic bowl or wooden rice bucket and cover with a bamboo mat. In a warmer climate or during the summer, leftover rice may need to be refrigerated if not used the same day. Leftover rice can be used in many ways: plain, fried, made into rice balls, sushi, and croquettes. For basic reheating, we like to steam it in a small cast-iron skillet with just a tablespoon or two of water on top. Put on the cover, simmer for two to three minutes, and serve.

Health Note
For better health, when using leftover rice, it should be warmed up on cool or cold days. In warmer weather, it may be eaten at room temperature.

*"They who would have
the very best bread
should certainly wash
their wheat, and
cleanse it thoroughly
from all impurities,
before they take it to
the mill; and when it
is properly dried, it
should be ground by
sharp stones which will
cut rather than mash
it: and particular
care should be taken
that it is not ground
too fine. Coarsely
ground wheat meal,
even when the bran is
retained, makes de-
cidedly sweeter and
more wholesome bread
than very finely
ground meal."*
— *Rev. Sylvester
Graham, A Treatise
on Bread 1837*

Wheat

Wheat is the main grain grown in North America today, and the Grain Belt stretching from New York to Kansas, and from Saskatchewan to the Dakotas, supplies much of the world's supply. *Hard red winter wheat* makes for stronger, firmer flour and is used primarily for bread and baked goods. *Soft durum wheat* is ideal for noodles, dumplings, and pasta. In addition to these foods, wheat is also used to make *seitan* (a dynamic fresh food made from wheat gluten, soy sauce, and kombu stock), and *fu*, (dried wheat gluten cakes or sheets).

Grinding your own wheat berries at home is ideal. Next best is obtaining stone-ground organically grown whole wheat flour at the natural foods store or co-op. Stone-grinding distributes the oil from the germ and preserves the nutrients which are often destroyed by modern high-speed mills.

As noted in the introduction, eating whole grains and their products in whole form is best for day to day consumption. Several times a week, for variety and enjoyment, we like to have good quality bread and baked goods, as well as noodles or pasta, and seitan and fu. Indigestion, dyspepsia, constipation, and poor intestines have been identified as the national affliction from colonial times to the present. Eating too many delicious flour products, especially hard baked ones like bread, pies, cakes, and cookies, is a primary cause of digestive troubles, skin problems, and a rigid way of thinking. Eating whole wheat and whole wheat products in moderation is a key to continued health.

Wheat Berries with Rice

By themselves, cooked whole wheat berries are hard and require thorough chewing to digest. As a result, most people prefer to consume the berries mixed with another whole grain such as brown rice, whole oats, or barley. This is one of several basic combinations. It has just enough wheat to give the rice (or other grain) variety and a chewy texture. Soft spring wheat berries are preferred since they are easier to cook and to chew, especially if you roast or soak them prior to cooking.

2 cups brown rice
1/2 cup wheat berries

4-5 cups spring water
pinch of sea salt per cup of grain

Combine rice and wheat berries and pressure cook or boil as for regular brown rice.

Ben Franklin's Bread

In a letter to a French friend in 1785, Ben Franklin wrote, "The Flour of Mayz [corn], mix'd with that of Wheat, makes excellent Bread, sweeter, and more agreeable than that of Wheat alone." The addition of rye flour, as in the following recipe, makes traditional New England "Thirded Bread."

1/2 cup sourdough starter
1 cup whole wheat flour
1 cup cornmeal
1 cup rye flour
2 cups spring water (approximately)
1/2 teaspoon sea salt

To make starter, combine 1 cup of wholewheat flour and enough water to make a thick batter. Cover with damp cloth and allow to ferment for 3 to 4 days in a warm place.

To make bread, combine flour and salt and mix well. Add sourdough starter and enough water to form a ball of dough. Knead about 300 to 350 times, adding flour as needed as dough becomes sticky. Oil bread pans lightly with sesame or corn oil. Divide dough in half and shape into loaves. Make a shallow cut in the top of each loaf, brush with oil, and cover with a warm, damp cloth. Allow to set for 6 to 8 hours in a warm place. Bake at 350 degrees for an hour and a half. Let cool and slice.

• Raisins, walnuts, and a little sweetener such as barley malt or amasake can be added if desired.

• It's generally better to make the bread in the morning and let it rise during the warmth of the day, rather than making it at night and baking it in the morning.

"But how do you make the sourdough?" Mrs. Boast asked.

"You start it," said Ma, "by putting some flour and warm water in a jar and letting it stand till it sours."

"Then when you use it, always have a little," said Laura. "And put in the scraps of biscuit dough, like this, and more warm water," Laura put in the warm water, "and cover it" she put the clean cloth and the plate on the jar, "and just set it in a warm place," she set it in its place on the shelf by the stove. "And it's always ready to use, whenever you want it."

— Laura Ingalls Wilder, By the Shores of Silver Lake

"We had a splendid breakfast of flapjacks, or slapjacks, and whortleberries."
— *Nathaniel Hawthorne, American Notebooks*

In pioneer days, the sourdough starter was known as the firkin. *The firkin was kept in a special crock in the chuckwagon to make biscuits and hotcakes without yeast, and it kept for years.*

"No, Jud," I said sincerely, "I meant it. It seems to me I'd swap my pony and saddle for a stack of . . . brown pancakes with some first crop, open kettle, New Orleans sweetening."
— *O Henry, The Pimienta Pancakes*

East West Bread

Combining rice and wheat—the archetypal East West grains— is as American as George Washington, whose mother made him waffles prepared with hot boiled rice added to wheat flour (see dessert chapter.) Kayu is the Japanese word for soft grain, and rice kayu bread is bread made with softly cooked rice. George Ohsawa introduced this recipe, and it has become a favorite in macrobiotic households and restaurants around the world.

2 cups whole wheat flour
1/8 to 1/4 teaspoon sea salt
2 cups brown rice, softly cooked

Mix the flour and salt together. Add the soft rice and form the dough into a ball. Knead the dough 350 to 400 times, adding a little more flour from time to time to prevent sticking. Oil an 8-inch-square pan with a little sesame oil and lightly dust the pan with flour. Shape the dough into a loaf and place it in the pan, pressing down around the edges to form a rounded loaf. With a sharp knife, make a shallow slit in the top center of the dough. Place the loaf in a warm place, such as a warm radiator or a pilot-lit oven, and let sit for 8 to 10 hours. Occasionally moisten the damp towel with warm water to prevent drying. After the dough has risen, bake in a pre-heated 300- to 250-degree oven for about 30 minutes. Increase the temperature to 350 degrees and bake for another hour and 15 minutes. When done, remove and place on a rack to cool.

• Add raisins or roasted seeds into the dough for a sweeter or crunchier bread.

Pennant-Winning Pancakes

Pancakes are the archetypal American breakfast treat. Originally made of small cakes of unleavened cornmeal or wheat dough, they were prepared on a flat bakestone in the oven or on a griddle in an open hearth.

1 cup wholewheat pastry flour
1/4 teaspoon sea salt
1 teaspoon corn oil
1 teaspoon rice syrup or maple syrup
1 cup spring water

Mix dry ingredients and stir quickly until batter is about the consistency of cake batter. Pour into pre-heated skillet oiled with corn oil. Cook until you see bubbles on the top and the top surface looks somewhat dry. Then turn over and complete cooking on the other side. Serve warm. Top with barley malt, a warm berry sauce thickened with kuzu, or natural fruit preserves.

• Baking powder and baking soda may be added if desired.

• Hearty buckwheat pancakes can be made by combining about half buckwheat flour with half whole wheat flour.

Texas Three-Grain Muffins

Made with wheat, corn, and millet and seasoned with chickpea miso, these muffins are sweet and delicious. In Texas-style weather, you may even want to add a little apple juice.

1 cup whole wheat flour
1 cup cornmeal
1/2 cup millet, cooked
1/4 cup onions, diced
1 heaping teaspoon, chickpea miso
1 tablespoon (or less) corn oil
spring water and/or apple juice (optional)

Combine ingredients, ladle into oiled muffin tins, and bake in moderate oven for about 30 minutes.

Apple Pecan Muffins

These muffins are a big hit morning, noon, or night.

2 cups whole wheat flour
1 cup oat flour
1 1/2 tablespoons corn oil
1/4 teaspoon sea salt
1 3/4 cup apple juice
spring water
1 large apple, diced
pecans to garnish

Combine ingredients, put in an oiled muffin tin, and garnish with pecans. Bake in a moderate oven (350 degrees) for 1 hour.

In Praise of Bread

"Let [the artist] relish the taste of fair water and black bread."
— *Emerson*

"I made a study of the ancient and indispensable art of bread making, consulting such authorities as offered, going back to the primitive days and first invention of the unleavened kind, when from the wilderness of nuts and meats men first reached the mildness and refinement of this diet."
— *Thoreau*

"We had bread and fruit for dinner. I read and walked and played till suppertime. We sung in the evening. As I went to bed, the moon came up very brightly and looked at me."
— *Louisa May Alcott, Diary, age 10*

Noodles with Watercress and Tofu

8-ounces of whole wheat noodles (udon)
4 ounces tofu, cut into small cubes
1/2 bunch of watercress
soy sauce to taste
spring water

Steam or boil tofu in separate pan. Watercress should be dropped into boiling water for 1 to 2 minutes and removed; if cooked longer, it becomes tough and bitter. Cook the udon in 4 to 5 quarts of rapidly boiling water until done but not soggy. Drain and rinse in cold water. Place in serving bowls with squares of tofu on top and place the cut watercress as garnish. Pour light soy sauce broth over for seasoning and serve hot.

Fried Noodles with Ginger

16 ounces whole wheat noodles (udon)
3/4 cup cabbage, shredded
1/2 cup carrots, cut into matchsticks
4 ounces tofu, cut into small squares
1/2 cup onion, cut into half-moons
scallions, thinly sliced
1 teaspoon ginger, grated
sesame oil
spring water

Place about one gallon of water in a large pan and bring to a rolling boil. Add noodles, cook for about five minutes, add two cups of cold water (this is the cold shock method), and cook a few more minutes. Drain and rinse in cold water.

Cut the vegetables and set aside. Add a small amount of sesame oil to the skillet and heat. Add the vegetables and tofu and sauté quickly, leaving them crisp. Add the noodles and a small volume of liquid. Cover and simmer for two to three minutes. Then mix the noodles in with the vegetables, adding soy sauce to taste. At the end, a small amount of grated fresh ginger or scallion may be added to each serving. The adventurous may prefer a slight sprinkling of red pepper.

• Seitan may be substituted for tofu for variety, and different vegetables may be used, though it's best to avoid those that are watery such as bok choy, mung bean sprouts, etc. If broccoli is used, it should be cut in thin pieces.

• Other tasty combinations: Mushrooms, yellow squash, broccoli, onion, carrot, cauliflower (just a few slices), and a hint of garlic.

• Mock Fried Noodles can also be made by water-sautéing. Put sliced cabbage and thinly sliced carrots in a skillet with 2 to 3 tablespoons of water and simmer until tender, about 5 minutes. Then put cooked and rinsed noodles on top and steam for a few minutes. Add a few drops of soy sauce and stir. This gives a nice oil-like consistency for those who have to watch their oil intake.

Yankee Doodle went to town,
Riding on his pony,
He stuck a feather in his cap,
And called it macaroni.
— Yankee Doodle

Noodle and Chickpea Salad

This is a crispy, light, very delicious dish that we enjoyed at our home in Dallas. It may be served warm or cool.

1 cup chickpeas, cooked with kombu
1 onion, diced
1 carrot, diced
1 stalk celery, sliced thinly
1 cup whole wheat elbow or ribbon noodles, cooked
1/2 cup whole wheat couscous, cooked
spring water

Dressing
1 teaspoon tahini
1 teaspoon umeboshi vinegar or umeboshi paste
1/2 cup spring water

Boil beans until tender. Dice vegetables and blanch for 1 to 2 minutes in 1 inch of boiling water in a saucepan. Cook the elbow noodles and the couscous separately. (Follow instructions on the package, usually about 5 to 10 minutes). Then mix the chickpeas, vegetables, noodles, and couscous and serve with dressing.

Corn, Fu, and Celery Casserole

This light, sweet dish is another Southern favorite.

3 ears of fresh corn with the kernels removed
3 rings of fu
1 stalk celery
spring water

pinch of sea salt
1 level tablespoon kuzu

Soak fu until soft and cut into small pieces. Strip kernels of corn from the cob with a knife and cut the celery. Put the celery on the bottom of a casserole dish or large saucepan, then the corn, and finally the fu. Bring to a boil. Add a pinch of sea salt and cook for about 10 minutes. At the end, dissolve kuzu in cold water, add a dash of umeboshi vinegar to balance the sweetness, and stir into fu and vegetables to thicken.
• A piece of sourdough bread may be substituted for fu if it isn't available in your area.

Tofu Noodle Casserole

This casserole is also made with elbow noodles and has a crispy, nutty taste.

1-2 cups elbow or shell noodles
1/2 cup onion, thinly sliced or diced
1 cup carrots, diced
1/2 cup celery, thinly sliced
1 cup broccoli, sliced
2 1/2 cups spring water
pinch of sea salt

Sauce
8 ounces tofu
1 teaspoon red miso
1 teaspoon umeboshi paste
2 teaspoons tahini
soy sauce
spring water

Bring spring water to a boil and add a pinch of sea salt. Add the noodles and cook about ten minutes (cooking time will vary with thickness of noodles). Boil the vegetables separately until done but still crisp. Separately crumble the tofu, add the ume paste, miso, tahini, and enough water to form a paste (3 to 4 tablespoons). Combine the cooked noodles, vegetables, and the sauce and gently mix. Put in a baking dish and bake in a moderate oven about 350 degrees for 10 minutes.

"I refuse to believe that trading recipes is silly. Tuna-fish casserole is at least as real as corporate stock."
— Barbara Grizzuti Harrison, article in McCalls 1975

Ecology Note
In U.S.D.A. studies, organic wheat farmers in New York and Pennsylvania used 30 percent less energy per acre than conventional farmers using chemical fertilizers and pesticides.

Homemade Seitan

Seitan is also known as wheat gluten or wheatmeat. It is a high-protein food traditionally enjoyed in China, Japan, and the Far East. Its dynamic taste and strong energy make wonderful cutlets, veggie burgers, kebabs, and other "meaty" dishes.

Seitan is now widely available in natural foods stores, but the homemade variety is fresher and more tender.

2 cups whole wheat flour (hard winter wheat preferred)
4 to 5 cups spring water
3-inch piece of kombu
1/4 cup soy sauce
fresh ginger

Place flour in a large bowl. Add enough water to make it the consistency of a cookie dough. Knead until it forms a smooth ball. Cover with warm water and let sit for at least 10 minutes.

Knead again in the soaking water until the water becomes cloudy. Then remove the dough and knead it in a bowl of cold water. Keep repeating this procedure, rinsing with warm water then cold water, until the bran and starch are washed out and the dough is a smooth, glutinous ball. (Save part of the rinse water to thicken other dishes if desired.)

Separate the ball into 5 or 6 smaller pieces of dough. Drop balls in boiling water to which soy sauce, kombu, and a few slices of fresh ginger have been added and simmer covered for 30 to 40 minutes. When cooled, you may store the seitan with the liquid in a jar in the refrigerator for several days.

Seitan with Sauerkraut and Onions

Sauerkraut gives seitan a rich, satisfying taste, without being too salty.

8 ounces of seitan, sliced into 1-inch strips
1 onion, sliced
1-2 tablespoons sauerkraut

Put a few drops of sesame oil in a hot skillet, sauté the onion for about five minutes, and add the seitan and sauerkraut on top. Cook for another few minutes, then mix, and serve.

"The best bread-makers I have ever known watch over their bread troughs while their dough is rising, and over their ovens while it is baking, with about as much care and attention as a mother watches over the cradle of her sick child."
— Sylvester Graham

Seitan au Mochi Gratin

Mochi—pounded sweet rice—added to casseroles makes a rich, crunchy, delicious topping—something like melted cheese. This is one of our favorites, again combining seitan and sauerkraut.

8 ounces seitan, sliced into strips
2-3 tablespoons sauerkraut
1-2 carrots, sliced thinly and lightly boiled
mochi, sliced into 1/4 x 2 x 3-inch strips
spring water

Brush skillet with oil, slice sauerkraut and put a small layer across the pan, add a second layer of lightly boiled carrots, and a layer of seitan, and then cover with sliced mochi. Steam with 2 to 3 tablespoons of water on top of the stove until mochi is melted. Serve warm.

Barley

The Pilgrims brought many seeds with them on the *Mayflower*, but only barley came up. For many years, barley supplemented corn as the principal grain in New England and was used in cereals, soups, and stews, in making bread and baking, and in making beer. The fertile Connecticut River Valley was more hospitable than the rocky soil of Cape Cod and much of the rest of New England and by the mid-seventeenth century supplied the Mass Bay with thousands of bushels. Later, Scandinavians and other immigrants introduced hardy winter barley which grew during the cold months and adapted more readily to the environment.

Today a variety of organically grown barleys is available. We prefer the heavier ones that have not been pearled for regular use. Pearling is a form of refining in which the aleurone, or outer layer of endosperm, is removed. Pearled barley, however, should not be confused with pearl barley, or *hato mugi*, a grain traditionally grown in the Far East which has many medicinal uses.

Barley gives light, upward energy and is very calming and cooling. With whatever foods it is combined, it gives a more soothing vibration. We have rice with barley (see rice section) as our main grain once or twice a week and use barley in many ways.

Hearty Barley Stew

1 cup barley
l medium onion, diced
l medium carrot, diced
l-2 cups buttercup squash, cut into small chunks
1 handful green beans, thinly sliced (optional)
3-4 cups spring water

Wash and cut vegetables, setting aside in separate bowls. Wash barley. Layer in a sturdy pot with a lid the onions, carrots, squash, and barley. Add water by gently pouring into the pot along the side. Reduce flame and cook until barley is almost done. Then add the slivered green beans and a pinch of sea salt. Cook for another 10 minutes. Serve in individual bowls garnished with scallions or parsley or in a family-sized bowl as the occasion requires.

Millet

Millet is eaten around the world, from China, Africa, and Hunzaland where it is the traditional staple, to India, Central Europe, and Canada where it is a supplemental crop. Millet comes in many types and colors. The common American variety is yellow; many Asian and African varieties are red. Millet's small, compact grains and ready adaptation to cold, northern environments make it a very strong, energizing grain. In fact, it is more energizing than rice, and we use it often, by itself, or cooked together with rice, especially in the autumn and winter and on cooler days. Millet also stimulates creativity and in our experience leads to many practical insights and discoveries. Until the sixteenth century, about 90 percent of all human inventions—from farming implements to the compass, from printing to silkweaving—came out of China, particularly the millet-growing regions. Millet arrived in the New World with the early colonists and it was planted along with corn. In this country, it is sometimes known as Indian grass, hog grass, or Turkish wheat. In modern society, the use of millet in cooking has declined; it is used primarily as birdseed. In the era to come, it will be rediscovered and honored as one of humanity's priceless treasures.

"It seems that not only did a significant percentage of the African slaves originate in millet-raising societies, but an equally significant percentage may have been involved in millet farming immediately before embarking."
— *Robert Hall, "Savoring Africa in the New World"*

Fluffy Millet

1 cup millet
3 cups spring water
pinch of sea salt

Place millet and water in a saucepan with the salt. Cover pan, bring water to a boil, and reduce heat. Simmer over low flame until soft and fluffy, about 30 minutes.
   • Various vegetables such as carrots, butternut squash, cauliflower, or onion may be added for variety.

Millet with Onions and Yellow Squash

This is a light, sweet, moist dish we enjoyed in the summer and early autumn in Texas.

1 small onion, diced
1 yellow squash, sliced
3-inch strip of wakame, pre-soaked
1/2 to 2/3 cup millet
2 cups spring water
miso to taste

Layer onion, squash, and millet and bring to a boil, turn flame to low, and cook for about thirty minutes. Just before done, add diluted miso, and simmer for 3 to 4 minutes.

Golden Millet-Squash Porridge

This very sweet and delicious dish turns a deep orange and makes a wonderful breakfast cereal.

1 cup millet
1/3 butternut squash, cut into chunks
pinch of sea salt
1 teaspoon soy sauce
3 cups spring water

Combine ingredients and pressure cook or boil for thirty minutes. Serve with a garnish of scallions or parsley.
   • A nice variation is soft millet cooked with parsnip and carrots.

"Eating no meat, [the enslaved Allmuseri of Africa] were easy to feed. Disliking property, they were simple to clothe. Able to heal themselves, they required no medication. They seldom fought. They could not steal. They fell sick, it was said, if they wronged anyone. As I live, they so shamed me I wanted their ageless culture to be my own..."
— *Charles Johnson, Middle Passage*

Millet with Rutabaga

l cup millet
l small rutabaga, cut into chunks
3-4 cups of water
pinch of sea salt

Layer the rutabaga and millet, and pour water gently along the sides. Place over fire and when the water is warm, add a pinch of salt. Cook for about 40 minutes. Garnish with scallions.

Deep Fried Millet-Rice Balls

leftover rice cooked with millet
sesame oil
kanako (soybean powder) or unbleached flour

Form millet-rice into balls by pressing them with your hands, much like you make rice balls. These should not be too large; otherwise, the inside will not be warm when cooked. Experiment but try to make them about 2-inches in diameter initially.

In a separate deep fryer or saucepan, put about 3 inches of sesame oil. The pan should not be too full as the oil tends to bubble up once the grain balls are added. Heat the oil over a medium sized flame, then gently lower one ball at a time into the hot oil. It's best to wait a minute or two after adding each ball so that the temperature of the oil remains relatively hot. As they begin to brown, you can turn them gently with wooden chopsticks. When they are light brown and crisp on the outside, remove them from the oil and let them drain on a paper towel to remove excess oil.

Serve millet balls warm with a splash of soy sauce and a small side dish of grated daikon or grated red radish to aid in digesting the oil.

Oats

Oats arrived in America with an English sea captain who settled in one of the islands off present-day Massachusetts in 1602. His fields flourished, and the Pilgrims, who arrived almost two decades later, followed his example. As in Scotland, where it is a

---

Mormon Doctrines and Covenants

14. All grain is ordained for the use of man and of beasts, to be the staff of life, not only for man but for the beasts of the field, and the fowls of heaven, and all wild animals that run or creep on the earth. . . .

18. And all saints who remember to keep and do these sayings, walking in obedience to the commandments, shall receive health in their navel and marrow to their bones.

19. And shall find wisdom and great treasures of knowledge, even hidden treasures.

20. And shall run and not be weary, and shall walk and not be faint.

principal grain, oats have been enjoyed in America ever since as a nourishing breakfast porridge, a thickening agent for soups and stews, and in flour form as a tasty ingredient for bread, muffins, and cookies. At home we enjoy whole oats on cold (and not so cold) mornings and also occasionally have Scotch oats and oatmeal. Like barley, oats give a nice upward energy and are very energizing.

Old Fashioned Oatmeal

Whole oats, like our grandmothers used to make, are very warming and delicious. Ideally, they are cooked in a heavy saucepan overnight over a low flame. If time is a factor, it can be made more quickly by cooking from 1 hour to 3 hours. Here is a quick method for modern households.

1 cup whole oats
4 cups spring water
1/4 teaspoon sea salt

Wash grain and soak for several hours. Place in a pressure cooker with water and sea salt. Bring to pressure, reduce heat, and cook for 1 hour. Garnish with roasted nori.

Whole Oats and Whole Barley

This combination of grains makes a delicious, chewy morning cereal.

1 cup whole oats
1 cup whole barley
9-10 cups spring water
1/4 teaspoon sea salt

Wash grains and soak for several hours. Place in a large pot over fire and bring to a boil. Place flame deflector over burner, reduce flame, and simmer for several hours until grains are soft and creamy.

"It's not the horse, but the oats that pull the cart."
— Traditional Proverb

Quick and Tasty Oatmeal

Rolled oats are quick, convenient, and good for on the road or visiting other people.

1 cup rolled oats
2 1/2 cups spring water
pinch of sea salt
1-2 tablespoons raisins

Place oats, raisins, and salt in a saucepan and bring to a boil. Reduce heat and simmer, covered, for 15 to 20 minutes.

Rye

Today rye is best known as the basis of dark ethnic breads, the main ingredient in a type of whiskey, and the title of J. D. Salinger's book, *The Catcher in the Rye.* For many centuries, rye played a prominent role in European and early American cooking. New England's famous brown bread, a staple for generations, was originally made of rye and cornmeal. Later, the Dutch cultivated rye extensively and used it liberally in their cereals, breads, and baked goods. We enjoy rye for its chewiness. Because it is harder than most grains, we use it sparingly and usually in combination with other foods.

Rice with Rye

By itself, rye is hard and so usually it is combined with other grains. We like rice cooked with about 20 percent rye.

2 cups brown rice
1/2 cup rye
4 cups spring water
pinch of sea salt

Grains should be pre-soaked or the rye should be roasted, as it is difficult to chew. Place grains in a pressure cooker, add water and sea salt. Bring to pressure, lower the flame, and cook for 50 minutes.

Health Note
Finnish men have one-third the colon cancer of American men, yet eat as much fat. Medical researchers found that the main protective factor was the high amount of whole rye eaten by the Finnish men.

Corn

Corn comes in many varieties and colors. *Flint corn*, which the Northern Indians and Pilgrims used, has hard kernels, matures early, and takes a lot of grinding. *Dent corn*, favored by native people in the South and Southwest, has soft kernels, matures late, and is easier to grind. It received its modern name from the small dent on the top of each kernel after drying. It is used for making *masa*, cornmeal, and corn flour. *Flour corn*, with its soft starchy kernels, is also used primarily for baking. *Popcorn*, a traditional native snack, explodes when heated owing to its hard outer layer. *Sweet corn*, with the largest proportion of sugar to endosperm, is the most widespread type available today. It is usually yellow or white. Traditional blue, red, black, speckled, and other colored corn are slowly being revived and are available in some natural foods stores or by mail order. In our home, we enjoy corn year round, fresh in the summer and fall, and dried or ground into meal or flour in the winter and spring. However, because most corn today is hybrid, including organic corn, and not as vitalizing as traditional standard or open-pollinated varieties, we usually serve another whole grain at the meal in addition to corn. Grinding your own corn, of course, is ideal. Next best is obtaining *masa* that has been made from whole corn or stoneground cornmeal or corn flour which has not been degerminated.

In addition to the usual ways of preparing corn and making dough, native peoples traditionally leavened it with ashes (made of juniper, cedar, or other fragrant wood) and by chewing. This masticated corn, mixed with ashes and salt, and left to ferment by the hearth was considered the best leavening. Its Aztec name was *chica*, and macrobiotic friends today who are accomplished chewers may wish to experiment with this method.

Fresh Corn on the Cob

Fresh corn on the cob is the quintessential American dish. It has been enjoyed by the Native Peoples, settlers in New England and Virginia, and every generation of Americans since. Benjamin Franklin wrote to his wife how much he missed Indian corn and defended it in a letter to a London newspaper which had cast aspersion on American cuisine. The infant country's other ambassador, Thomas Jefferson, grew it in his garden in Paris. Fresh corn on the cob can be boiled, steamed, baked, or grilled. Traditionally it was eaten fresh from the

"It's up to you. I have nothing here. I live simply. All I have is my planting stick and my corn. If you are still willing to live as I do, and follow the road plan which I shall give you, you may live here and take care of the land. And you will have a long, happy, and fruitful life."
— *Massau, Hopi Creator*

fields and cooked in its husk. The silky tassles retained the natural sweetness of the grain. Sometimes it was soaked in the husk so that the steam produced by roasting would enable the kernels to absorb the flavor of the burnt husks. In macrobiotic households today, small pieces of fresh umeboshi plum or umeboshi paste are customarily rubbed on fresh corn to give a tangy, slightly salty taste.

4 ears fresh corn in the husk
umeboshi plum

Place corn in oven and bake for about 30 minutes over medium to hot heat. Husk and serve. Take an umeboshi plum and rub the fleshy part on the corn or use umeboshi paste.

• Fresh corn may also be grilled for about 15 minutes on a hot stone or griddle.

• In a saucepan, fresh corn may be boiled or steamed in a small volume of water (1/2 inch) for about 7 to 10 minutes on a medium flame.

Creamy Corn Grits

Grits have been a favorite from the time of the Jamestown colonists to Jimmy Carter's presidency. Their name is believed to be a contraction of "groats" or "good groats." They are light, quick to prepare, and nourishing. The white corn variety is favored in the South, and the yellow corn variety in the North. We are partial to Southern style and enjoy grits about once a week for breakfast.

1 cups grits
3 cups spring water
pinch of sea salt

Add grits and salt to boiling water. Cover saucepan, reduce flame, and simmer for about ten minutes. Serve with sliced scallions, parsley sprigs, or roasted pumpkin seeds for garnish.

• Add a drop or two of unrefined corn oil for a richer, smoother taste.

• A teapoon of miso diluted in water may also be added the last two minutes of cooking for stronger seasoning.

• Leftover grits can be reheated or fried into small fritters.

On the First Thanksgiving Day

On the first Thanksgiving Day,
Pilgrims went to church to pray.
Thanked the Lord for sun and rain,
Thanked him for the fields of grain.
Now Thanksgiving comes again:
Praise the Lord as they did then;
Thank him for the sun and rain,
Thank him for the fields of grain.
— Traditional Hymn

"We had the first of a very relaxed and informal series of meals with our family. Earlier, when Rosalynn was visiting the White House, some of our staff asked the chef and cooks if they thought that they could prepare the kind of meals which we enjoyed in the South, and the cook said, 'Yes, Ma'am, we've been fixing that kind of food for the servants for a long time.'"
— Jimmy Carter, White House Diary

Corn Grits with Fresh Corn

1 cup grits
3 cups spring water
1 ear of fresh corn with the kernels removed
chickpea miso to taste

Combine grits and fresh corn and salt in boiling water, reduce flame, and simmer about 10 minutes. Add diluted miso to taste the last 2 or 3 minutes of cooking. Serve with garnish of sliced scallion or toasted black sesame seeds.

Southern Style Cornbread

Cornbread is another Southern favorite. Traditionally it was made with just cornmeal, salt, and water and baked in shallow pans and cut in squares. When it came North, Yankee households added sugar and wheat flour and often milk and eggs. In many parts of the South today, basic unsweetened cornbread is still the rule.

This basic style of making cornbread results in a moister, chewier texture than most modern cornbread recipes. It's especially appreciated by those who are older or who have difficulty chewing.

1 1/2 cups cornmeal
1/2 cup whole wheat pastry flour
1/4 teaspoon sea salt
2 tablespoons corn oil
3 cups spring water

Pre-heat oven to 375 degrees. Lightly oil an iron skillet. Heat water in separate pan. Mix cornmeal, pastry flour, and sea salt in mixing bowl. Add corn oil and work into flour mixture with fork or fingers until the oil is evenly distributed. Pour hot water into the mixture. Stir quickly and pour into skillet. Cook for 35 minutes or until the top is lightly browned.

Sweetened Cornbread

Cornbread is naturally sweet, but because today's cornbread mixes are sweetened with sugar, some people are used to a sweeter flavor. Here's a recipe using all natural ingredients.

1 1/2 cups cornmeal
1/2 cup whole wheat flour
1/4 teaspoon sea salt
1 tablespoon corn oil
2 tablespoons brown rice syrup
3 cups spring water

Combine ingredients with water into a batter, pour into a baking dish, and bake at 375 degrees for 35 minutes.

Millet Cornbread

2 cups cornmeal
1 cup whole wheat flour
1 small onion, diced
1 tablespoon sesame or corn oil
1 cup pre-cooked millet
1/4 teaspoon sea salt
3 cups spring water

Combine ingredients, mix with water to form a batter, spread into baking pan, and bake in hot oven (350 to 400 degrees) for about 35 minutes.
  • For variety, add 1 cup fresh corn in place of the millet.

Hopi Bread

The blue-grey tissue-like bread eaten by the Hopi of the South-west is made of blue corn and is known as piki. *Ground finely and leavened with wood ashes, the cornmeal is mixed with boil-ing water. Then it is formed into a dough that is spread thinly on a hot rock or baking stone which has been oiled with crushed sunflower or squash seeds. After cooking, Piki is rolled or folded and eaten.*

2 cups fine blue cornmeal
1 cup boiling spring water
1 cup cold water
2 tablespoons of ash (optional)
cold water to moisten

Add boiling water to cornmeal, stirring constantly to prevent lumping. Mix ash (traditionally from the juniper tree) into cold water and add to mixture, continuing to stir. Add additional

"His earliest memory was of swinging on a rung of the ladder to the loft. As he put his early sensations to-gether into a narra-tive, he recalled (mov-ing backwards in time) mimicking farm animals, splash-ing into the creek without having to take off any clothese (because all he had on was a shirt), and be-ing fed 'corn-meal mush' with an oyster shell for a spoon."
— William S. McFeely, Frederick Douglass

"The sprouts of corn are like little children. If we don't sing to them, they may turn their faces away and stop growing."
— *Hopi farmer*

cold water to desired consistency of batter. Ladle batter with a spoon onto hot oiled skillet. When brown around the top and outside, separate from skillet around the sides. Remove with pancake turner, roll up, and keep covered until all are done and ready to serve.

Tortillas with Vegetables and Tofu Sour Cream

Tortillas are the flat bread of the Southwest. Traditionally, they are made with masa, *or whole corn dough. In the natural foods store, ready-made tortillas made with organic cornmeal are widely available. These are not as hearty as the original but are enjoyable from time to time, filled with beans or vegetables from land and sea. Here is one of our favorite combinations. This dish is a nice accompaniment to brown rice and black beans.*

4 corn tortillas
1/2 cup broccoli, sliced
1/2 cup onions, thinly sliced
1/2 cup cauliflower, sliced
1/2 cup yellow squash, thinly sliced
sesame oil
soy sauce to taste

Tofu Sour Cream
1 cup tofu
1 teaspoon sweet rice vinegar
1/4 teaspoon sea salt
1/4 teaspoon umeboshi paste or 1 small umeboshi plum

Cut vegetables in very thin slices so they will cook quickly. Brush the skillet lightly with sesame oil and stir-fry the vegetables, adding soy sauce just before they are done. Warm tortillas in iron skillet. Place vegetables inside tortillas and roll. Spoon tofu sour cream over the tortillas and garnish with chopped scallions.

To prepare tofu sour cream, crumble the tofu and blend with above ingredients in 1/4 cup of spring water until smooth. Simmer 2 to 3 minutes over low flame.

• Vegetables may be varied in this dish. Arame is very good in tortillas.

For you these Tamales, these heavy Tortillas, This offering of Tortillas, many Tortillas, Tortillas wrapped in leaves, a heavy offering of Wrapped Tortillas, cut in two, cut in three, For many days, for many years.
—*Lacadone Prayer*

Whole Corn Arepas

Arepas are corn balls made of masa that have been boiled, baked, or fried. A staple throughout the Southwest and Central and South America, they are easy to prepare and make excellent travel food. We usually pan-fry them in a skillet without oil, but for a richer taste a little sesame or corn oil can be used.

4 ounces masa (whole corn dough)
spring water to moisten
sea salt to taste

Divide masa into four parts, add salt and moisten with water, and form by hand into small ovals about 2 inches in diameter. Place in hot skillet, lower flame, cover, and simmer for about 10 to 15 minutes. Turn over with a spatula or with cooking chopsticks and let other side cook for another 10 or 15 minutes. Serve warm.

Hominy

Hominy is more coarsely ground than grits, though sometimes it takes the form of whole soaked, deskinned corn kernels. It takes its name from the original native name *rockahominie*. Hominy makes a tasty morning porridge.

Hoecakes a la Thoreau

One of the simplest and oldest corn recipes, hoecakes are made by cooking fresh corn in the husk directly in the ashes or coals of a hot fire. Originally they were made outdoors in the fields on hoes and other farm implements. Thoreau made hoecakes out of cornmeal when he lived on Walden Pond and savoured their piney flavor.

Hush Puppies

Hush puppies are corn balls that have been deep-fried. Traditionally in the South they are eaten with fried fish.

"Bread I at first made of pure Indian meal and salt, genuine hoecakes, which I baked before my fire out of doors on a shingle or the end of a stick of timber sawed off in building my house."
— *Thoreau, Walden*

I sang there—I dreamed there—I was suckled face downward in the black earth of my western cornland.
I remember as though it were yesterday how I first began to stand up.
All about me the corn—in the night the fields mysterious and vast—voices of Indians—names remembered—murmurings of winds—the secret mutterings of my own secret boyhood and manhood . . .
And all this in the long cornfields.
And then in the fall, the crackling of corn leaves, the smells, sights and sounds.
The corn stood up like armies in the schocks.
— Sherwood Anderson, from Mid-American Chants

Zuni Water Balls

The Zuni and other native peoples of the Southwest enjoyed boiled cornbreads and dumplings. Anthropologist Frank Cushing learned this recipe when he lived with the Zuni in Arizona in the late nineteenth century.

1 cup fine cornmeal
1 cup coarse cornmeal
sea salt
cold water

Mix equal parts of the two meals or flours, add salt and water, and by kneading form a stiff dough. Divide into small round balls and add to boiling water. Instead of disintegrating, the balls will become harder with cooking. When the water becomes pasty, pour the cornballs and fluid into a bowl of pottery or other serving dish. Customarily served with a brine sauce, they can be dipped like sushi in a little soy sauce for taste.

Corn Dumplings

Another Zuni dish, these were made, according to Cushing, "by hulling corn, then grinding it with water, precisely as colors are ground by artists with oil." The fine, sticky batter, seasoned with lime, was wrapped in broad corn shucks, carefully folded over, tied at the ends, and then boiled. When done, the batter resembled a hard gelatin. Cushing notes that the Zunis cooked these dumplings in large quantities, since they took intricate preparation, and when cold they could be reheated by roasting on the embers or baking in the hearth.

Corn Polenta

Polenta is a casserole made of corn and vegetables. It is popular in Europe as well as parts of this continent. This is a typical dish, whose ingredients are limited only by the imagination of the cook.

l cup cornmeal
3 to 3 1/2 cups waer
l carrot, diced
l onion, diced

pinch of sea salt or soy sauce to taste

Lightly roast cornmeal in skillet; slowly add water and stir to keep from sticking. Bring to a boil, stirring frequently until thickened. Add carrots and onions, lower flame, and simmer for 30 minutes. You may need to continue stirring during this time. Toward the end of cooking, add sea salt or soy sauce for seasoning. This may be served hot as a porridge or poured into an oiled dish and allowed to cool. Once cool, it can be sliced and pan-fried in sesame oil until golden and served with a nice sauce.

Salmon Croquettes

Salmon is traditionally eaten in the Pacific Northwest, Alaska, and other colder regions of North America. These croquettes, made with rice, millet, and cornmeal, temper the strong yang energy of this red-meat fish, but will still make you want to leap around and be outdoors for the rest of the day. Makes 5 to 6 medium-size croquettes.

1/2 cup fresh salmon, pre-cooked
1 cup rice with millet, pre-cooked
1/4 cup celery, minced
1/4 cup scallions, sliced
cornmeal
sesame oil

Crumble the salmon into small pieces, mix in the rice cooked with millet, the celery, and the scallions. Add a few spoonfuls of cornmeal. Mix and shape into patties. Pan-fry on both sides in a small amount of oil over a medium-high flame.

Serve with grated daikon and mustard sauce. The mustard sauce is made with mustard and soy sauce with a few spoonfuls of water.

• For variety, serve with a sweet and sour sauce (see recipe in chapter 5).

Health Note
The two healthiest communities in North America are the Tarahumara Indians of Mexico, noted for their marathon running and their traditional diet of corn, beans, and squash, and modern macrobiotic people.

In Boston, Dr. Castelli, director of the Framingham Heart Study, found that people eating macrobiotically had healthier hearts than trained atheletes. "What a person eats everyday is a very important aspect of how his or her health will be everyday as well as in later life. Supporting this view is the fact that macrobiotic people studied had a [total cholesterol to HDL cholesterol ratio] ratio of 2.5 and Boston marathon runners were at 3.4, ratios at which rarely, if ever, is coronary heart disease seen. Studies and observations such as these are a clear indicator that people need to take a critical look at their diet with the intention of making changes now."

Wild Rice

Known as *menominee* or "good grain" among the Chippewa and Winnibegos, wild rice grows in the freshwater lakes and ponds of the upper Great Lakes region. It is traditionally harvested by hand from tall marshy grasses by the women and girls of the community and used in special dishes for ceremonial occasions. Freshly picked wild rice has a black color tinged with purple and when cooked has a slightly smoky aroma. Because of its scarcity and high cost, wild rice is used sparingly. In our home in western Massachusetts, as in many kitchens across the nation, wild rice is served on Thanksgiving and other holiday events. It may be prepared by itself, cooked with brown rice or other grains, or be added to soups, stews, and casseroles for extra taste, color, and fragrance.

Wild Rice Croquettes with Miso-Tahini Sauce

These croquettes are very chewy and delicious. The wild rice gives them a wonderful fruity flavor that is very different from wild rice that is boiled or pressure-cooked.

2 cups brown rice and 1/2 cup wild rice, pressure cooked together
1/2 carrot, grated
1 scallion, finely sliced
2 tablespoons whole wheat pastry flour
sesame oil

Sauce
1 tablespoon miso
4 tablespoons tahini
1/4 cup spring water

Mix rice, wild rice, grated carrot, and sliced scallions together with pastry flour. Form into balls and then mold into patties about 1/2-inch thick. Pan-fry in sesame oil until each side is browned.

For sauce, mix miso and tahini. Gradually add water to form sauce. Heat gently over low flame for a few minutes. Grated daikon can be served as a condiment.

Buckwheat

Buckwheat is the hardiest of the cereal plants. A member of the same family as sorrel, rhubarb, and dock, it is native to Siberia, Mongolia, Russia, and other northern regions. Its name comes from *bockweit*, the Dutch word for "book wheat," in honor of the Holy Bible whose inspiration, it was said, guided this wonderful plant to their land. Dutch and German settlers brought buckwheat to New Amsterdam and Pennsylvania.

In America, buckwheat is known by various names such as Antelope Brush, Bee's Bonnet, Napkin Ring, Indian Tobacco, Whisk Broom, Spotted Turban, and Desert Strumpet. Today buckwheat grows wild in many parts of the country, and few people who see its pretty white flowers and heart-shaped leaves realize how strong and energizing a food it produces. We enjoy *kasha*—toasted buckwheat—and *soba*—traditional Japanese style noodles made with 50 percent or more buckwheat flour—in the winter or on cold days. However, at other times, even a spoonful of this amazing grain can make us too yang. If we want to spend all morning cleaning house, move heavy furniture, chop wood, or do other hard physical activity, we cook buckwheat or soba. Otherwise, we respect its strong energy and use it wisely and in season.

Kasha and Cabbage

1 cup buckwheat groats
1 cup diced cabbage
2 1/2 cups spring water
pinch of sea salt

Roast buckwheat in a dry skillet for about 5 minutes, stirring gently to prevent burning, and remove from skillet. Place cabbage on the bottom of a saucepan, cover with the buckwheat, and slowly add water. Add sea salt and cover. Reduce flame and simmer for 25 to 30 minutes. Serve with chopped parsley, scallions, or toasted nori as a garnish.

"The buckwheat and Indian cornmeal are come safe and good. They will be of great refreshment to me this winter; for since I cannot be in America, everything that comes from thence comforts me a little, as being something like home."
— Ben Franklin, letter to his wife from London

The buckwheat cake was in her mouth,
The tear was in her eye.
Says I: "I'm coming from the South, Susanna, don't you cry."
— Stephen Foster, "Oh Susanna"

Sorghum

Though the world's third biggest cereal grain crop after wheat and rice, sorghum is almost unknown in America except as the source of molasses and as an animal feed called *milo*. Native to Africa, where it is the traditional staple in many regions, sorghum came West with slavery and grew in the West Indies and American South. Sorghum is also grown extensively in dry parts of China where it is known as *kaoling*. It is a very versatile grain and can be used for porridge and usual grain dishes, as well as ground into flour for bread and baked goods, and fermented into beer and wine. The basic recipe is 2 cups of water and a pinch of sea salt to 1 cup of sorghum.

Teff

Teff is a tiny grain native to East Africa. It is brown and when cooked looks something like chocolate. In Ethiopia teff is ground into flour, fermented for several days, and made into a traditional large, flat bread called *injera*. Teff has recently become available in natural foods stores in North America, and we have just begun to experiment with this unique grain.

Teff Cereal

Teff has a very soft consistency. The basic recipe makes a nice morning porridge. Sweetened it can be made into a pudding or dessert. Teff is also customarily used in a wide variety of breads and baked products such as cookies and muffins.

1/2 cup teff
3 cups spring water
pinch of sea salt

Place grain and salt in a saucepan, add water, and bring to a boil. Reduce heat and simmer until done, about 30 minutes.

Health Note
Whole grains and other foods high in complex carbohydrates are recommended for women and girls with premenstrual difficulties. Medical studies show "improved depression, tension, anger, confusion, sadness, fatigue, alertness, and calmness."

Amaranth

Amaranth is native to Central and South America and was identified by Columbus on his first visit to the Bahamas. It is remarkably adaptable, growing in almost any environment. At the Kushi Institute in Becket, its tall, wavy stalks and purple blossoms look out over fields of adjoining wheat and barley.

Amaranth has very fine, sand-colored grains and in cooking tends to add bulk or texture to other grains or foods.

Brown Rice with Amaranth

Amaranth has a nutty flavor, and we occasionally enjoy it in small volume cooked with rice.

1 3/4 cups short-grain brown rice
1/4 cup amaranth
4 cups spring water
pinch of sea salt

Add amaranth to rice and pressure cook or boil in the usual way.

Quinoa

The Incas called quinoa, their staple, "the Mother Grain," and it is traditionally grown in terraced fields in Peru, Equador, Bolivia, and other pacific coastal highlands of South America. Today it is also grown in the mountainous regions of North America including the Pacific Northwest, British Columbia, and Colorado and New Mexico.

Quinoa can be enjoyed by itself or mixed with other grains. It may also be used in baking and combined with beans, vegetables, and other foods.

Quinoa Porridge

We enjoy quinoa added to other grains or as a soft morning cereal.

1 cup quinoa
pinch of sea salt
3 cups spring water

Put grain and salt in a saucepan, add water, bring to a boil, reduce heat, and cook for about 30 minutes or until soft.

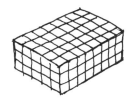

"For Purple Mountains Majesties"

3
Beans and Sea Vegetables

It is commonplace to talk about mountains of beans. Seaweed is not so given to metaphors, though occasionally it is used as in the Willa Cather quotation in the margin. Like the invisible ridges in the oceans, seaweed exerts a strong influence on the global ecosystem as a whole. By this token, aduki, kidney, and other purplish-red beans and nori, dulse, and other purplish seaweeds are poetically linked with the national image of towering terrestrial forces and swirling subterranean currents of life.

Relative to other foods, beans are more yin—slightly larger than grains, with more fat and protein—while seaweeds are more yang—more contracted than land plants, with higher concentrations of minerals and vitamins. Traditionally, beans and seaweeds are often cooked together to make balance. Just a small piece of kombu will soften and make more digestible an entire pot of beans. Gas—or flatulence—the major stigma of beans in modern society completely disappears with proper cooking, as well as general strengthening of the intestines and thorough chewing. Beans cooked in the macrobiotic style are

121

Cooking Times

Soft Beans such as lentils, mung beans, split peas 45 minutes (boiling) or 30 minutes (pressure cooking)

Medium Beans such as pinto, kidney, navy, lima, black, and turtle 2 hours (boiling) or 1 hour (pressure cooking)

Hard Beans such as adukis, chickpeas, and soybeans 2-3 hours (boiling) and 1 - 1 1/2 hours (pressure cooking)

Soak medium and hard beans from 1-2 hours for pressure cooking and 2-4 hours or overnight for boiling.

Add salt or other seasoning when beans are about three-quarters done and let cook in for at least 15 minutes.

A Gift of Beans Burned in the Name of the Gods

Here are the first beans!
I give them to you, oh Lord.
I shall eat them.
— Prayer by the Lacadone, descendents of the Maya

soft, tender, delicious, and satisfying.

Beans and seaweed (discussed in more detail further in this chapter) make up about 5 to 10 percent of the daily diet, about one or two small servings or side dishes. Small beans have less fat and protein than large beans and are easier to digest. The standard macrobiotic dietary approach recommends smaller beans such as adukis, chickpeas, lentils, and black soybeans for daily consumption and medium and larger beans such as pinto, navy, kidney, and lima for occasional use (altogether several times a month). Bean products such as tofu, tempeh, and natto are suitable for everyday use, while beans that have been partially processed (and thus lower in energy and nutrients) such as split peas fall in the infrequent category. While it is important to have a small volume of food from the bean category every day, too much should be avoided.

Preparing tasty and well-cooked beans is an art, and one that is quickly learned when animal products are not the main source of protein. Beans are usually soaked for several hours (see chart in the margin) to increase digestibility and reduce cooking time, with the exception of lentils, split peas, and other light beans which can be rinsed and cooked directly. Usually, we do not cook the beans in their soaking water, as this tends to give a bitter taste. In addition to cooking beans with a small piece of kombu (1 to 2 inches square as noted above), cooking beans without the lid on for a few minutes and skimming off the foam increases their digestibility.

Boiling is the basic way of preparing beans, especially the cold-shocking method (explained in the margin on next page). This gives strong uplifting energy. However, pressure cooking (which is usually reserved for whole grains) gives strong gathering energy and cooks quickly, reducing overall cooking time by 50 percent or more. We use it occasionally. Baking is another popular method, especially in traditional New England baked beans. We enjoy it on holidays and special occasions. Because baking is so yangizing, baked beans are customarily sweetened with a little barley malt, maple syrup, or other sweetener.

Beans may be seasoned with sea salt, miso, or soy sauce. We add the salt about 10 to 20 minutes before the end of cooking. We add miso or soy sauce about 3 to 4 minutes before serving and simmer gently. Variety in seasoning is important. We prefer to use sea salt for digestibility, sometimes adding a little rice miso or soy sauce for flavor.

Beans in modern society are often cooked with hot spices and herbs. While a tiny hint of spice may be appropriate in a hot, humid climate or at higher elevations, as a rule we do not spice our beans or any other foods in a four-season climate. Very rarely, on a scorching hot day in Dallas we might add a little chili powder to black beans for a cooling effect. Or in Santa Fe, New Mexico, which is at an elevation of 7000 feet, a pinch of herbs may help open the lungs. But these are exceptions. Spices and most herbs are extremely yin and historically have been used to balance meat, poultry, fish, and other strong yang animal food. Beans are generally yin to begin with and their energy is not offset with spices—they are made even more yin. In general, spices expand the nervous system, creating excitability and forgetfulness. In a tropical environment, they are cooling and relaxing and help to balance the penetrating year round heat. We prefer to avoid them in a temperate climate.

There are hundreds of beans native to North America, including pinto, red Mexican, and scarlet runner beans (which played a prominent role in Hopi mythology and dances). Early people such as the Narragansett baked beans in pits lined with hot stones and sometimes sweetened them with maple syrup. The Pilgrims learned this technique and gradually incorporated local beans into their diet. As in England, the main legume in America among the colonists continued to be peas. Pease porridge or pottage, made in heavy pots hung over the hearth fire, later gave way to an earthenware pot that retained the heat long after the beans had cooked. Boston baked beans—as this famous dish became known—grew out of the Puritans' commandment to refrain from cooking on the Sabbath. In this way, the beans remained warm from Saturday till Sunday evening without having to be reheated.

Chickpeas

Chickpeas—the staple bean of Southern Europe, North Africa, and the Middle East—were the first beans brought to the New World. They played a unique role in the continent's destiny. On his return voyage to Spain in 1493, Columbus ran into a terrific storm in the mid-Atlantic. Fearing that his ships would go down and all news of his findings be lost, he made a vow that if he were allowed to reach home, one of his crew would make a religious pilgrimage. The crew drew lots, made up of chickpeas, and Columbus himself drew the marked bean. Whether this was a portent of divine favor or a sign that he should incorporate more beans into his diet, the storm subsided and the small vessels safely made land.

The Shocking Method
This long, slow method of cooking beans, alternating hot and cold water, will bring out the beans' natural taste.

Put soaked beans in a cast-iron pot, add 2 1/2 cups of water per cup of beans. Bring to boiling very gradually and set a small lid on top of the beans that fits inside the pot.

The lid will jiggle when the water comes back to a boil. At this time, remove lid and gently add just enough cold water to stop the boiling. Pit the lid back in. Continue to "shock" beans like this until 80 percent done. Then add seasoning, remove cover, and cook until done, adding more cold water when needed. When beans are soft, turn up the heat to boil off any extra liquid.

Health Note
In traditional medicine, beans are said to nourish the kidneys. However, too many beans can tighten these organs. This is why we often cook beans together with sweet vegetables such as squash or carrots, onions, and parsnips.

"For this purpose, [Columbus]commanded as many chickpeas to be taken as there were persons in the ship, and that one should be marked with a knife, making a cross, and that they should be placed in a cap and well shaken. The first to put in his hand was the admiral, and he drew out the pea marked with the cross, and so the lot fell to him, and from that moment he regarded himself as a pilgrim."
— *Columbus's Journal, Feb. 14, 1493*

Chickpeas with Vegetables

This makes for a sweet, delicious, substantial winter stew. We serve it over millet, with broccoli on the side.

1 cup chickpeas, soaked
3-inch piece of kombu
1 small carrot, diced
1 small onion, diced
1/2 cup parsnips, sliced
1 cup cabbage, chopped
pinch of sea salt
1 tablespoon sweet barley miso (or soy sauce)
3-4 cups spring water

Pressure cook chickpeas with kombu for 45 minutes. Let pressure down. Add the vegetables and sea salt. Cook 10 minutes more or until vegetables are tender. Add miso at end and simmer gently for 4 to 5 minutes.

Lentils

Lentils are native to the Middle East and figure prominently in the Bible. Ordinary lentils are olive green or light brown in color, cook up quickly, and make delicious soups and stews. We are especially fond of baby green lentils which are about half the size of ordinary lentils and give a slightly different texture. Red lentils are also small and fine, cooking up like split peas. We enjoy them from time to time by themselves or combined with other beans and grains. See the soup chapter for basic recipes.

Aduki Beans

Adukis—the small red beans traditionally eaten in the Far East—contain less fat and protein than most beans and are extremely nourishing. A staple in macrobiotic households around the world, they are now grown organically in Ohio and other parts of North America. The Japanese variety (from the cold northern island of Hokkaido) gives very strong energy and, though more expensive, is recommended for medicinal use. We enjoy aduki beans several times a week: as soup, a side dish, cooked together with rice, in ohagis, or in other forms.

Aduki Beans with Squash and Kombu

This is a very sweet, delicious dish and one of the principal bean dishes recommended by Michio in his consultations.

2 cups squash, cut into cubes
1 cup aduki beans, soaked
3-inch strip of kombu
spring water

Soak kombu, cut into small squares, and put on the bottom of a saucepan. Wash and peel the squash (we prefer butternut) and place over the kombu. Layer soaked aduki beans over the squash. Add water by gently pouring into the saucepan until squash and beans are about half covered. Cook until soft but not mushy, about 60 minutes. If desired, add a small volume of soy sauce at the end.

Gale's Becket Baked Beans

New England baked beans were originally made with pea beans, Jacob's cattle, yellow eye, or soldier beans, but almost any small, hard bean will do. If a sweeter taste is desired—to help balance the yang method of baking—a little barley malt can be added. This recipe, using navy beans and ginger, is a Becket original.

1 cup navy beans (or other hard bean)
2-3 cups spring water
1/4 teaspoon sea salt
1 carrot, thinly sliced or diced
1 teaspoon fresh grated ginger
1-2 tablespoons barley malt
1 teaspoon mustard powder (optional)

Soak beans 6 hours or overnight. Pre-heat oven to 300 degrees. Pour out soaking water. (Beans cooked in soaking water often turn out bitter). Place beans in a large kettle with water and simmer gently for 30 minutes. Skim off froth and discard. Add salt, mustard powder, natural sweetener, and thinly sliced carrot. Pour into bean pot or heavy casserole with cover and place in oven, on the bottom rack. Bake 2 hours, and add additional soy sauce and ginger if desired.

• Instead of barley malt, brown rice malt, rice syrup, or barley malt powder may be added.

Ecology Note
"[The native peoples] plant a Bean in the same Hill with the Corn, upon whose Stalk it sustains itself [and] sow'd Peas sometimes in the Intervals of the Rows of Corn."
— Robert Beverley, The History and Present State of Virginia 1705

Health Note
Scientists report that a diet high in soybeans reduces the incidence of breast cancer in laboratory experiments. The active ingredient in the soybean, protease inhibitors, is also found in some other beans and seeds.

Soybeans

Soybeans are among the most nourishing and versatile beans. The staple of Eastern cooking for thousands of years, they are eaten primarily in the form of tofu, tempeh, natto, and other naturally processed products that reduce the beans' high fat and oil content and make them more digestible. In America, soybeans were first reported cultivated in 1804, and dried tofu was imported from Hong Kong to San Franciso in 1852. However, it took another century and the influence of Chinese, Philippine, and other Oriental immigrants for soy to enter the national consciousness. In the early part of the century, the Seventh Day Adventists began experimenting with soyfoods as a dairy replacement, and soybeans began to be grown extensively for oil and for use in livestock feed. In the 1940s, tofu was made by Japanese-Americans in detention camps in the West. In the '60s and early '70s, macrobiotics popularized miso, tofu, and tempeh—a traditional fermented soybean cake from Indonesia. Today these foods, made from organic soybeans grown in the United States, are available in natural foods stores and many supermarkets from coast to coast. They are being incorporated into school lunch programs and hospital diets as a healthy substitute for dairy foods. While tofu, tempeh, and other soyfoods can easily be made at home (see *Aveline Kushi's Complete Guide to Macrobiotic Cooking* for recipes), hundreds of shops—including many large soy dairies—are now making high-quality organic soyfoods available to millions of Americans.

Aveline Kushi's Soybean Stew

This rich, delicious, thick stew is one of Aveline's favorite dishes. The beans are soft and strengthening.

1 cup soybeans, soaked
3-inch piece of kombu
1 onion, diced
2 squares of dried tofu, pre-soaked in 1/2 cup water and 1/2 cup soy sauce
1 carrot, diced
2 1/2 to 3 cups spring water
1 teaspoon miso

Soak soybeans for 6 hours. Dice onions, dried tofu, and carrots.

Layer kombu, onions, tofu, and carrots in pressure cooker. Bring to pressure and cook for 30 to 40 minutes. Let pressure down, add sea salt, and simmer for 10 more minutes. Add puréed miso and simmer gently for several more minutes.

• Add trout or other white-meat fish at the end for a hearty fish stew or seitan for a different flavor.

Tofu

At first tofu looks and taste strange to most Americans, and so it did to us. But as you experiment and discover its ability to absorb flavors and tastes, assume different shapes, sizes, and textures, and combine well with many foods, you quickly become hooked. For an artistic cook, it is the raw material out of which many wonderful sculptures can be created. We use it often in soups, stews, in vegetable and noodle dishes, in sandwiches, and in sauces and dressings. Because it is more yin—soft, light, cooling, and relatively high in fat and oil—tofu should be cooked, if only for a minute or two, or marinated with miso or soy sauce. At the natural foods store or coop, there are often different types of tofu available. *Firm tofu* is harder and is used for dishes in which the cubes or slices are meant to keep their shape. *Soft or silky tofu* is usually puréed in a *suribachi* for sauces and dressings or crumbled by hand for scrambled tofu, casseroles, and other dishes in which foods blend together. *Dried tofu*—made at home or available ready-made in thin, dry cakes that are soaked in water—is more yang than fresh tofu. It has an entirely different taste and texture—both appealing—and is customarily used in hardy soups, stews, and root vegetable dishes.

Tofu Medley

8 ounces of tofu, cut in small squares
1 cup cabbage, diced
1 medium carrot, diced
1 small leek, thinly sliced
3-inch piece of kombu
1-2 teaspoons barley miso

Rinse the tofu and cut into small squares. Soak small strip of kombu and cut into squares. Place on the bottom of the pan. Add tofu, carrots, leeks, and cabbage which have been cut into sizes compatible with the tofu. Add water to cover and boil for

Storage Tip
Fresh tofu will keep for about a week submerged in an open container of water that is changed daily or every other day and kept refrigerated or in a cool place.

15 to 20 minutes. Remove some of the broth to purée the miso. Add the miso back into the pot. If you like, you may add a small amount of kuzu mixed with cold water to thicken the stew. Simmer for five minutes after adding the miso but do not boil. Serve warm with a main dish of whole grains or unleavened sourdough whole wheat bread.

Tofu with Vegetables

2-inch strip of kombu, soaked
8 ounces tofu, sliced into 1-inch pieces
1 small onion, cut into six pieces
4-6 broccoli flowerettes
1 carrot, cut in thin diagonal slices
4 slices nappa cabbage, cut in 1-inch strips
2 1/2 cups spring water
2 teaspoons miso

Place kombu and water in a saucepan, bring to a boil. Reduce heat and simmer several minutes. Remove the kombu. Drain and slice tofu. Place tofu, onion, broccoli flowerettes, and carrot into the water and cook over medium flame for 5 minutes. Add puréed barley miso and the nappa cabbage. Simmer for 3 to 4 minutes more. Serve in individual serving bowls with grated ginger and chopped scallions.

Fried Tofu Sandwiches

Children and adults will love these tasty sandwiches.

1 pound of tofu, sliced into 1/4-inch slices
1/2 cup soy sauce
1/2 cup spring water
1 teaspoon grated ginger
1 tablespoon lemon juice or rice vinegar
sesame oil
whole wheat bread and trimmings

Slice tofu and place in shallow dish. Mix remaining ingredients and pour over tofu. Marinate for several hours. Sauté in lightly oiled skillet for several minutes on each side. Serve on whole wheat bread with lettuce, sprouts, grated carrot, and cucumber or wrap in one and a half-inch strips of nori and serve as a finger sandwich.

Scrambled Tofu

This is another scrumptuous dish, especially good for breakfast and to introduce new friends to familiar looking foods.

1 pound of tofu
sesame oil
1/2 cup scallions, chopped
1 small carrot, cut into matchsticks
1/2 cup mushrooms, diced
1 cup of fresh corn kernels (when in season)

Heat a small amount of oil in a skillet. Add mushroom and sauté 1 to 2 minutes. Next sauté the carrots and corn and finally the scallions. Crumble tofu over vegetables. Reduce flame and simmer for 5 minutes. Season with soy sauce or chopped umeboshi plum, simmer again for 3 to 4 minutes, and serve.

Tofu Cheese I

Pickled tofu has the look, texture, and taste of cheese—without the saturated fat, cholesterol, and animal protein. Since tofu is high in vegetable-quality protein and fat, you may wish to pickle or marinate it from time to time and then fry it.

1 pound of tofu
1 pound of miso (approximately)

Spread a half-inch layer of miso on the bottom of a pie plate, shallow bowl, or stainless steel pan. Place tofu on top of the miso. Cover with remaining miso. Cover with cheesecloth or a plate and let sit for several hours. Before serving, scrape off the miso. (The miso may be kept and reused for this purpose.) Slice into 8 pieces, fry in a little sesame oil, and serve with rice or noodles or other dish.
  • Natto chutney miso imparts a nice flavor to the tofu.

Health Note
The Journal of the American Dietetic Association reported that in tests with preschoolers, the quality of tofu recipes in school lunch programs adhered more closely to national dietary guidelines than beef, chicken, eggs, and cheese and the children accepted the tofu well, preferring it to dairy and meat in several dishes including macaroni and cheese, lasagna, tuna casserole, and quiche.

"Need anything from the store? Bean curd? Tofu?"
— McGyver TV Series

Tofu Cheese II

Tofu cheese may also be made with seasonings other than miso and with a slightly lighter effect. This is a favorite.

1 pound tofu
2 teaspoons umeboshi paste
1 teaspoon tahini
1 teaspoon brown rice vinegar
12-inch square of good quality cheesecloth

Mash the tofu with a fork. Combine ume paste, tahini, and vinegar. Add umeboshi mixture to the tofu and combine very well. Put this in the middle of the cheesecloth and tie the corners or secure with a rubber band. Bring 1 cup of water to a boil and put the cheesecloth package in it. Reduce heat and simmer for 15 minutes. Remove tofu and drain well, then refrigerate to chill thoroughly. Open the package when you are ready to use it. Break it into clumps and use like feta cheese in salads, sandwiches, and casseroles.

Dried Tofu Stew with Vegetables

Dried tofu is slightly more strengthening than regular tofu. We especially enjoy it in late fall and winter with vegetables.

1 onion, diced
1/2 daikon, thinly sliced
1/4 head cabbage, shredded
1 carrot, thinly sliced
1/2 small buttercup squash, cut into cubes
3-4 squares dried tofu, cut into cubes
3-inch piece of kombu
1 teaspoon miso
1 tablespoon kuzu
3 cups spring water

Soak kombu, bring to a boil in the spring water, and cook for 5 minutes. Soak the dried tofu in a mixture of two-thirds water and one-third soy sauce for about 20 minutes. Add the tofu and the vegetables and cook for about 15 minutes until tender but not mushy. Season lightly with miso and if a thicker broth is desired, mix kuzu with cold water and add just before the end of cooking. Simmer 5 minutes to allow the mixture to thicken. Stir gently. Serve warm.

*Behold this compost!
Behold it well!
Perhaps every mite has
once form'ed part of
a sick person—yet
behold!
The grass of spring
covers the prairies,
The bean bursts noise-
lessly through the
mould in the gar-
den,
The delicate spear of
the onion pierces up-
ward,
The apple-buds cluster
together on the ap-
ple-branches,
The resurrection of the
wheat appears with
pale visage out of its
graves.
What chemistry!
— Walt Whitman*

Tofu Kebabs with Soy-Ginger-Kuzu Sauce

From Texas to Maine, macrobiotic families and friends enjoy tofu or tempeh kebabs at barbeques, picnics, and other special occasions. This recipe makes 4.

Kebabs
8 ounces firm tofu, cut into 8 cubes
8 carrot slices, cut on the diagonal
4 radishes, cut in half
8 broccoli flowerettes
spring water
sesame oil
soy sauce

Marinade
1 cup spring water
1 tablespoon barley miso
1 teaspoon rice vinegar
1/2 teaspoon mustard

Sauce
1 tablespoon soy sauce
1 tablespoon chopped scallion
2 teaspoons kuzu
3/4 cup spring water
1 teaspoon ginger juice

Marinate tofu pieces in mixture of spring water, puréed miso, rice vinegar, and mustard for at least 1 hour. (Tofu may also be marinated in equal parts of soy sauce and water.)

Remove from marinade, drain, and sauté lightly in a skillet brushed with sesame oil. Set aside. Wash and cut vegetables and boil one at a time in rapidly boiling water for 4 to 5 minutes until tender but crisp.

Alternate pieces of vegetables with tofu on a wooden skewer. Place in a platter or on individual serving dishes and cover with soy-ginger-kuzu sauce.

To make sauce, mix water, soy sauce, and scallion in a skillet. Before heating the water, dissolve the kuzu in water and add to the mixture. Bring to a boil, reduce the heat, and simmer until liquid becomes clear. Grate ginger and squeeze the juice into the sauce. Pour over kebabs and serve.

• Tempeh or seitan may be substituted for the tofu.

"Pounding beans is good to the end of pounding empires."
— Emerson

Tempeh

Tempeh gives a rich, dynamic taste, strong energy, and is a good way to digest beans. We use it several times a week in stews, cooked together with sauerkraut and cabbage, in cabbage rolls, in sandwiches, added to fried noodles or fried rice, and in other ways. Made traditionally with rice and soybeans, inventive American tempeh makers are now introducing tempeh made with millet, barley, and other grains and with other beans.

Chunky Tempeh Stew

1 cup onions, cut in chunks
2 cups butternut squash, cut in chunks
**2 cups rutabaga, cut in smaller chunks than the squash
    and carrots**
1 cup carrots, cut in chunks
2 cups cabbage, cut in chunks
2 cups bok choy, thinly sliced
4 cups spring water
1 pound tempeh, cut into 2-inch squares
2 tablespoons barley miso
1-2 teaspoons kuzu

Wash vegetables. Remove peeling from squash. Cut root and round vegetables into chunks. Slice bok choy thinly. Cut tempeh into 2-inch squares and sauté in skillet until brown on both sides. Layer onions, bok choy, cabbage, rutabaga, squash, and carrots in a large stew pot. Spread tempeh on top.

Half-cover with water (about 4 cups) and cook 30 minutes until vegetables and tempeh are almost done. Add sea salt and cook until vegetables are tender. Purée miso and add to pot. Dissolve kuzu in 2 tablespoons cold water and add to the pot. Stir and simmer 3 to 4 minutes.

Tempeh Squash Stew

This sweet, delicious thick stew is good anytime, but is especially warming in the fall or winter.

1 onion, cut in chunks
1/2 buttercup squash, cut in chunks
1 pound tempeh, cut in chunks

Health Note
Tempeh is a good source of Vitamin B_{12}, with an average serving containing from 50 to 210% of the recommended daily allowance. Other fermented soy products including miso, soy sauce, and natto, also contain Vitamin B_{12}, as do sea vegetables.

Tempeh is also an excellent source of calcium—higher than any other bean or bean product.

1/2 cup cabbage, sliced
2 to 2 1/2 cups spring water
1 teaspoon miso
1 teaspoon kuzu

Boil tempeh and vegetables together for 10 to 15 minutes. Add diluted miso and simmer for 3 to 4 minutes. Add a little kuzu diluted in cold water at the end for thickening.

Tempeh-Leek-Carrots in Kuzu Sauce

8 ounces tempeh, cut into squares
2 leeks, thinly sliced
2 medium carrots, thinly sliced
spring water
1-2 teaspoons kuzu

Cut the tempeh into squares and brown in an oil-free iron skillet or brush the skillet lightly with oil. Remove from skillet. Wash and cut the leeks and carrots and sauté them slightly and then place the tempeh on top. Add water to partially cover. When the vegetables are tender and the tempeh is done, remove them from the skillet. Using the leftover broth, add kuzu (dissolved in cold water) and stir until thickened. Season with soy sauce to taste. Serve over the tempeh and vegetables.

• A small clove of garlic cooked with the leeks makes a nice addition to this stew.

Tempeh Melt

The mochi gives this dish the texture and taste of grilled cheese. It tastes better when prepared in an iron skillet or heavy pot that has a lid.

8 ounces tempeh, cut into 1 x 2-inch squares
1 large onion, diced
1/2 cabbage, shredded
1-2 carrots, cut into matchsticks (optional)
1/2 cup sauerkraut (adjust to taste and family's condition)
8 ounces mochi
sesame oil
spring water
soy sauce

*Health Note
During World War II, prisoners of war in the Pacific who ate tempeh were less susceptible to dysentery and other tropical diseases.*

Cut tempeh into squares and sauté on both sides using a small amount of sesame oil. Remove from pan. Layer onion, cabbage, carrots, and tempeh in skillet, half cover with water, and cook over low heat for 20 minutes. Add the drained sauerkraut over the tempeh. (If desired, season lightly with soy sauce.) Cut mochi into thin slices and place on top of the vegetables. Cover so the heat will soften the mochi, giving the look of melted cheese. Serve immediately in the skillet.

Sticky Natto

Natto, a fermented soy product that looks like a cake of tempeh with long, sticky strands, is excellent for digestion. Because of its unique, strong odor, some people do not like natto. Others, ourselves included, really enjoy it.

While it can be made at home, we generally purchase natto in the natural foods store and warm it in a skillet with a few teaspoons of water or sesame oil for 5 to 10 minutes. It is nice served with a garnish of sliced scallions and seasoned with soy sauce. Fresh grated ginger may also be added at the end of warming. Stronger condiments such as mustard may also be used occasionally with natto.

Black Soybeans

Well cooked black soy beans are very strengthening and deli-
cious. We enjoy this dish often.

2 cups black beans
1/4 teaspoon sea salt per cup of beans
5-6 cups spring water

Wash and soak the beans overnight in water to which sea salt has been added to keep the skins from peeling. Cook, uncovered, until the foam arises. Discard the foam, then cover, and continue cooking for 2 1/3 to 3 hours. Skimming the foam helps prevent gas when eating the beans.

Add root vegetables 20 to 30 minutes before beans are done and season with soy sauce or purée the mixture for black bean soup.

• Add a small volume of barley malt for a sweet flavor.
• In Texas we added a little chili powder to this dish for a cooling effect.

Kidney Bean Surprise

This dish gives a nice red, orange, and green color and a soft, rich taste. We enjoyed it often while living in Texas.

1 cup kidney beans, soaked
3-inch piece of kombu
1 medium carrot, diced
1/4 teaspoon sea salt
2 1/2 to 3 cups spring water

Soak beans overnight. Pressure cook with kombu. After 45 minutes add chopped carrots and sea salt and cook for another 10 minutes without the top on.
•Add celery, onions, parsnips, or other vegetables as desired.

Red Beans and Ricey Yours,
—Louis Armstrong's salutation at the end of his letters

Sea Vegetables

Known by many names—seaweed, sea vegetables, sea holly, sea grass, sea lettuce—plants from the sea have been an integral part of humanity's diet from time immemorial. Today they are eaten primarily in Japan, China, Korea, Hawaii, and other Asian and Polynesian societies. But historically, seaweeds are an important article of diet in Europe, Africa, the Middle East, Australia, and North and South America. Native peoples from Alaska to the Caribbean islands, from the Atlantic seaboard to the California coast, traditionally harvested common edible varieties including dulse, tangle (kombu), kelp, and sea palm.

In a way, the European discovery of the New World can be attributed to seaweed. Columbus constantly monitored the seaweed his ships encountered along the way, and he used the sighting of rockweed on September 17, 1492, to convince his mutinous crew that land was close at hand. On Cape Cod, the Pilgrims learned the value of seaweed from the Narragansetts who used it steaming corn, baking clams and seafood, and in other types of cooking. In the 1800s, dulse—the native purple-red seaweed—had become so popular that dulse chips that had been fried, baked, or deep-fried were hawked in the street by vendors and sold at railroad stations. Before baking powder was introduced, many immigrants from Europe continued to use the refined ash of *barilla*, a Spanish seaweed, to leaven their bread. In Louisiana and other parts of the deep South, Irish moss was

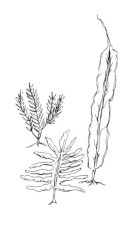

used in Southern and Creole cooking as a thickener in soups and stews, as a cooling gelatin, and as a base for medicinal drinks and beverages. On the West Coast, seaweed and rockweed continued to be used in coastal and riverine cuisines by the gold diggers, the Oregon Trail pioneers, and their descendents. In the 1880s, Park Davis, and Co. introduced tangle—a common name for kombu—into the pharmaceutical trade as a secret ingredient against obesity.

In the twentieth century, the fortunes of Neptune's harvest faded in North America, Europe, and other industrial regions as dairy food spread, refined table salt (fortified with iodine extracted from seaweed) replaced natural sea salt, and the modern artificial vitamin, mineral, and supplement industry grew. In fact, the rich taste and smooth, creamy texture of dairy food eclipsed the subtle flavor and irregular texture of seaweed. Even today, many people who embark on macrobiotics find it hard at first to enjoy seaweed. With time, however, as the taste buds naturally rebalance by eating grains and vegetables and the body discharges old dairy deposits, sea vegetables become one of the most satisfying—and most anticipated—foods in the macrobiotic way of eating.

In our home, we use sea vegetables daily—in miso or other soup, as a small side dish, as a small square cooked with grains or beans, in noodle broth, cooked together with land vegetables, in gelatins, in sushi, in medicinal beverages, and in other forms. Sea vegetables are an incomparable source of minerals and vitamins. Unlike plants that grow on land, plants in the sea constantly bend and sway creating strong, flexible energy that is especially nourishing for the heart and circulatory system and for the brain and nervous system. The sea is an age-old symbol of the unconscious. Eating sea vegetables and sea salt daily enables us to plumb the secrets of natural order and attain new levels of awareness.

Modern macrobiotics reintroduced sea vegetables to North America, and until recently most of the seaweed available was imported from Japan. However, as its benefits became recognized, individuals and families began to forage their own and native seaweed companies sprang up on both coasts. Today delicious, high-quality kombu, kelp, nori, dulse, and other sea vegetables—including sweet kombu, sea palm, ocean ribbons, and other varieties found in North American waters but not in the Orient—are available. Pioneers such as Larch Hanson, founder of Maine Sea Vegetables, and Betsy Holiday and Victor Marren of Ocean Harvest, are supplying America with this buried treasure. In modern food, seaweed is beginning to reappear in everything from ice cream to hamburgers. By the new century, we hope that this wonderful food source will be available in whole form in supermarkets, restaurants, hospitals, and schools. It is truly one of our nation's most precious heritages.

Wakame or Alaria

The most frequently used sea vegetable in miso soup, wakame is a long, thin green seaweed that cooks up relatively quickly. It may also be used in salads, ground into a condiment, and used in other ways. Known as alaria or escalenta in the West, the central ribbons of wakame were traditionally removed and served like string beans. Twelve species are found on the North Atlantic coast from northern Massachusetts to Labrador, some up to 20 feet long.

Wakame-Cucumber Salad

1 cup wakame
1 large cucumber, quartered lengthwise and sliced
1/4 cup red radish, thinly sliced
1 tablespoon brown rice vinegar
1/4 to 1/2 teaspoon sea salt

Rinse wakame, soak for 10 minutes, drain, and cut into small pieces. Place one-half inch of water in a saucepan and bring to a boil. Simmer radishes for 1 minute and remove. Simmer wakame for 1 to 3 minutes and remove. Mix sea salt with rice vinegar and add to wakame, cucumbers, and radish. Put in pickle press for 1 to 2 hours. Remove, rinse off excess salt, and serve.

Kombu or Tangle

Known as tangle, wrack, oarweed, and kelp in the West and as kombu ("delight") in the East, the Lamanaria family of seaweeds is one of the largest and most nourishing. It was traditionally used in the British Isles and in Russia, where it was customarily fried and served with cabbage and beets. We use kombu daily cooked in small squares with whole grains and beans and with vegetables, especially *nishime* dishes. Please see these recipes for ways to incorporate this monarch of the ocean in your daily cooking.

Storage Tip
Sea vegetables should be stored in a clean, dry area or in a sealed container if the air is humid.

Don't refrigerate kombu after you've used it in a broth. Dry it and you can use it again.

*Soaking Time for
Sea Vegetables*
Agar agar: none
Arame: rinse
Dulse: rinse
Hiziki: 5"
Irish moss: 20-30"
Kombu: 3-5"
Nori: none
Ocean Ribbons: 5"
Sea Palm: 30"
Wakame: 3-5"

*Cooking Time for
Sea Vegetables*
Agar agar: 5-10"
Arame: 30-40"
Dulse: 5-10"
Hiziki: 45-60"
Irish moss: 30"
Kombu: 35-40"
Nori: 1"
Ocean Ribbons:10-
    15"
Sea Palm: 25-30"
Wakame: 5-10"

Nori or Laver Garnish

*Known in the West as laver and in the East as nori, this sea-
weed was a staple of whaling ships in the nineteenth century.
On long voyages, it often served as the only fresh green vegetable. On the East Coast, it is found off shore from Virginia to the
Arctic. Among the native peoples of the Northwest, red laver
was the main source of salt. Today natural foods stores carry
laver from the Atlantic Ocean and a wide variety of nori from
the Pacific and Japanese coastal waters.*

1 sheet nori

Roast a sheet of nori by quickly passing it over a flame for several seconds until it changes to a greenish color and becomes
crisp. Crumble in your hands by rubbing between the palms.
Store in a tightly closed container and use as a garnish for soups
and grains.

Arame with Sweet Vegetables

*Arame is a long, thin black sea vegetable that has a mild, sweet
taste. It is customarily prepared as a side dish or added to
soups and stews.*

1 3/4 ounces arame
1 leek, sliced
1 carrot, cut into matchsticks
spring water
soy sauce
brown rice vinegar

Brush skillet with oil, sauté the leek for a minute, and then the
carrot for 1 to 2 minutes. Add pre-soaked arame on top, half-
cover with water, and cook for about 30 minutes. Season with
soy sauce to taste (about 1 to 2 teaspoons) and a few drops of
rice vinegar. Simmer for a few more minutes and serve.
   • For variety, use scallions and lotus root, onions and corn-
on-the-cob, or carrots and tempeh.

Arame with Onions and Dried Tofu

2 handfuls of arame
2 squares of dried tofu
1 medium onion, cut into half-moons
sesame oil
soy sauce
spring water

Rinse the arame by dipping it into a pan filled with water. Let drain for a few minutes to let the moisture soak in. In the meantime, soak the tofu in a liquid of half soy sauce and half water for 15 minutes. Peel the onion and slice it lengthwise into thin half-moons. Sauté it in sesame oil for a few minutes. Squeeze the liquid from the tofu and cut it into small lengthwise strips. Add the tofu and arame and a small amount of the soy sauce flavored soaking water. Cook for about 25 minutes.

Taste to see if additional soy sauce is needed. At the very end of cooking, you may add a slight amount of juice from grated ginger for additional seasoning.

Hiziki with Vegetables

Hiziki has one of the strongest tastes among sea vegetables, and its long, black strands cook up thicker and blacker than arame. However, once you get used to it, it is very delicious and strengthening.

1 3/4 ounces hiziki
1 onion or leek, sliced
1 carrot, sliced
1-2 teaspoons soy sauce

Rinse and soak the hiziki a half hour, then drain, and cut into smaller pieces. Slice onions and carrots and layer in a skillet with the hijiki on top. Cook for 30 minutes. Season with soy sauce and simmer for a few minutes longer and serve.

• Hiziki may also be cooked with tempeh, lotus root, and other vegetables.

Health Note Kombu, nori, and other sea vegetables in the daily diet may protect women from breast cancer, according to researchers at Harvard School of Public Health.

Sweet Kombu Sesame Condiment

Also known as sweet tangle and broadleaf kelp, sweet kombu is harvested off the California coast and is distributed by American seaweed companies. We particularly enjoy it in this condiment.

6-inch piece of sweet kombu
1/2 cup unhulled sesame seeds

Roast the sweet kombu in a 300-degree oven for 8 to 10 minutes until crunchy. Wash and drain sesame seeds and roast in a skillet over medium flame, stirring constantly. Pour on plate to cool. Grind the kombu and seeds together in a *suribachi*. Serve on top of rice or beans.

Sea Palm with Vegetables

This sweet temperate-climate seaweed flourishes in the Pacific from Vancouver Island to central California. Its graceful blades make it one of the most visually appealing seaweeds and thanks to native harvesters, it has become a favorite in macrobiotic cooking from coast to coast.

2 cups dried sea palm
1 tablespoon sesame oil
1 clove garlic, crushed
1 onion, sliced in half-moons
1 yellow squash, thinly sliced
soy sauce to taste

Soak sea palm in 4 cups of warm water for 30 minutes. Drain and cut into 3-inch pieces. Heat oil, add onions, garlic, and yellow squash one at a time, sautéing about 1 minute each. Add sea palm and sauté it slightly. Add soaking water until vegetables and sea palm are about half-covered. Cover and cook for 25 to 30 minutes, adding additional water as necessary to keep the mixture moist. Season with soy sauce and simmer a few minutes longer. Sprinkle with toasted sesame seeds before serving.

Health Note
In Canada in the early 1960s, scientists discovered that kelp and other seaweeds from the Pacific and Atlantic Coasts in the diet could reduce by 50 to 80 percent the amount of radioactive strontium absorbed through the intestine and eliminate it from the body.

"The evaluation of biological activity of different marine algae is important because of their practical significance in preventing absorption of radioactive products of atomic fission as well as in their use as possible natural decontaminators," McGill University researchers in Montreal concluded.

Delectable Ocean Ribbons

Like an underwater willow tree, ocean ribbons (Lessionopsis littoralis) grow in the Pacific Basin amid sea palm and mussel beds. Their long, delicate blades give a nice sweet taste and cook up quickly like wakame. The following recipe is adapted from Ocean Harvest, a West Coast seaweed company.

2-3 strands ocean ribbons
1 1/2 cups winter squash, cut in large chunks
1 large onion, cut into 6 crescents
soy sauce to taste

Rinse and soak the ocean ribbons in water to cover for 5 minutes. Peel onions and slice. The squash should be about 2 inches in diameter. Place seaweed in the bottom of a heavy saucepan with 1 inch of water. Place the onions and squash on top, cover tightly, and bring to a boil over high flame. Reduce flame to medium and cook 10 minutes. When vegetables are nearly done, season to taste with soy sauce. Toss the ingredients top to bottom, lower flame, cook several minutes more, and serve.

Deep Purple Dulse

The most popular seaweed in the British Isles and Canada, dulse was known in Ireland as "dillisk" and in Iceland as "sol" where it was customarily chewed raw until displaced by tobacco and chewing gum. In Scotland, it was served as a popular snack. Today it is still dried, salted, and enjoyed as a crisp, crunchy snack in Nova Scotia, Labrador, New Foundland, and other maritime provinces of Canada. We enjoy it in salads, fried, boiled, sautéed, and cooked in other ways.

1/2 ounce dried dulse
1 medium carrot, thinly sliced
1 small onion, thinly sliced
1 cup spring water

Pour water into a pan and bring to a boil. Reduce heat, add onions and carrots, and cook until soft. Remove with strainer. Wash the dulse and soak for 2 to 3 minutes. Remove from water and cut into small pieces. Add to the carrots and onions, mix and serve.

Irish Moss

Known as Carragheen, Irish moss took its name from County Carragheen in Ireland where housewives in the Middle Ages discovered that its thickening properties made a tasty pudding. Immigrants brought it to America until 1835 when J.V.C. Smith, a former mayor of Boston, discovered that it grew locally and native harvesting began. See the medicinal cooking section for a recipe.

Agar Agar

Agar-agar comes in the form of flakes, cakes, or powder and is used as a thickener and for making gelatins. We include a recipe for delicious seaweed fruit kanten in the dessert section.

Common North
American Seaweeds

Angel Wing
Bead Coral
Bladder Wrack
Bull Kelp
Color Changer
Dainty Leaf
Feather Boa
Fir Needle
Green Confetti
Honeyware
Hooked Rope
Leaf Coral
Mermaid's Fan
Nail Brush
Oyster Thief
Pointed Lynx
Popping Wrack
Red Fringe
Ribbon Kelp
Sea Brush
Sea Comb
Sea Lace
Sea Whistle
Tangle
Veined Fan
Whiptube

"Across the Fruited Plain"

4
Vegetables

Several years ago, Masanobu Fukuoka, the natural farmer, came to Becket and taught that the key to a happy marriage was growing and preparing a wide variety of fresh vegetables. Of course, whole grains and beans, he said, provide the foundation of good health and a clear, peaceful mind, but vegetables were the secret to harmony between man and woman—and by extension, to parents and children and other family relations. Lack of fresh, seasonal vegetables cooked in delicious and attractive ways quickly leads to boredom, cravings, and the desire to eat out. Eating out of the home leads to separation, first mental and psychological, and later physical, as family members consciously or unconsciously become attracted to someone else and their cooking.

Traditionally, America's fruited plains are homeland to many marvelous plants—both wild and domesticated—and the cooking of native peoples, African-Americans, the early health reformers, and Southerners, in general, reflected this cornucopia of vegetables. Fall- and winter-season squash come in dozens of varieties, as do fresh beans, turnips, cabbages, leafy greens, and sprouts. Vegetables have been largely ignored in modern cooking and are usually overcooked. Recently, however, the virtues of a low-fat, low-calorie diet have popularized salad bars, stir-fries, and vegetarian and semi-vegetarian entrées.

"The greatest delight which the fields and woods minister is the suggestion of an occult tradition between Man and the vegetable."
— Emerson

"We should treat every tiny grain, every piece of vegetable, as a spiritual manifestation, and should never waste them in the process of choosing, preparing, cooking, and eating"
— Michio Kushi, The Book of Macrobiotics

143

"Pray, how does your asparagus perform?" — *John Adams, letter to Abigail Adams*

Health Note
Orange and yellow vegetables are high in beta-carotene, a nutrient that has been shown to be protective against certain cancers and coronary heart disease. Carrots, squash, rutabaga, and pumpkins are high in beta-carotene, as are green leafy vegetables including kale and collard greens.

The rules of thumb in macrobiotic vegetable cookery are simple:
• Eat locally grown vegetables (or vegetables grown in a similar climate and environment)
• Eat vegetables in season (or pickled or dried naturally)
• Every day have at least one serving of root vegetables, round vegetables, and leafy green or white vegetables.
• Two-thirds of our vegetables should be cooked The rest, if desired, may be eaten raw, or lightly boiled or pressed, in salad.
• In a temperate climate, including most of the United States and Canada, avoid vegetables of tropical or subtropical origin.

People eating a strong yang meat-centered diet are attracted to raw salads, potatoes, tomatoes, eggplants, avocados, and other very yin vegetables. In macrobiotic cooking, everyday vegetables include winter squash (butternut, buttercup, acorn, and others), carrots, onions, cabbage (green, Chinese, nappa, and others), broccoli, cauliflower, turnip, radish, daikon, lotus root, rutabaga, parsnips, Brussels sprouts, bok choy, collard greens, kale, mustard greens, scallions, leeks, parsley, and watercress. For occasional use, once or twice a week or in season, we enjoy other common garden vegetables including celery, green peas, cucumber, fresh beans, mushrooms (common and shiitake), summer squash (yellow, zucchini, patty pan, and others), chives, endive, escarole, lettuce, sprouts, and others.

Traditionally, many wild plants have been eaten in North America such as cattails, wild onions, purslane, and prairie turnip. Today macrobiotic families sometimes forage and use burdock, dandelion greens, milkweed, and other common varieties in cooking. However, wild plants tend to have strong energy and can lead to a tight, overly contracted condition if used in large volume or too frequently. In the past, some macrobiotic friends have reasoned that wild foods are more natural than their domesticated cousins and incorporated them into their daily diet—with wild, unpredictable results. We very much respect the energy of these foods and encourage you to use them wisely in small condiment-sized volume once a week or less until you are familiar and comfortable with their effects.

The standard method of cooking vegetables is boiling. This produces the most centrally balanced energy and the sweetest results. In turn, boiling is commonly divided into three types: long-time, medium, and quick boiling. Long-time boiling (known as *nishime* in the East) is used for root vegetables and typically includes a skillet of different foods, half-covered with water, and cooked over medium flame for 20 to 40 minutes. Medium boiling typically is used for a single vegetable such as cauliflower and takes 5 to 10 minutes. Quick boiling also is used primarily for single vegetables and lasts from 30 seconds to about 1 to 3 minutes.

Sautéing is another frequent method for preparing vegetables. The two basic types are water-sautéing with a small volume of water, and oil-sautéing with a teaspoon of oil or the pan lightly brushed with oil. In addition, there is stir-frying (especially tasty when prepared in a wok which can coat each piece with a little oil better than a skillet). Tempura and deep-frying, which involve more oil and produce very crisp and delicious vegetables, are used for holidays and special occasions, perhaps once a month or more frequently in cold weather, as they give strong energy and a dynamic taste.

We don't usually pressure cook vegetables because we use this strong method for preparing grains and often beans. In terms of overall variety for a meal, it is important that different cooking methods be used. Similarly, we will occasionally bake a vegetable casserole or bake a squash in cold weather. But as an everyday method of cooking, baking is too yangizing. We enjoy broiling, barbecuing, and other more yang methods from time to time. On the yin side, steaming is a quick, easy way to prepare vegetables. This can be done either in a Western metal steamer inside a saucepan or in an Eastern bamboo steamer that fits over a kettle. Steaming gives light, upward energy, and we favor it on warmer days, in the spring and summer, and for greens and lighter vegetables.

Vegetables are usually seasoned toward the end of cooking, typically about 10 minutes before the cooking is completed in the case of sea salt, and 3 or 4 minutes in the case of soy sauce or miso, and then left to simmer until done.

Ordinarily, we cook with a low to medium flame for calm, peaceful energy. With root vegetables or longer cooking, we will simmer. With stir-fries and sautéed vegetables, we will cook often with a medium or even high flame for strong, active energy. Varying the flame in this way will also reduce monotony and stimulate those who eat your food.

Vegetables provide color and are an easy way to make the meal more attractive. From red radishes to deep-orange and yellow squashes to white radishes, purple turnips, brown mushrooms, and deep green broccoli and other leafy greens, the cook has a large palette to work from. Quick boiling, in which vegetables are dipped in bubbling water for just a minute or two, will bring out the vegetable's deepest colors—in sharp contrast to the modern custom of overcooking vegetables until their hues fade away along with their taste and texture.

In this chapter, we include a selection of our favorite vegetable recipes including salads.

"Plants can exist alone; but neither animals nor men can exist without plants. Without plants, or when their balance is disturbed, the quality of life and existence declines."
— Basil Johnson, Ojibway Heritage

Health Note
Cruciferous vegetables are protective against colon cancer, the leading malignancy in the United States. Cruciferous vegetables include cabbage, Brussels sprouts, cauliflower, and broccoli.

Cooking Tip
Daikon and ginger root help the body to discharge fat. Dried daikon is especially good for dispersing deep accumulations of fat in the inner organs, while fresh grated daikon is customarily served at the meal to help digest fat and oil from fish, tempura, or deep-fried dishes.

New England Boiled Vegetables

The classic boiled New England dinner consisted of a large pot of carrots, onions, beets, and other vegetables hung over an open hearth which simmered gently for hours. The food was then served altogether in one dish. The result is similar to a boiled Far Eastern dinner in which vegetables are layered in a saucepan and allowed to cook slowly over time in a little water and their own juices. In Japan, this method is known as Nishime-style boiling. In macrobiotic cooking today, we often make boiled vegetables. In the fall and winter, this is an especially warming dish.

1 or 2 leeks
1 small butternut squash, cut in squares
1 rutabaga, cut in squares
1/4 head green cabbage, cut in chunks
6-inch piece of kombu
pinch of sea salt or few drops of soy sauce

Soak the kombu for 10 minutes then cut into 1-inch squares and place on the bottom of the pan. Wash the other vegetables and peel the squash.

Wash the leeks after cutting them in half lengthwise so that the dirt is easily removed. Cut into strips. Cut the squash and rutabaga into large squares and the cabbage into chunks. Layer the leeks, squash, rutabaga, and cabbage on top of the kombu. Add salt or soy sauce. Add enough water to cover about one-third of the vegetables; too much water will make a soggy dish. Cover and bring to a boil then reduce heat and cook over a low flame for about 20 minutes. Mix lightly and serve warm.

Onion's skin very thin,
Mild winter coming in.
Onion's skin thick and tough.
Coming winter cold and rough.
—American Proverb

Squash and Onion Nishime

2 onions, cut in chunks
1 large butternut squash, cut in large chunks
6-inch piece of kombu
spring water

Soak kombu in a bowl of water until soft, then slice into 1-inch pieces, and place on the bottom of a saucepan. Cut onions into half lengthwise and then each half into three or four pieces, depending on the size of the onions. Peel the butternut squash and cut into large chunks. Place the onions on top of the kombu and the squash on top of the onions. Add water to half-cover the onions (about 1/2 inch). Bring the water to a boil, cover, and reduce the flame. Simmer for 25 to 30 minutes or until the vegetables are almost done. Sprinkle lightly with soy sauce and simmer a few minutes more. (Liquid should be almost gone and the vegetables should be tender but not mushy.) Mix vegetables gently and serve.

Sautéed Parsnips and Carrots

Parsnips are one of the sweetest vegetables, especially after the first frost. Native people and colonists, including Martha Washington, used them as vegetables, as pie filling, and as fritters. This Texas-style dish, combining parsnips and carrots, makes crispy, sweet, delicious chiplike vegetables.

**1 cup parsnips, cut in half-moons
1 cup carrots, cut on the diagonal into thin slices
1 teaspoon sesame oil**

Sauté the parsnips and carrots in a little oil until tender but still crisp, stirring gently. Add a pinch of salt if desired. Serve.
• Sautéed Chinese cabbage and snowpeas, or snowpeas with cubes of tofu, are also nice prepared in this fashion.

Pacific Stir-Fry

This style of cooking is popular in California, the Pacific Northwest, and increasingly around the country. In addition to serving stir-fried vegetables as a side dish with rice and beans, they are delicious as a sandwich in pita or pocket bread.

**1 cup mushrooms, thinly sliced
1/2 cup celery, thinly sliced
1/2 cup carrots, cut in matchsticks
1 cup nappa cabbage, thinly sliced
1/2 cup pea pods or 1/2 cup bean sprouts
1 tablespoon sesame oil
pinch of sea salt
soy sauce to taste**

Cut the vegetables. Brush a warm skillet or wok with a small amount of sesame oil. When the oil is hot, add the vegetables and a pinch of sea salt. Vegetables should sizzle when placed in

Cooking Tip
If you heat the skillet first, you need less oil when sautéing vegetables, while if you put the oil in the pan before turning the heat on you will need more oil.

Also, those who must watch their oil intake can lightly brush the skillet with an oil brush kept for this purpose.

For those who can't have oil, vegetables may be water-sautéed by adding a quarter-inch or so of water to the pan, covering it, and letting the steam cook the food.

the pan. Stir gently with chopsticks while sautéing. They should be done in 5 to 10 minutes. If more seasoning is desired, add soy sauce 3 minutes before vegetables are done and continue cooking.

Stewed Onions with Miso

Onions are one of the sweetest vegetables, if properly cooked. This is one of our favorite onion dishes.

6 medium onions
spring water
2-3 teaspoons miso
1-2 teaspoons kuzu
parsley or scallions

Brush warm skillet with sesame oil. Wash and peel onions and place in skillet whole, adding enough water to half-cover them. Purée miso in 2 to 3 tablespoons of water and pour on top. Cover and bring to a boil. Lower heat and simmer about 30 minutes until onions are transparent. Remove the onions. Thicken the remaining liquid with kuzu and pour over the onions. Garnish and serve.

Sweet Vegetable Casserole

We don't ordinarily bake vegetables, but the strong energy of baking in the following recipe is somewhat offset by the more yin vegetables and beans. This is a Texas favorite.

1/2 cup onions
1/2 cup corn
1/2 cup carrots
1/2 cup celery
1 cup pinto or kidney beans
2 cups rice or millet, cooked
pinch sea salt

Cut vegetables in small, uniform pieces and layer onions, corn, carrots, and celery on the bottom of a casserole dish. Cover with pre-cooked pinto beans or kidney beans, sea salt, and leftover rice or millet. Add half an inch of water and bake for 20 minutes.

"There is nothing like a farm, being alone in the fields, with the vegetables, the corn, the wheat."
— Roy Hobbs (Robert Redford) in The Natural

Who loves a garden still his Eden keeps Perennial pleasures plants, and wholesome harvest reaps.
— Bronson Alcott

Ecology Note Researchers at Rutgers University in New Jersey report that organic garden produce has as much as three times the mineral content and other nutrients as chemically grown produce.

Cooked Greens

Known as "garden sass" (i.e. sauce) or "a mess o' greens" in traditional American cookery, green leafy vegetables include collard greens, kale, mustard greens, turnip greens, watercress, chard, and other varieties. When properly cooked, these plants are tender and delicious. Traditionally enjoyed throughout the South, they are becoming popular in the North as people today eat more salads and less animal food. Modern macrobiotic cooking makes use of most greens, including daikon greens, carrot tops, and other greens not usually found in the supermarket.

Collards and kale cook up sweetly, while turnip greens, mustard, daikon, and some others are on the bitter side. To offset the bitter taste, we sometimes use a little sea salt or soy sauce on the greens when boiling or steaming. The water that greens cook in (usually just a half inch) is rich in minerals and vitamins and may be added to soup stock if it's not too bitter and the greens are organically grown. In American folk tradition, this liquid was known as "potlikker" and considered a special treat.

Tender Collards

In season and properly cooked, steamed collards and other greens are so juicy and tender, they melt in your mouth.

1 bunch of collard greens
spring water

Wash the collard greens thoroughly. You may use a metal or bamboo steamer or simply put in a saucepan with about half an inch of water on the bottom.

Fold each collard leaf so that the outer stem is visible and cut it away from the leaves. Then cut the stems in small pieces and steam them a few minutes before adding the leaves which have been sliced in 1/2 to 1-inch strips. Steam over high flame for 4 or 5 minutes until the vegetables are tender. Place in a dish and serve.

• Turnip greens, bok choy, kale, cabbage, and many other leafy green and white vegetables may be prepared in this manner.

"Gave up spinach for Lent."
— *F. Scott Fitzgerald*

"Kentucky pioneer women, in the eighteenth century, collecting spring greens in a new country, made it a rule to watch cattle. From the plants which the cows ate, they chose the more appetizing to feed their families."
— *John Bakeless, America as Seen by Its First Explorers*

Cooking Tip
Vegetables lose vital energy when cut, so it's better to use a small, whole vegetable in cooking rather than using part of a larger one and storing the rest until later.

The Mushroom is the Elf of Plants—
At Evening, it is not—
At Morning, in a Truffled Hut
It stopped upon a Spot.
— Emily Dickinson

Health Note
Shiitake mushrooms are excellent to reduce cholesterol in the body. Medical tests have also shown they have a strong anti-tumor effect.

Mustard Greens with Onions

Sweet rice vinegar, sweet vegetables, and soy sauce help sweeten bitter greens.

1 onion, diced
1 bunch mustard greens
sweet rice vinegar
soy sauce

Layer onions and greens in a saucepan or steamer. Steam for 5 minutes. Add a few drops of sweet rice vinegar and soy sauce for seasoning and steam 2 to 3 minutes more. Mix and serve.

Stuffed Squash Turkey with Seitan-Mushroom Gravy

Hubbard, the largest of the squashes, is traditionally used in macrobiotic households and educational centers for Thanksgiving dinners and other harvest festivals. Aveline Kushi started this custom in Boston in the early 1960s. Figure about a half pound of squash per person. Along with friends, we enjoyed this recipe at our home in Dallas for Thanksgiving in 1987.

5 pounds hubbard or golden squash

Stuffing
2 cups whole wheat bread crumbs
1 cup celery, diced
1/2 cup mushrooms, sliced
1 parsnip, cut into quarter-moons
1 medium carrot, finely diced
1/4 cabbage, cut in small squares

Gravy
1 onion, diced
1 cup seitan, cut into cubes
1 cup mushrooms, thinly sliced
arrowroot or kuzu
miso or soy sauce
rice vinegar

Cut squash in half, take out seeds, and pre-bake 30 to 45 minutes over low heat (300 to 350 degrees). Water-sauté the bread crumbs and vegetables for a few minutes in a little water in a skillet and put stuffing inside the partially baked squash. Bake for an additional 15 minutes.

To make gravy, sauté the onions in oil, add mushrooms and seitan, water, and a little arrowroot or kuzu to thicken. Add miso or soy sauce to season and a drop of rice vinegar. Place in individual serving or dipping dishes.

Pure and Simple Carrots and Onions

2-3 carrots, thinly sliced
1 onion, thinly sliced
spring water

Slice carrots and onions and place in separate bowls. Pour 1 inch of water into a pan and bring to a rolling boil. Cook the onions in the water for 2 to 3 minutes and remove with a skimmer. Do the same with the carrots. Mix and serve.

• Boiled cauliflower and broccoli flowerettes served with carrot flowers make a nice presentation.

• Boiled peas and yellow squash are colorful in the late spring and summer.

• Boiled watercress is nice by itself or as a topping for a steaming bowl of noodles.

Savory Succotash

Succotash, a combination of corn, beans, and vegetables, was served at the first Thanksgiving and included sun-dried corn kernels, small dried pea beans (seasoned with bear fat), and large chunks of stewed squash and pumpkin. Today it is often made with corn and lima beans.

1 large onion, minced
2 cups lima beans, cooked with kombu
2 cups corn, cut from the cob (3-4 small ears)
1 cup carrots, minced
2 cups spring water
2 pinches of sea salt

Layer onions, corn, carrot, and limas in a saucepan. Add water and sea salt. Cook over medium-low heat for 15 to 20 minutes. Garnish with chopped parsley or scallions.

Cooking Tip
Native peoples in North America ate a wide variety of wild vegetables including the roots of arum or arrow leaf, the young shoots of cattails or bullrushes, ground nuts, Jack-in-the-Pulpit (treated with wood ashes, boiled, dried, and ground into meal), the greens from pigweed or purslane, wild sunflowers, and the roots of various lilies and other edible water plants.

*I love his cabbage,
  gravy, hash
Daffy 'bout his succo-
  tash,
I can't do without my
  kitchen man.
—Bessie Smith,
"Kitchen Man"*

Fresh Lotus Root

The lotus flower, a symbol of enlightenment, is famous in Far Eastern mythology, but it is the lotus root that is the most nourishing part of the plant. This long, segmented root has hollow chambers, which are customarily sliced and cooked, giving a unique symmetrical design and shape to the dish. Fresh lotus is not always available (though can often be found in Oriental food markets). In this case, dried lotus root, commonly found in natural foods stores, may be used. Lotus is particularly beneficial to the lungs and is traditionally given to help relieve breathing difficulties or coughs.

In North America, the native water lily is similar to the Oriental lotus root and figured in the cooking and home remedies of native peoples.

lotus root
1 cup spring water
pinch of sea salt or 1/2 umeboshi plum

Wash the lotus root well and remove ends and any soft spots and slice into quarter-inch rounds. Prepare a stock of spring water and a small pinch of sea salt or umeboshi plum cut into small pieces. Bring to a boil. Add the lotus rounds and simmer uncovered for 10 to 12 minutes. Serve with umeboshi pieces or garnish with parsley.

Cabbage Delight

Cabbage is one of the most versatile vegetables. In some countries, such as China, it is often the only fresh vegetable available, and cooks have learned to prepare it in imaginative ways. The most basic method, however, is boiling. This recipe is from Amelia Simmon's American Cookery, *the first American cookbook.*

1 cabbage
sea salt
spring water

"If your cabbage is large, cut it into quarters; if small, cut it in halves; let your water boil, then put in a little salt, and next your cabbage with a little more salt upon it; make your water boil as soon as possible, and when the stalk is tender, take up your cabbage in a colander, or sieve, that the water may drain off, and send it to table as hot as you can."

Peas Supreme

Peas were the main vegetable of the Pilgrims and early New Englanders. On his maternal grandmother's side, Alex's family was named Pease, and his grandparents, farmers in Ohio, grew many garden vegetables and both lived into their late nineties.

In American Cookery, *Amelia Simmons advises, "All Peas should be picked carefully from the vines as soon as dew is off, shelled and cleaned without water, and boiled immediately; they are thus the richest flavored."*

2 cups of fresh peas
pinch of sea salt
spring water

Shell peas by hand and place in a saucepan with about a half-inch of water. Add sea salt, bring to a boil, reduce flame, and simmer for about 10 minutes until tender.

Vegetable Kimpira

Kimpira (or kinpira*) is a Far Eastern cooking style in which root vegetables cut into matchstick slices are sautéed in a little oil. It gives strong energy and a crispy taste. In macrobiotic homes, carrots and burdock are the most common kimpira, but other combinations are also used.*

1 carrot, cut into matchsticks
1 onion, thinly sliced or cut into half-moons
sesame oil

Wash vegetables and cut. Brush skillet with oil. Sauté vegetables for 2 to 3 minutes. Add water to lightly cover bottom of the skillet. Cover and cook until vegetables are almost done. Add several drops of soy sauce and cook for several minutes more. Boil off excess liquid. Mix and serve.
  • Turnip, lotus root, and rutabaga may also be used in this dish.
  • If you are using burdock, cook it a while before adding the carrots.

May 16. First dish of pease from earliest patch.
May 26. A second patch of peas comes to the table.
June 4. Windsor beans come to table.
June 5. A third and fourth patch of peas come to table.
June 13. A fifth patch of peas come in.
July 13. Last dish of peas.
July 18. Last lettuce from Gehee's.
July 23. Cucumbers from our garden.
July 31. Watermelon from our patch.
August 3. Indian corn comes to table. Blackeyed peas come to table.
— Thomas Jefferson's Garden Book, 1774 entry

Daikon with Daikon Greens

1 small daikon, cut in 1/2-inch rounds
daikon greens, cut in 2-inch pieces
kombu or sesame oil
soy sauce

Wash and slice daikon and greens. Brush skillet with oil or put a few 1-inch pieces of soaked kombu on the bottom of the pan. Place daikon rounds in pan (or on kombu). Add enough water to cover. Cook for 25 minutes. Add greens and a splash of soy sauce. Cook for 5 minutes more.

Baked Acorn Squash

Baked squash is a fixture in New England and other colder regions of the country. This casserole-like recipe, in which the squash in baked and puréed and served in its skin, is made sweeter and tangier than usual by adding a little rice syrup and nutmeg or cinnamon.

1 squash for every 2 persons
sesame oil
rice syrup
nutmeg or cinnamon (optional)

Pre-heat oven. Wash squash and cut in half lengthwise. Brush shallow pan or baking dish with oil and place squash halves face down in pan. Add water to a depth of one-half inch and bake in a 375-degree oven for about 1 hour 15 minutes (time will vary depending on the size of the squash).

When tender, remove from oven. Remove seeds and discard. Scrape out inside of squash and mash with a potato masher or purée in a food mill. Add 1 to 2 tablespoons of rice syrup per squash half and a sprinkle of nutmeg or cinnamon if desired. Mix into the squash and return this mixture to squash halves before serving. Garnish with chopped parsley.

Health Note
Common nightshade vegetables such as white potato, tomato, eggplant, and peppers are associated with rheumatism and arthritis. In medical studies, the Journal of the International Academy of Preventive Medicine reports that when 5000 arthritis patients avoided these foods, 70 percent experienced progressive relief from aches and pains.

Steamed Delicata Squash

Delicata, the long, slender winter squash with a pale yellow skin and green stripes, is the most delicate of the squashes (as its name implies) and has a mildly sweet flavor. We enjoy it steamed by itself.

1 delicata squash, sliced into 1/2-inch rounds
spring water

Wash and slice squash. Remove seeds from each slice. Put in steamer with water in the pan below (or in a pan with a half-inch of water) and steam 8 to 10 minutes until tender when tested with a chopstick or fork. Remove, arrange on a platter, and garnish with chopped parsley.

Abigail Adams' Squash Rolls

This recipe is based on a traditional dish made by Abigail Adams, wife of Revolutionary War leader and later president John Adams and an ancestor of Alex's on his mother's side. At the home in Braintree, Massachusetts, Abigail farmed, gardened, and tended the crops while her husband was away at war and serving as Ambassador to England.

whole wheat pastry flour or oat flour
1/2 pound winter squash, cut into small squares
sea salt

Wash, dry, and peel winter squash (buttercup or butternut are nice) and slice into small squares. Sprinkle lightly with sea salt and steam until tender. Purée or mash with a fork or potato masher. Add enough flour to enable you to shape into small rolls. Steam 15 to 20 minutes over low heat until thoroughly cooked or pan-fry with a small volume of oil in a skillet, turning once to brown both sides.

• For holidays and special occasions, you can deep-fry the squash rolls and serve with a little soy sauce and grated daikon. They are very crunchy and delicious.

"Scallions—the greatest cure for a batting slump ever invented."
— Babe Ruth quoted in Leo Durocher's Nice Guys Finish Last

Health Note
Root vegetables such as carrot, burdock, lotus root, and jinenjo (traditional Japanese mountain potato) are good for strengthening sexual vitality.

Fried Okra

Okra, a podlike vegetable native to Africa, arrived in America in the sixteenth century and has become a distinctive vegetable in Southern cooking. This is usually fried after dipping in a batter of equal parts cornmeal and unbleached white flour and water and seasoned with sea salt.

Vegetable Tempura

Tempura is a crispy, delicious style of cooking which originated in Portugal, was adopted by the Japanese, and is now enjoyed in the United States, Canada, and around the world.

Food is dipped in a special batter, deep-fried in oil at high temperature, and served with a dipping sauce and condiments.

While all foods, including grain, beans, fish and seafood, can be made into tempura, vegetables are the principal food cooked in this unique way.

Vegetables
carrots, cut into matchsticks
burdock, cut into matchsticks
onions, sliced thinly or cut into half-moons
winter squash (butternut, buttercup, etc.), thinly sliced
broccoli, cut into flowerettes
corn on the cob, cut into 1-inch rounds
mushrooms, whole

Batter
1/2 cup whole wheat flour
1/2 cup unbleached white flour
1 tablespoon kuzu
pinch of sea salt
1 cup spring water (approximate)

Dipping Sauce (per person)
1 tablespoon soy sauce
1 tablespoon kombu stock (or spring water)
pinch of grated ginger
1/2 teaspoon grated daikon
1 teaspoon mirin (optional)

Tempura batter should be prepared after the vegetables are cut, just before cooking. Make fresh batter everytime you prepare

"A Chinese vegetable peddler, Tu Charley, a well-known character in the Yuba River back in the 1890s . . . carried fresh cucumbers, tomatoes, beans, melons, and other produce in a horse-drawn wagon, traveling periodically between Marysville and Sierra City, a distance of over one hundred miles in hilly terrain . . . adapting an ancient Chinese practice to the California environment."
— Sucheng Chan,
The Bitter-Sweet Soil

tempura, as it changes consistency when stored.

Combine dry ingredients in batter, stirring in the liquid and mixing lightly. The mixture should have the consistency of cake or pancake batter.

Heat 2 to 3 inches of sesame oil to about 350 degrees in a saucepan. Drop a small bit of batter into the oil. If it sinks to the bottom, then rises quickly to the top, the oil is ready.

Dip the vegetables into the batter and then place in the hot oil using chopsticks or a skimmer. They should be ready in 1 to 3 minutes. Drain on a paper towel.

To make dipping sauce, mix the ingredients together. The dipping sauce is served individually in small cups or bowls. At the table each person dips the tempura in the sauce before eating. You may also wish to serve a small volume of grated daikon or ginger on the side to help digestion.

Deep-Fried Vegetables

Vegetables and other foods may be fried in hot oil without a batter. Pieces of seitan or tempeh, thinly sliced carrots, parsnips, and winter squash are a few of the foods that can be prepared in this way. Simply cut the different items, dip into a pan or skillet with 1 to 2 inches of hot sesame oil for a few minutes, and serve with grated daikon or turnip to aid in digestion.

Salad

When we think of salad today, we think of raw salad. But originally, salad was lightly boiled or pressed with sea salt (hence its root *sal* or salt). Through the mid-nineteenth century, American cookbooks often included recipes for fresh vegetables prepared as salad in these ways. As meat eating and other animal food consumption increased, raw vegetables became popular. By mid-twentieth century, vegetable cookery practically disappeared from the kitchen table, and salad meant lettuce, tomatoes, and possibly a few slices of cucumber or celery.

Thomas Jefferson was especially fond of salads and grew many fresh vegetables. At Monticello he cultivated thirty kinds of peas, five types of endive, and many lettuces.

Here are just a few of the many ways you can make delicious, healthful salads. For a wider selection, please see Aveline and Wendy Esko's delightful book, *The Wonderful World of Salads* (Japan Publications, 1990).

"We might go through the entire list and find each vegetable possessing its especial mission of cure, and it will be plain to every housekeeper that a vegetable diet should be partly adopted, and will prove of great advantage to the health of the family."
— *The White House Cook Book 1887*

Health Note
Green leafy vegetables
including broccoli,
collards, daikon
greens, kale, mustard
greens, turnip greens,
parsley, and water-
cress are high in cal-
cium. Recent medical
tests found that the
calcium in green leafy
vegetables was ab-
sorbed by the body
more efficiently than
milk. Vegetarian and
macrobiotic women
have about half the
bone loss (leading to
oseteoporosis) of wom-
en eating the Stan-
dard American Diet.

Fresh Garden Salad

Fresh salads are cooling and delicious, especially on a warm summer day. Lettuce and other delicate greens are best torn with the hands rather than a knife.

1 head of lettuce
1 ear of corn with the kernels removed
1 cucumber, thinly sliced
4-5 red radishes, thinly sliced
1 box of sprouts
1 carrot, shredded
1 celery stalk, diced

Boil the fresh corn kernels in a little water in a saucepan for 2 to 3 minutes and let cool. Arrange lettuce on a serving place and arrange the cucumber and radishes in an attractive circle or spiral. Put the sprouts in the center in small bunches or around the perimeter or both. Sprinkle corn kernels and celery over the salad. Add the shredded carrot to the center and/or four directions Serve with a dressing made of tofu and umeboshi, miso and brown rice vinegar, or soy sauce and ginger. Add a little mirin for a sweet taste.
   • Seasonal vegetables may be added to or substituted to this basic salad, including watercress, parsley, shredded red cabbage, and slices or cubes of tofu, tempeh, or seitan.

Summertime Rice Salad

Leftover grains, beans, and noodles go well in salads. They give a strong, rich taste to the salad (and may serve as the principal dish in the meal), at the same time complementing the color and texture of the lighter vegetables.

2 cups brown rice, pre-cooked
1 cup carrots, diced
1 cup green peas
1/2 cup celery, diced
1/4 cup sliced scallions or parsley

Boil the carrots, celery, and peas separately in a saucepan with a little water until tender. Drain and allow to cool. Add these to the leftover rice, along with the celery and mix well. Garnish and serve.

Plimouth Plantation Boiled Salad

In macrobiotic households around the country, lightly boiled salads are served frequently. These are made by boiling each ingredient separately for 30 seconds to a minute or more, then combining, and serving with or without a soy sauce dressing. While boiled salad is often thought of as an Oriental dish, it was also traditionally made in the West. The Pilgrims made boiled salad as a vegetable side dish. This recipe is adapted from a sweet-and-sour combination still served at seasonal dinners on Cape Cod.

1 cabbage (about 2 pounds)
1/2 teaspoon sea salt
1/2 cup currants
1 tablespoon rice syrup
2 tablespoons rice vinegar

Discard withered outer leaves and cut the heart of the cabbage into quarters. Fill saucepan one-quarter full with water. Add salt and bring to a boil. Add cabbage, cover, and cook over a medium flame for about 10 minutes or until tender. When done, drain off excess liquid. Chop cabbage while still in pot with a wooden spoon, and add the currants, rice syrup, and vinegar. Simmer gently for another 5 minutes and serve.

Marinated Salad

Fresh vegetables may be marinated for a short time in sea salt, soy sauce, brown rice vinegar, umeboshi vinegar, or mirin. Seasoning them in this way removes some of the liquid and makes them crispier and sweeter. Various combinations include:

• Red radish, sliced or cut into flower shapes, and marinated with umeboshi vinegar. This creates a beautiful pink dish.

• Cucumber, sliced and sprinkled with a pinch of sea salt, and marinated for 5 to 10 minutes.

• Turnips marinated with soy sauce, sea salt, or brown rice vinegar for 30 minutes.

• Daikon, cut in matchsticks or rectangles, marinated with sea salt for 30 minutes. After softening, squeeze out excess water from the daikon and let sit for a short time in soy sauce, mirin, or brown rice vinegar

"It was good to know that there were turnips enough in the cellar to last all winter long. There would be boiled turnips, and mashed turnips, and creamed turnips. And in the later evenings, a plate of raw turnips would be on the table by the lamp. They would peel off the thick rinds and eat the raw turnips in crisp, juicy slices."
— *Laura Ingalls Wilder,* On the Banks of Plum Creek

Health Note
Older people who eat plenty of garden vegetables and other fresh foods have a lower risk of developing cataracts, the leading cause of blindness, according to studies at Brigham and Women's Hospital in Boston.

Pressed Salad

Pressing is another traditional way of preparing salads. Use a salad or pickle press especially designed for this or put in a dish and cover with a small saucer or plate and a rock or other heavy weight.

2 cups Chinese cabbage, thinly shredded
1/4 cup celery, sliced
1/2 cup red radishes, sliced
1 teaspoon sea salt

Slice vegetables and put in a bowl. Sprinkle sea salt over and mix lightly. Put in a pickle press and tighten the top so that pressure is applied to the vegetables. Let sit for 2 hours. Remove lid, pour off the liquid and place vegetables in a dish for serving.
   • If vegetables are too salty, they may be rinsed in cold water prior to serving.

Hot Climate Vegetables

Sweet potatoes, yams, cassava, manioc (yucca), taro, and other tropical or subtropical vegetables are traditionally eaten in Mexico, the Caribbean, Hawaii, and extremely hot, humid zones of the continental United States.

Poi

Poi is made from the roots of taro, a type of hairy potato that grows in the tropical latitudes. The thicky, fleshy root is traditionally baked, peeled, and pounded into poi, which has the consistency of bread dough. It is then eaten in the form of thick pudding in Hawaii and other parts of Polynesia.

"Each of them brought to [us] what they had to eat, which is bread of 'niamas,' that is, or roots like large carrots which they grow, for they sow and grow and cultivate this in all these lands, and it is their mainstay of life."
— *Columbus, description of yams*

"I took a bite [of roasted yams], finding it as sweet and hot as any I'd ever had, and was overcome by such a surge of homesickness that I turned away to keep my control."
— *Ralph Ellison, Invisible Man*

*"America, America,
God Shed His Grace
on Thee"*

5

Seasonings,
Condiments,
Pickles & Sauces

Like particles of sunshine, seasonings, condiments, pickles, sauces, dressings, and garnishes bathe the entire meal in a new light. Though small and often invisible, these ingredients largely govern the overall taste, visual harmony, and satisfaction we experience from our daily food. The New World, it should be recalled, was newly discovered as a result of Europe's quest for Oriental spices.

Modern cooking uses spices, seasonings, and sauces to arouse the senses, disguise and cover up foods, and alter tastes. In macrobiotic cooking, we use healthful, simple substances to bring out the natural flavor in the food.

Seasonings

Natural salt is the most basic seasoning. Native people evaporated it from the Great Eastern Sea, the Great Western Sea, the Great Salt Lake, and from salt licks such as those on the site of

*"You can travel 50,000 miles in America without once tasting a piece of good bread. Americans can eat garbage, provided you sprinkle it liberally with ketchup, mustard, chili sauce, tobasco sauce, cayenne pepper, or any other condiment which destroys the original flavor of the dish."
— Henry Miller*

present-day Buffalo, New York, where herds of bison once flocked to stretch their long tongues.

The first Europeans used salt imported from Spain. The salt we use today comes from off the coast of Baja California. It is a simple white variety that retains the natural balance of trace minerals that are removed in commercial table salt. Some macrobiotic friends use a heavier white variety (which clumps as opposed to flowing freely) or a light or dark grey sea salt. In our experience, these contain too high a mineral content and can lead to tight kidneys, cravings for sweets, and other symptoms of an overly yang condition.

Usually just a pinch (the amount of salt that can be grasped with the thumb and index finger) is used per cup of dry grain in cooking whole grains. Beans require slightly more. A pinch of sea salt on melons, berries, or apples brings out the natural sweetness of the fruit—a time-honored practice among American farmers and homesteaders.

We also use miso and soy sauce for seasoning. They are fermented soy products and have a base of sea salt. As noted in the miso soup section, two-year barley miso is the standard for daily miso soup, with rice miso and hatcho (all soybean) miso used occasionally. For sauces, dressings, and lighter dishes, we will use all of the other misos from time to time, including red miso, mellow barley, white miso, yellow miso, chickpea miso, and others.

Soy sauce (also called natural shoyu) gives a unique flavor to clear soup, noodle broth, steamed greens, and other dishes. The first commercial soy sauce factory opened in Indiana in 1928. Today there are several modern processing plants in the United States, but like their counterparts in Japan, they use chemically-grown soybeans, table salt, and artificial methods. We use good quality organic soy sauce from Erewhon, Eden, Westbrae, and other major macrobiotic suppliers. Recently there have appeared a low-sodium variety and real tamari (a wheat-free soy sauce), which we find either too weak or too strong for daily cooking.

Once again, tried, true, simple basic ingredients are the best. The natural foods market is fair game for the great American tradition of hucksters and promoters. Today there are almost as many varieties of soy sauce, rice cakes, and other basics as corn flakes and ice cream!

Among oils, toasted dark sesame oil and unrefined corn oil are the staples in most American macrobiotic households. Dark sesame has a wonderful smoky aroma and flavor and makes delicious sautés, stir-fries, tempuras and deep-fries, pancakes and flat breads, and other dishes. For a lighter taste, we use corn

"Salt is the magician."
— George Ohsawa

Health Note
In the 1970s, Harvard Medical School researchers reported that macrobiotic people in Boston had the most ideal blood pressure of any group studied in modern society and that the use of sea salt did not increase blood pressure.

oil—for example, in biscuits and muffins and most baked goods. Light sesame is also good quality and we use it for sauces, dressings, and occasional frying when dark sesame is unavailable or imparts too strong a taste. Other unrefined vegetable cooking oils, including safflower, sunflower, and olive oil, are used sparingly and add a unique bouquet to special dishes.

Usually only a small amount of oil is needed to coat the skillet. Often a teaspoon will do, or sometimes we use an oil brush and lightly brush the surface of the pan. For richer dishes, we might use a tablespoon or more of oil, depending on the volume and number of people to be served. The modern American practice of using excessive oil is unhealthy. When we think of fat and oil, we think of red-meat, dairy, and other heavy animal food. But actually, most of the fat and oil consumed today is in the form of soft oils, including salad dressings, mayonnaise, and the oil in which French fries, potato chips, and other snacks are fried. These can have just as harmful effect on the heart and other organs as hamburgers and hot dogs.

Other seasonings that we use include umeboshi plums, fresh grated ginger root, rice vinegar, umeboshi vinegar, sauerkraut brine, mirin (fermented sweet brown rice sweetener), grated daikon, grated radish, lemon juice, orange juice, and other traditionally used and commonly consumed seasonings.

Umeboshi are a variety of plum that have been salted, aged, and fermented for several years or more. They have a wonderful salty, sour flavor and are used for seasoning, as a condiment, and medicinally. A traditional staple in Japan, they were brought over or imported by the first generation of macrobiotic teachers in the 1950s and 1960s. In California, Junsei and Kazuko Yamasaki have started growing and distributing native grown umeboshi plums, and Noboru Muromoto, another macrobiotic pioneer, has developed apriboshi from apricots.

Ginger root has a hot, spicy flavor and gives a warm, pungent taste to fried rice, noodles in broth, and other dishes. We use it gingerly. In America, it has traditionally been used in teas and beverages (including ginger ale) and medicinally. Armand Hammer, the entrepreneur, got his start by cornering the world ginger market to sell a patent home remedy in which ginger was the chief ingredient.

Brown rice vinegar, made from whole grain rice, makes delightful sauces and dressings, giving a unique sour flavor to salads, sushi, and other dishes. It is less acidic than apple cider vinegar and may be combined with oil, salt, and sweet and spicy items. Sweet rice vinegar is also available, made from sweet brown rice.

Grated daikon aids digestion and is customarily taken to bal-

Cooking Tip
Among condiments, salt is the most contractive, followed by miso, and soy sauce. Among misos, short-term (white, red, yellow misos) are more salty than long-term misos (aged 2 to 3 years), which are softer on the kidneys.

"Like a salt plum, she makes his mouth water."
— Maxine Hong Kingston

ance foods high in fat and oil such as fish and seafood, deep-fried foods, tempura, and mochi.

Among native peoples, corn silk or corn hair was a popular seasoning. The long fine strands were removed from the corn husk, dried before the fire, and added to foods in the cooking pot for seasoning. It served to thicken the broth as well as give a pleasant flavor. No doubt, there are other traditional seasonings to be rediscovered and readapted to the modern macrobiotic kitchen.

Condiments

Most people think of ketchup or pickle relish when they think of condiments. This is because the modern diet, based on animal food, is so excessively yang that some form of strong yin is needed to offset it. Tomatoes, peppers, spice, vinegar, and other ingredients of tropical origin are customarily used today. Interestingly, ketchup was not originally made with tomatoes. It was made with walnuts or mushrooms or with oysters or anchovies. Not until the mid-nineteenth century when tomatoes became plentiful were they introduced into relish. Today this form of strong yin has displaced more moderate substances from the dining table. Condiments balance the meal by allowing each person to add a little more seasoning, flavor, or texture according to his or her needs and taste. For family cooking, this is essential since usually children require less salt, miso, soy sauce, and other seasoning than adults. Generally, the cook prepares the meal according to the taste of those with the least needs and the balance is made up for with condiments. Regular condiments used in modern macrobiotic cooking include umeboshi plums (just mentioned), sesame seed salt (*gomashio*), sea vegetable powder, *tekka* (root vegetable mixture of miso, sesame oil, burdock, lotus root, carrots, and ginger root), salty kombu, toasted green nori sheets or nori flakes, miso cooked with scallions or onions, beefsteak (*shiso*) leaves, dulse, roasted sesame or sunflower seeds, and others.

Sesame Seed Salt (Gomashio)

Sesame seed salt, or gomashio as it is known in the Orient, is made from roasted sea salt and sesame seeds. Its bitter taste is good for the heart. Gomashio also provides calcium and helps digest grain. The proportion of salt to sesame seeds is very important. Too much salt can create tightness and an overly yang

Health Note
University of Wisconsin researchers report that mice given fermented soy sauce experienced 26 percent less induced cancer than mice on a regular diet. Soy sauce "exhibited a pronounced anticarcinogenic effect," the scientists concluded.

"Put an extra condiment into your dish, and it will poison you. It is not worth the while to live by rich cookery."
— Thoreau, Walden

condition. The first macrobiotic cookbooks and classes in America recommended 1 part salt to 8 to 12 parts sesame seeds. Today, the Kushis recommend 1 to 16 to 1 to 18 as standard. Freshly made sesame seed salt is a delightful condiment for rice and other grains, as well as soups, casseroles, and vegetable dishes.

The following recipe results in a ratio of 16 parts sesame seeds to 1 part sea salt. For 18 to 1, add 2 more teaspoons of sesame seeds.

1/3 cup black sesame seeds
1 teaspoon sea salt

Wash seeds, discarding any that float to the top. Pour into a strainer and let them drain. Dry-roast the sea salt in a frying pan for a short time until it becomes shiny. (Roasting releases moisture and a chlorine from the salt.) Then pour into a *suribachi*, grind, and set aside.

Roast the damp seasme seeds over medium heat. While roasting, move the seeds back and forth in the pan with a rice paddle or wooden spoon. Shake the pan occasionally to promote even roasting and avoid burning. The seeds are done when they crush easily between the thumb and index finger and give off a nutty fragrance.

Add the roasted sesame seeds to the roasted, ground sea salt. Slowly grind the seeds in a circular motion with a wooden pestle until the seeds are half-crushed and coated with oil.

Allow the gomashio to cool and then store in an airtight glass or ceramic container.

• For variety, seeds may be prepared with miso or soy sauce or seaweed powder. Roasted sesame seeds may also be used as a garnish without salt or other seasoning.

Sea Vegetable Powder

A very tasty, strengthening condiment can be made by grinding sea vegetables into a fine powder and sprinkling on grains and other dishes.

1 ounce wakame (about half a standard package)

Bake wakame on a cookie sheet or a pyrex baking dish in a 350-degree oven until it breaks apart when pressed. This may take 10 to 20 minutes depending on the thickness of the wakame. Place roasted wakame in a *suribachi* and grind finely.

Health Note
Good quality sea salt should have a slightly sweet taste. Put a pinch on your tongue, and if it is bitter, it contains too many minerals.

Salt should be cooked in the food, not taken raw (except on fresh fruits). The body transmutes salt, miso, or soy sauce more easily when it has been cooked.

Excessive salt and condiments are the main cause of overeating and attraction to sweets and other strong yin foods and beverages.

Some of the wakame may not easily be ground into a powder. In this case, remove the wakame from the *suribachi* into a strainer and shake it lightly so the powder will sift through and the harder pieces will remain in the strainer. Those may be used later in soups. Put the fine wakame powder in a condiment jar on the table.

• Kombu or dulse powder may also be made this way.

• Any of these sea vegetables may be combined with roasted sesame seeds for a different condiment.

Nori Condiment

5-6 sheets nori, cut into 1-inch pieces
1/2 cup spring water
1 teaspoon soy sauce

In a suacepan, cover nori with water. Bring to a boil, cover, and reduce to low heat, Simmer for about 30 minutes until the liquid evaporates and a thick paste remains. Add soy sauce a few minutes before the end of cooking. Cool and store in a glass jar.

Shiso Condiment

Shiso leaves are customarily used to wrap umeboshi plums. A tasty condiment can be made with just the leaves themselves.

4 teaspoons shiso leaves

Chop shiso leaves very finely and dry-roast in a skillet until crisp. Place in a *suribachi* and grind slightly.

Carrot Top–Miso Condiment

2 cups carrot greens, finely chopped
1 onion, diced
sesame oil
1-2 teaspoons miso, puréed in small volume of water
1/4 to 1/2 cup spring water

Cut the carrot tops very fine and sauté in a little oil with a pinch of sea salt for 3 to 4 minutes. Add water to almost cover, then add the miso, cover, and simmer for about 10 minutes. Remove cover, cook off some of the remaining liquid, and serve.

Miso and Scallions

This condiment is very pungent, warming, and helps cleanse the liver.

1 bunch scallions with roots
1-2 teaspoons miso
spring water
rice vinegar (optional)

Finely chop scallion, including the roots and greens. Layer the roots and then the scallions in a saucepan and make a place in the center. Purée the miso and put in the hollow space. Add water to cover, cover, and simmer 5 minutes. A touch of rice vinegar may be added if desired. Mix well and serve.

Miso and Roasted Walnuts

*This is a very delicious condiment, almost like can*dy.

1 cup walnuts
1 tablespoon miso
1/2 teaspoon rice vinegar

Roast walnuts in the oven or in a skillet. Then chop into smaller pieces and crush in a *suribachi*. Stir in miso and rice vinegar.

Pickles

Like ketchup, our modern notion of pickles is limited. We think mainly of cucumber aged in dill, vinegar, garlic, or other spices. Traditionally, almost all garden vegetables were pickled, as well as many fruits, nuts, and other foods. Carolina housewives made pickles with cabbage, onions, mushrooms, walnuts, and fresh beans to complement their dishes. The Pennsylvania Dutch were fond of pickling beets in ginger. America's first cookbook includes a recipe for watermelon pickles. On the Western prairie, frontier housewives served *chow-chow*, a homemade vegetable relish.

In the latter half of the nineteenth century, Henry J. Heinz developed mass pickling, replacing vegetables stored in brine in mason jars and stone crocks with bottled and canned pickles

"Pickles are wicked, thunder and lightning! They'll burn you inside out, slip you through the looking-glass, and that's fine, too,"
— **Hannah Bond, article in East West Journal**

produced by high steam pressing techniques. At the Columbia Exposition in Chicago in 1893, he exhibited 57 varieties, and his six-story giant electric pickle sign lit up New York until 1906.

In modern macrobiotic cooking, we enjoy a wide variety of pickles. Instead of spices, vinegar, and other yin, we use soy sauce, miso, umeboshi juice, rice bran, and other more balanced ingredients. Such pickles help us to digest grains and vegetables, and we like to have a small condiment-size amount daily.

Traditional Chippewa Condiments

Corn Silk
Pumpkin Blossoms
White Pine Moss
Dried Squash and
 Pumpkin
Milkweed
Woodbine
Aster
Aspen
Sweet Acorns
Basswood
Lichen or Reindeer
 Moss

Turnip and Kombu Salt Pickles

Quick salt pickles, made in the morning, may be eaten in the evening or be left to ferment for several days. Long-time pickles may be aged for several weeks. A small pickle press (available in natural foods stores) is useful to apply pressure, or the same effect can be produced by placing pickles in a bowl and covering with a saucer and a stone or other weight.

We like to use fresh, firm vegetables and let them ferment in a cool, dark place.

2 cups turnips, quartered and thinly sliced
6-inch piece of kombu, soaked and very thinly sliced
1 teaspoon sea salt

Place sliced turnips in a pickle press or bowl. Add the sliced kombu and mix together. Add sea salt and mix well. Screw down top of pickle press or place weight on saucer in a bowl. Let ferment for 1 to 2 days or more. If the water from the pickles rises above the pressure plate or saucer, release some of the pressure. Pickles will keep about 2 to 3 weeks stored in a cool place.

• Other nice salt pickles are Chinese cabbage; mustard greens; turnip or daikon greens; cauliflower, broccoli, or carrots; and cucumbers with several sprigs of fresh or dried dill.

Quick Soy Sauce Pickles

3-inch piece of fresh daikon
2 red radishes
soy sauce
spring water

Slice the daikon into 1/8-inch slices and then cut into matchsticks. Slice the radishes into thin rounds. Place in a bowl or glass jar and cover with a mixture of 50 percent soy sauce and 50 percent water. Let sit for 2 to 3 hours. Remove and serve.

If the pickles taste too salty, you can rinse them to remove excess soy sauce. The mixture can be used several times, varying the vegetables, to make this type of pickle.

• Other tasty combinations are: onions and carrots (cut thin), cauliflower and broccoli, and ginger and Chinese cabbage.

Long Time Soy Sauce Pickles

1 cup mixed vegetables (cauliflower, carrot, celery, peas, red radish, etc.)
1 cup soy sauce
1 cup spring water

Combine equal parts of water and soy sauce and place in a small glass jar. Thinly slice root or round vegetables and place in the liquid. Keep in a cool place for 3 to 5 days and serve.

Parsnip Miso Pickles

Miso pickles are very delicious but salty, so they should be eaten in tiny volume. Root vegetables such as carrots, daikon, turnips, ginger, lotus, and parsnips are wonderful pickled in miso. Press them first with a little salt for several hours or a day or two to take out excess water, or boil them for a few minutes before putting in the miso. Aging ranges from 3 days to 1 week, depending on the vegetable and type of cutting (thin slices are ready more quickly).

1 parsnip, thinly sliced
miso paste

Slice and boil parsnip for several minutes and let cool. Put in a jar and cover completely with miso paste. Cover the jar (no weight is needed) and store in a cool place for 3 to 5 days.

Umeboshi Pickles

5-6 whole umeboshi plums
vegetables, thinly sliced
spring water

Health Note
In the Far East, umeboshi plums have traditionally been taken to balance extremes and strengthen the blood. Modern scientific experiments show that umeboshi are high in citric acid, which serves to neutralize and eliminate harmful lactic acid in the body, and in picric acid which stimulates the liver and kidneys to cleanse the blood.

Place plums into a quart of water and simmer for a few minutes. until the water turns pink. Let cool and pour into a jar. Add vegetables so they are completely covered with liquid. Cover jar with cheesecloth and secure with a rubber band. Let sit for 3 to 5 days, stirring each day, then serve.

Mustard Green Pickles

1 large bunch mustard greens
1/2 cup soy sauce (or 1/4 cup soy sauce and 1/4 cup spring
**   water)**
2 tablespoons roasted sesame seeds
2 tablespoons rice syrup
1/2 teaspoon grated ginger

Wash greens and cut into 1-inch pieces. Pack firmly into quart jar. Sprinkle on sesame seeds. In saucepan, bring soy sauce, ginger, and rice syrup to boil. Cool, pour over greens. Cover and place in the refrigerator. Pickles will be ready the next day.

Cooking Tip
Kuzu root powder is the main thickener used in macrobiotic cooking. Always dissolve kuzu in cold water before adding to other liquids when preparing kuzu drinks, sauces, or puddings.

Sauces and Dressings

Natural foods tend to cook themselves. Most of the time, we enjoy whole grains, beans, vegetables, and other dishes just as they are, with a minimum of adornment. From time to time, however, for variety and enjoyment, we like a little richer cooking. There are many wonderful sauces and dressings that are made in macrobiotic kitchens across America today.

For thickening, we use kuzu root and arrowroot powder. Kuzu, used traditionally in Japan, is the root of a prolific vine that was introduced to the United States in the late nineteenth century as an ornamental. Kuzu has proceeded to multiply throughout the South, where as the dreaded kudzu vine it has taken over fields, farms, shopping malls, and other zones of life. Unbeknownst to its detractors, the root is an incomparable thickener, prized throughout the Orient for its use in regular and medicinal dishes. Japanese businessmen, aware of the value of this "white gold," have recently announced joint ventures to rid the South of this prolific nuisance.

Native peoples used pumpkin and squash blossoms to thicken their food. In colonial American cooking, arrowroot served as the chief thickener. Imported from the West Indies, it was used to thicken porridges, soups, stews, and other dishes and given to children and invalids. Later, arrowroot plantations were established in Georgia, but Abolitionist boycotts of slave labor spelled their end. Tuckahoe, a green plant found in eastern bogs and swamps, was another popular natural thickener. In fact, its name came to be associated with Virginians east of the Blue Ridge who used it in their cooking to make porridges, puddings, and sauces and to starch their ruff collars. The commercial development of baking powder, baking soda, and other chemical additives brought an end to the use of natural substances until modern macrobiotics.

Many other wonderful sauces and dressings can be made using tofu, umeboshi, nuts and seeds, and other plant-quality ingredients. Here are some of our favorites.

Scallions with Miso-Vinegar Dressing

1 bunch scallions
1 tablespoon miso
1 tablespoon brown rice vinegar
1/2 cup spring water
2 tablespoons sesame seeds, coarsely crushed

Cook scallions whole and then cut in 1-inch pieces. Mix miso, vinegar, and water and pour over scallions. Sesame seeds can be added. Also fresh tofu can be lightly boiled and mixed in for a creamy dressing.

Tofu-Parsley Dressing

This makes a smooth, light dressing, and its pastel green color adds a soft hue to the dinner table.

16 ounces tofu
1 cup spring water
1 cup chopped parsley
2 teaspoons umeboshi paste
1 teaspoon mellow barley miso

Crumble tofu and place in a blender with remaining ingredients. Blend until smooth. Taste and adjust seasoning. Serve over boiled vegetables or greens. Store remainder in covered jar in the refrigerator.

"Among southern rural folk, kudzu came to be known as the 'mile-a-minute vine' . . . One legend tells of a man who planted kudzu behind his barn, and its branches grew fast enough to beat him back to the house. Another asserts that the tale of Jack and the Beanstalk was but a slightly exaggerated account of a boy who was careless with kudzu."
— Bill Shurtleff and Akiko Aoyagi, The Book of Kudzu

Health Note
Ginger root can benefit the heart and circulatory system by slowing blood clotting.

Grated and dissolved in tea, it shows an intense anti-cough effect, lowers fever, and reduces pain.

Powdered, it is beneficial for treating motion sickness.

Sesame Tahini Dressing

3 tablespons sesame tahini
1 tablespoon lemon juice (or brown rice vinegar)
2 tablespoons chickpea or mellow barley miso
1/2 cup spring water
1 teaspoon sesame oil
1 tablespoon chopped parsley

Mix all the ingredients except water in a *suribachi*. Then add water gradually or use a blender.

Poppy Seed Dressing

Poppy seed dressing is a traditional favorite in Texas, especially among the Germans who settled in the hill country near Austin. Here is a macrobiotic version.

1/3 cup rice bran oil
2 tablespoons sweet rice vinegar
4 teaspoons stoneground mustard
2 tablespoons rice syrup
3 tablespoons poppy seeds
1/2 cup onion, diced and pre-cooked
1/4 teaspoon sea salt
2-3 tablespoons spring water

Mix all ingredients except the water in a blender and purée. If too thick, add a few tablespoons of water and blend again. Taste and adjust seasoning if necessary. The dressing should have a mildly tart taste with an essence of sweetness. Simmer a few minutes. Let cool and store in a glass jar in the refrigerator.
 • If rice bran oil is not available, try 2 parts light sesame to 1 part olive oil.

Sweet and Sour Sauce

This sauce may be served over tempeh, rice, noodle dishes, or stir-fried vegetables. For a thicker sauce, increase the amount of kuzu.

1 cup apple juice
1/2 cup spring water

pinch of sea salt
1/2 teaspoon rice vinegar
1 rounded tablespoon kuzu
1 tablespoon soy sauce

Place juice, water, rice vinegar, and salt in a saucepan and bring to a boil. Add soy sauce and reduce heat. Simmer mixture for a few minutes. Dissolve kuzu in a few tablespoons of cold water and add to the other ingredients, stirring gently until it thickens.
• You may substitute the water that the vegetables have been cooked in for the apple juice or water.

Alice's Cranberry Applesauce

This is a tasty sauce for Thanksgiving or other special occasions courtesy of Alice, a good friend living in Becket.

1 cup cranberries, washed
2 cups apples, chopped
1 cup apple juice
pinch of sea salt
rice syrup to taste
1 1/2 teaspoons kuzu

Place cranberries, apples, apple juice, and sea salt in a saucepan. Cover and bring to a boil. Reduce flame and simmer for 15 to 20 minutes until the cranberries are soft. Add a little rice syrupt if too tart. Dissolve kuzu in a little cold water and add to sauce. Cook and stir until thickened and clear.

Garnishes

Garnishes stimulate the appetite, add a hint of color to the meal, and are often the crowning touch of a wonderful meal. We enjoy the following:
• Chopped scallions (both the white and green parts and the root) on noodles and pasta, tempeh, natto, and fish and seafood.
• Grated daikon for fish and seafood, mochi, buckwheat noodles and pasta, tempeh, and natto.
• Grated ginger for soups, noodle and pasta dishes, fish and seafood.
• Small squares or strips of nori (cut with scissors) on noodles or rice and other grain.

• A slice or two of fresh carrot (cut in chrysanthemum shapes) on vegetables and casseroles.

• Parsley sprigs, kale leaves, or other green leaves on various dishes.

• Roasted sesame seeds, sunflower seeds, or other seeds and nuts on grains, salads, and casseroles.

• Infrequently, grated horseradish, lemon peel or orange peel, red pepper, freshly ground black pepper, green mustard paste, and other traditionally used garnishes.

"And Crown Thy Good With Brotherhood"

6
Snacks and Desserts

From the earliest days, Americans have had a pronounced sweet tooth. Native peoples enjoyed maple syrup over popcorn, cornmeal (Indian pudding), baked beans, and other staples. They also sweetened dishes with birch syrup, basswood, aster, and other tree and flower saps and with various sweet corn preparations. The Pilgrims adapted squash and pumpkins to breads, pies, and other baked goods. John Chapman, a vegetarian and Swedenbourgian mystic better known as Johnny Appleseed, spread apple trees across the continent, whose harvests provided generations of pioneers with baked apples, apple pie, apple fritters, and other apple-based sweets. In the South, rice pudding, rice custard, rice jelly, and other rice dishes were popular. Parsnips, carrots, and other naturally sweet vegetables graced many dessert plates. Persimmons, cherries, rhubarb, berries, melons, nuts, seeds, and other edibles came in many varieties and figured in endless cakes, cobblers, cookies, jams, preserves, gelatins, and other treats, as well as being enjoyed by themselves. The old-fashioned names of sweet American desserts—grunts, slumps, cobblers, pandowdies, jumbles, puffards, and wonders—strike us as quaintly today as the names of Packards, Studebakers, and other bygone automobiles.

Until sugar came into widespread use, maple syrup, honey,

"Every fruit has its secret."
— D. H. Lawrence

175

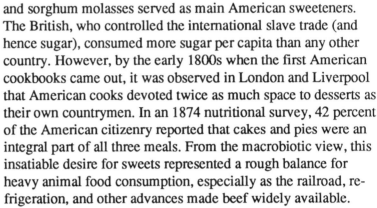

and sorghum molasses served as main American sweeteners. The British, who controlled the international slave trade (and hence sugar), consumed more sugar per capita than any other country. However, by the early 1800s when the first American cookbooks came out, it was observed in London and Liverpool that American cooks devoted twice as much space to desserts as their own countrymen. In an 1874 nutritional survey, 42 percent of the American citizenry reported that cakes and pies were an integral part of all three meals. From the macrobiotic view, this insatiable desire for sweets represented a rough balance for heavy animal food consumption, especially as the railroad, refrigeration, and other advances made beef widely available.

Between 1880 and 1915, sugar consumption doubled and continued its spectacular conquest of America and the modern world. (In 1970 per capita consumption reached 120 lbs. compared with 38 lbs. in 1880). With the advent of modern macrobiotics, the pendulum began to turn. Dentists, doctors, and other health care professionals (as well as parents and teachers with hyperactive children) have become well aware of the harmful effects of sugar, honey, chocolate, and other simple sugars. (Interestingly, chocolate, at whose shrine millions of modern people worship, was a staple among the ancient Aztecs and appears to have contributed to the wild hyperactive mentality and final collapse of the Empire.)

Today, milder sweeteners, including barley malt, rice syrup, and amasake (made from complex sugars in whole grains), are becoming popular across the continent. In macrobiotic homes, centers, restaurants, food stores, and other enterprises, delicious crisps, crunches, puddings, pies, cakes, and other desserts are prepared daily using good quality ingredients.

The recipes that follow are a combination of old American standbys traditionally made without sugar and modern macrobiotic snacks and desserts.

"Witness the natural recipe for plum pudding. Take a pound of every indigestible substance you can think of, boil into a cannonball, and serve in flaming brandy."
— *Harriet Beecher Stowe criticizing British sweets*

Seeds and Nuts

Seeds and nuts make tasty snacks. Seeds contain less fat than nuts. However, because of their oil content, seeds and nuts are often lightly roasted with (or sometimes without) sea salt or soy sauce.

Sunflower, squash, and pumpkin seeds are native to North America and were given to Spaniards and other colonists by native peoples as a gift of peace. Sesame seeds originally came from Africa, where they were known as *bennes*, pounded into a paste, and mixed with grain. The Pilgrims ate groundnuts the first hard winter on Cape Cod. Walnuts, hickories, butternuts, and chestnuts were prized for their oils.

At the Tuskeegee Institute, George Washington Carver introduced dandelion greens, chicory, watercress, and other plant foods. The peanut, however, proved to be the most popular. He once cooked a nine-course meal including peanut soup, peanut mock chicken, peanut bread, peanut salad, peanut as a vegetable side dish, peanut ice cream, peanut candy, peanut cookies, and peanut coffee. In Africa, where they were known by the Bantu as *nguba* (hence goober peas), peanuts served as a vegetable and prepared dried or roasted in a creamy sauce. Today, peanaut butter is still spread on fresh corn in the Carolinas.

Roasted Seeds

1-2 handfuls of seeds (pumpkin, sunflower, or sesame)
pinch of sea salt or few drops of soy sauce

Gently rinse the seeds, drain in a strainer for 5 to 10 minutes, and place in a dry skillet. Gently stir the seeds over a medium flame for 5 to 10 minutes, picking up the pan by the handle and shaking it from time to time. When done, seeds will have darkened slightly, turned crisp, and give a delightful, fragrant aroma. Toward the end of roasting, lightly season with sea salt or soy sauce to make them more digestible and delicious.

Tangy Fruit Compote

Dried fruit, cooked and thickened with kuzu root, is one of the simplest, quickest, and most delicious desserts.

1 cup dried apples, apricots, peaches, or pears
pinch of sea salt
spring water
1 tablespoon kuzu

Place fruit in a saucepan and add enough water to half-cover the fruit. Add sea salt and bring to a boil. Cover and simmer on low flame for about 20 minutes or until tender. Dissolve kuzu in several tablespoons of cold water, add slowly to cooked fruit, stirring with a wooden spoon. Compote is done when liquid thickens slightly and is clear. Remove from pan and serve.

"The autumnal leaves and nuts were clattering down everywhere. Shellbarks, hickory nuts, and chestnuts strewed the ground, and grapes, muscadines, persimmons, and various wild autumnal fruits were plentiful. It was delightful to observe the women and children wallowing in the dry leaves in the evening, and gathering such quantities of nuts as to require assistance to get them into camp."
— Gideon Lincecum, Early American Naturalist

Cooking Tip
You may prefer to roast seeds and grains in a stainless steel pan rather than a cast-iron skillet as the heat is easier to adjust.

Gale's Apple Surprise

This fruit dessert has a smoother, richer texture than when agar or kuzu is used alone. We had this in Dallas a few days before moving to Becket, and it was very relaxing.

Health Note
A medical study found that women with PMS (premenstrual syndrome), including symptoms of nervous tension, mood swings, irritability, anxiety, and insomnia, ate two and a half times as much sugar as women without PMS or with mild cases.

1 apple
1 teaspoon raisins
1/2 cup apple juice
1/2 cup water
1 tablespoon agar agar flakes
1/2 tablespoon tahini
1 teaspoon kuzu
pinch of sea salt
spring water

Peel and core apple and cut each half into 4 slices and each slice into thirds. Heat apple juice and water in a saucepan. Add agar flakes in this liquid and simmer until they dissolve. Add apples, raisins, tahini, and sea salt and cook over low flame 5 to 10 minutes until fruit is tender (but not mushy). Mix kuzu in a few teaspoons of cold water and add to the fruit, stirring gently until it becomes transparent. Serve warm or at room temperature.

Southern Apple Crisp

This is a delicious apple crisp, made crispier by sautéing the apples in a little oil.

6 apples
1/3 cup pecans
1 cup rolled oats
sesame oil
pinch of sea salt
1/2 cup spring water
2 tablespoons arrowroot flour
1/2 cup rice syrup
1/4 cup barley malt

Peel, core, and slice apples. Roast pecans and rolled oats separately in skillet. Lightly sauté the sliced apples in sesame oil with a pinch of sea salt. Put in baking dish. Mix arrowroot flour in water and pour over ingredients. Mix rice syrup and barley malt with rolled oats and pecans. Sprinkle over apples. Bake 20 to 25 minutes in preheated 375-degree oven. Remove cover for last 5 minutes to make top crispier.

Baked Pears with Kuzu-Raisin Sauce

This is a sweet, smooth, relaxing dessert.

3 Anjou pears (or 1/2 pear per person)
1/2 cup apple juice
1/2 cup spring water
2 tablespoons raisins
1 teaspoon kuzu
rice syrup

Cut and core pears and slice in half. Put in a baking dish with apple juice, water, and raisins. Bake 20 minutes. Then mix kuzu in cold water and thicken the remaining liquid. Add rice syrup to taste, simmer, and serve in serving bowl.

Strawberry Kanten

Strawberries are native to North America and have been enjoyed from earliest times. The Iroquois observed an annual strawberry festival to commemorate the renewal of yearly growth. This is one of our favorite strawberry recipes, a delicious, mild, light refreshing gelatin.

In the Far East, gelatins (known as kanten) *were traditionally made with agar-agar, a seaweed that is processed into flakes or powder.*

1 cup strawberries, freshly sliced
2/3 cup apple juice per person
1/3 cup spring water per person
1/4 cup amasake
2 tablespoons agar agar flakes
1 teaspoon kuzu

Slice strawberries, add fluids and amasake, put in agar flakes, and simmer until the agar has dissolved. Then dissolve kuzu in a few spoonfuls of spring water and stir in fruit mixture until it thickens. Pour into molds or dessert bowls and let cool.

• For variety, use blueberries, peaches, apples, cantaloupe, or other seasonal fruit, singly or in combination.

"That lady must be a wretched cook indeed who cannot make apple dumplings, mince pie, or cake palatable without the additon of poisonous substances."
— Amelia Jenks Bloomer 1842

"She had only to stand in the orchard, to put her hand on a little crab tree and look up at the apples, to make you feel the goodness of planting and tending and harvesting at last."
— Willa Cather, My Antonia

"The pie is an English institution, which, planted on American soil, forthwith ran rampant and burst forth into an untold variety of genra and species. Not merely the old mince pie, but a thousand strictly American seedlings from that main stock, evinced the power of American housewives to adapt old institutions to new uses.

"Pumpkin pies, cranberry pies, huckleberry pies, cherry pies, green-currant pies, peach, pear, and plum pies, custard pies, apple pies, Marborough-pudding pies—pies with top crusts, and pies without—pies adorned with all sorts of fanciful flutings and architectural stripes laid across and around, and otherwise varied, attested the boundless fertility of the feminine mind, when once let loose in a given direction."
— *Harriet Beecher Stowe, Oldtown Folks*

Sinfully Delicious Walnut-Strawberry Cookies

The word "cookie" comes from the Dutch word koekje *meaning little cake. There are many delicious cookies that can be made in the macrobiotic kitchen with good-quality ingredients. Here is one of our favorites.*

1/2 cup ground walnuts
1 cup ground rolled oats
1 cup whole wheat pastry flour
pinch of sea salt
2/3 cup brown rice syrup
2 tablespoons corn oil
5 ounce strawberry jam (sugar-free or naturally-sweetened)
1/2 teaspoon almond extract
1 teaspoon vanilla extract

Grind walnuts by putting them between wax paper and rolling with a rolling pin. If they're not fine enough, then put them in a blender. Grind rolled oats the same way. Measure the cup after they are ground. Add walnuts, oats, flour, and sea salt together in a bowl.

In a separate bowl, mix the rice syrup, corn oil, strawberry jam, and extracts. Pour the liquid ingredients into the dry ingredients and mix until dry ingredients are moistened. Let cool for 30 minutes. Then on an oiled cookie sheet, drop a tablespoon of batter per cookie and bake in a 350-degree oven for 20 minutes. Makes 15 to 18 cookies that are about 3-inches in diameter.

Apple Pie with Kuzu-Apple Juice Glaze

Pies originated in England as meat pies. In the American colonies, apples and other fruit replaced beef and mince meat as the main filling.

4 apples, thinly sliced
1 1/3 cup apple juice
1/3 cup raisins
1/2 teaspoon cinnamon (optional)

1/2 teaspoon lemon juice
2 tablespoons kuzu

Crust (for a Single 8-Inch Pie)
1 1/2 cups whole wheat pastry flour
1/4 cup corn oil
1 tablespoon barley malt
1/4 teaspoon sea salt

Prepare crust first by mixing salt into the fresh pastry flour, then adding oil until flour begins to bead. Sprinkle barley malt over this mixture, slightly mix, and add enough water to make a thick ball of dough. Quickly roll out between two sheets of wax paper or on a board used for pie crusts. Cut into a circle which is about 9-inches wide and place into lightly oiled glass or stainless steel pie pan. Pierce the bottom of the pie crust and sides lightly with a fork so the crust will not puff up and let the liquid from the pie filling go under it.

Meanwhile, combine apples, 1/3 cup of apple juice and raisins and bring to a boil. Cover and simmer 15 minutes. Mix in cinnamon and lemon juice. Remove from heat and allow to cool. Combine kuzu and remaining 1 cup of apple juice, stir until dissolved, and bring to a boil. Simmer about 1 minute or until transparent and thickened. Spoon apples into crust and pour glaze over. Bake for about 40 minutes.

Squash Pudding

1 butternut squash (3-4 cups puréed)
3 tablespoons agar agar flakes
1 tablespoon barley malt
1 teaspoon tahini
1/8 teaspoon sea salt
1 tablespoon arrowroot powder

Boil squash for about 30 minutes or until done, peel, and purée in a handmill. Put back in saucepan on stove, add agar agar powder, barley malt, tahini, and sea salt. While simmering, mix arrowroot in water and add to squash. Simmer 5 to 10 minutes more. Place in dessert bowls and let set.

Over the river and through the wood, Now Grandmother's cap I spy! Hurrah for the fun! Is the pudding done? Hurrah for the pumpkin-pie!
— Old School Reader

Squash Pie with Millet Crust

Millet makes a firm chewy crust, a nice alternative for those who are careful of hard baked wheat products.

3-4 cups buttercup squash
sea salt
1 tablespoon agar agar
spring water
1 tablespoon barley malt

Crust
1 cup millet
1 cup spring water

Boil the squash with a pinch of sea salt. Put in hand mill and purée. Add agar agar flakes dissolved in a little water and the barley malt. Cook, stir, and dissolve agar agar for 5 minutes. For the crust, cook the millet and press it in a pie tin. Bake for 10 minutes, then add the squash filling, and bake for another 20 minutes.

Open Sesame Pumpkin Pie

Open Sesame, the macrobiotic restaurant in Brookline Village, makes one of New England's best pumpkin pies, as generations of Kushi Institute students can testify.

2 quarts puréed squash or pumpkin
1 tablespoon agar agar powder
2 tablespoons arrowroot
1 teaspoon sea salt
1 to 2 teaspoons cinnamon
1 cup barley malt
1/4 cup tahini

Crust (for 2 pies)
1/2 quart pastry flour
pinch of sea salt
1 cup corn oil
1 cup apple juice

Cook squash in very little water and blend. Mix arrowroot, agar agar, and cinnamon in cool water and add to puréed squash.

"Early in the afternoon the bushel baskets and all the pails were full, and Father drove home. They were all a little sleepy, soaked in sunshine and breathing the fruity smell of the berries.

"For days Mother and the girls made jellies and jams and preserves, and for every meal there was huckleberry pie or blueberry pudding."
— *Laura Ingalls Wilder, Farmer Boy*

Combine ingredients, roll out dough, and form crust about 1/4-inch thick. Add filling to crust, top with walnuts, and bake at 300 degrees for 40 minutes.

Lemon Tofu Creme Pie

Often we crave foods that we grew up on and don't know how to create a healthy, satisfying substitute. This is one effort in that direction. This is recommended for occasional use only.

Filling
6 ounces lemon juice (about 6 lemons)
rind of 1 lemon
2 cups organic apple juice
2 cups rice syrup
1 teaspoon vanilla
4 ounces fresh soft tofu
pinch of sea salt
4 heaping tablespoons agar agar flakes
4 tablespoons arrowroot

Tofu Creme
1 1/2 cups of soft fresh tofu
1/4 cup tahini
1/4 cup rice syrup or barley malt
1 teaspoon vanilla extract
1 teaspoon almond extract (optional)
pinch of sea salt
1/4 cup apple juice

Squeeze the juice from the lemons and strain the seeds out. Grate the rind on a fine grater. Put lemon juice, lemon rind, apple juice, rice syrup, vanilla, crumbled tofu, and sea salt into a blender and blend. Pour into a pan and add the agar flakes. Cook gently for five to ten minutes, making sure all the agar is dissolved. Then dissolve arrowroot in small amount of water and add to mixture to thicken. Pour into dessert dishes and let set until firm.

To make tofu creme, combine ingredients in blender and spread on top of lemon filling when it is firm. Slivered, toasted nuts may be added to garnish.

• The effects of the electric blender are greatly lessened if the food is allowed to sit for several hours before eating.

Melon Creme Pie

This is a very unique, delicious, creamy pie. It has a subtle taste and hardens nicely.

4 cups cantaloupe, diced
pinch of sea salt
spring water
1 cup apple juice
3-4 chunks tofu (about 4 ounces)
4-5 tablespoons agar agar

Water-sauté the cantaloupe for about 10 minutes. Put in blender or food mill and purée with apple juice and tofu. Put mixture back in pan on the stove, add agar agar, simmer until dissolved, and pour in pie plate until hardened.

Zesty Indian Pudding

"Pudding" is an Old English word originally meaning a simple dish with softly cooked grain and chopped vegetables or fruits. If made with a thick crust it became a pudding pie. Following the Crusades, when spices and sugar entered Europe, rich puddings began to appear made with sweetened almond milk and colored with saffron. In colonial New England, the favorite was Hasty Pudding, a pudding that could be prepared quickly and which often included maple syrup and molasses, cinnamon and nutmeg, raisins and apples, and was served with cream. The main ingredient, cornmeal, eventually led to puddings of this kind being called Indian pudding.

"The family had been living on corncakes and sorghum molasses for three days."
— *Willa Cather, My Antonia*

1 cup cornmeal
2 1/2 to 3 cups apple juice
2 tablespoons raisins
pinch of sea salt
1/4 cup roasted, chopped walnuts
1/4 teaspoon lemon zest (grated lemon peel)
1 tablespoon pearl barley malt (or other sweetener)

Roast walnuts in oven or skillet and chop. Place cornmeal, salt, and raisins in a saucepan and gradually stir in apple juice. Bring to a boil, reduce heat, and simmer for 15 to 20 minutes, stirring occasionally until mixture thickens. Stir in pearl barley malt and nuts. Simmer a few minutes longer and serve warm.

Rice Pudding

American Cookery, *the first cookbook written by an American, included six recipes for rice pudding. Here is one of our own.*

2 cups long-grain rice, cooked
3/4 cup apple juice
3/4 cup spring water
2 tablespoons raisins
1-2 teaspoons tahini (optional)
2 tablespoons rice syrup
pinch of cinnamon
pinch of sea salt
1 tablespoon kuzu

Put the rice, raisins, sea salt, and cinnamon in a saucepan. Add apple juice, water, tahini, and rice syrup. Cook over low flame for 25 minutes. Dissolve kuzu in cold water and add to the other ingredients and stir so it will thicken the mixture. This will only take a few minutes. Remove to dessert dishes and let sit until ready to serve.

• Top with roasted, slivered almonds or walnuts if desired.

"And it's lovely rice pudding for dinner again."
— A. A. Milne,
When We Were Very Young

Heavenly Gingerbread

Gingerbread is another traditional American favorite. It was originally made from stale bread crumbs, red wine, and black licorice. Here is a macrobiotic version that is so delicious you will think you've died and gone to heaven.

2 cups whole wheat flour
2 teaspoons baking powder
1 teaspon cinnamon
1 teaspoon ginger
1/2 teaspoon nutmeg
1/2 teaspoon sea salt
2/3 cup rice syrup
1/3 cup rice syrup or barley malt
1/4 cup corn oil

Malt Syrup Icing
1/2 cup barley malt or rice syrup
1/2 cup rice syrup

1 tablespoon tahini
1/4 teaspoon vanilla
1 teaspoon kuzu
chopped nuts (optional)
spring water

Pre-heat oven to 350 degrees and oil muffin tins or cake pans. Combine dry ingredients in mixing bowl and mix. Combine sweeteners, corn oil, and water and stir into dry ingredients. Pour into oiled muffin tins or cake pans and bake for 25 to 30 minutes (for muffins) or 35 to 40 minutes (for cake). Test by inserting knife tip into center of cake. If it is relatively clean when removed, then the cake is done. Or if you touch the top of the cake with a finger to make an indentation and it quickly springs back to its original shape, then it is done.

To make icing, mix sweeteners with tahini and vanilla and add gradually about a half cup of water until the icing reaches the desired thickness. Dissolve kuzu in cold water and add to mixture. Stir gently as the icing thickens. Add nuts at the last minute. Also, grated lemon peel or orange peel may be added for a distinctive flavor.

Mock Banana Pudding with Parsnips

Parsnips are one of the sweetest vegetables and have traditionally been used in America to make wonderful desserts. This dish tastes like banana pudding

1 cup parnips, cut into 3/4-inch cubes
1/2 butternut squash, cut into small chunks
1 cup of apple juice
1 cup spring water
pinch of sea salt
1 cup couscous, pre-cooked

Wash, peel, and cut parsnips and squash and place in a pressure cooker. Mix a cup of apple juice with a cup of water and pour this over the vegetables. Add a pinch of sea salt. Pressure cook for about 15 minutes. Then you can either mash the vegetables or purée them in a pressure cooker. When puréed, put back in a pot and add a small amount of couscous. Cover and let it simmer in the puréed squash until tender. Mix and serve in individual serving bowls.

• A small amount of grated lemon or lemon juice may be added to the parsnips before cooking or a hint of cinnamon for a slightly different flavor.

• The pudding can be turned into a pie by adding a crust of couscous made with half apple juice and half spring water or of millet made with half pear juice and half water.

Grape Couscous Cake

This makes a purple, sweet, very cooling dessert, resembling a cheese cake with a crumbly taste.

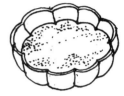

2 cups grape juice
1/2 cup spring water or apple juice
pinch of sea salt
1/2 cup amasake
2 heaping tablespoons agar agar
1/2 cup whole wheat couscous

Mix apple juice, grape juice, and amasake and bring to a boil with a pinch of sea salt. Add agar flakes and boil until they are completely dissolved, stirring occasionally. Add couscous, simmer 2 to 3 minutes more, and let sit 5 minutes while couscous expands. Pour into baking dish and let sit until jelled.

Sweetened Chestnut Purée

Chestnuts are naturally sweet and can be eaten by themselves or combined with sweeteners for a lovely snack or dessert.

1/2 cup spring water
1/2 cup barley malt or 1 cup amasake
1/2 pound dried chestnuts

Soak chestnuts for several hours. Combine water, sweetener, and chestnuts in a 2-quart saucepan. Bring to a boil over medium heat, lower the heat, and simmer about 30 minutes until the chestnuts are very soft. Remove from the pan and let cool slightly. Purée in a food mill while still warm.

• This purée will keep in the refrigerator for up to a week but should be warmed before eating.

Sweet Corn Pudding

This Zuni delicacy was made of yellow cornmeal with some of the batter which was sweetened by previous chewing and fermentation or by adding dried flowers. The batter was then skillfully wrapped in dried green corn leaves made flexible for cooking by immersing in hot water. The small crescent-shaped pieces of dough were then boiled or occasionally baked. The leaves brought out their succulent taste, making them the sweetest cooked food known to the Zuni. Other sweet dishes were made with licorice-root or wild honey. Macrobiotic friends today who are accomplished chewers may want to experiment with this dish.

Popcorn

"[Popcorn] is the national addiction: warmth on chilly winter nights, innocence on Saturday afternoons, the essence of hearth, home, and blissful abandon."
— Patricia Linden, article in Town and Country 1984

Chief Massasoit brought popcorn to Governor Bradford in Plymouth in 1621. Since the first Thanksgiving, it has been a perennial favorite. We enjoy it at parties and holidays, including the traditional stringing of popcorn for the Christmas tree. Neither oil nor salt is necessary for cooking and seasoning.

1 tablespoon popcorn

Take three kernels of popcorn and place in a saucepan or pot. Cover lightly and heat on low to medium flame. When the three kernels have popped, the pan is hot enough to add the remaining kernels. Cover lightly, place a flame deflector beneath the pot, and cook until there are no more popping sounds and nearly all the kernels have popped. One tablespoon of kernels will make about two and a half cups of popcorn. Serve or store in a sealed container in a cool dark place.

Parched Sweet Corn

This was a popular Indian snack made from dried seed corn parched in oil and salted. It is sold in natural foods stores today as cornnuts. This recipe makes about 2 cups.

2 cups sweet dried corn
4 tablespoons corn or sesame oil
sea salt or soy sauce to taste

Place dried corn in a large colander and pour boiling water over them. Drain on cheesecloth or a paper towel. Lightly oil skillet, add the corn, and stir continuously until each kernel is lightly browned. Add sea salt or soy sauce.

Amasake Pudding

1 quart amasake
3 rounded tablespoons kuzu
pinch of sea salt
roasted, slivered almonds

Pour amasake into a saucepan. Dissolve kuzu in several tablespoons of cold water and stir into the amasake. Add salt and stir gently but constantly while bringing mixture to a boil over low heat. Simmer several minutes more. Pour into individual serving dishes. Garnish with 1 teaspoon of slivered almonds per serving.
  • For a different taste, add a couple of level tablespoons of grain coffee mix (such as Cafix) along with the kuzu.

George Washington's Rice Waffles

When he was a little boy, Washington's mother made the future leader of the Republic rice waffles with native Virginian brown rice and whole wheat flour. They make a delightful breakfast, snack, or dessert. Our modern statesmen should dine so well!

1 cup brown rice, softly cooked
whole wheat flour
pinch of sea salt
spring water

Add pre-cooked or leftover rice that has been warmed to flour, a pinch of salt, and enough water to make dough. Oil waffle iron, ladle dough on top, close, and cook for 5 or 10 minutes or until done. Serve with barley malt, rice syrup, pearl barley malt, or fruit preserves.

"I don't think a really good pie can be made without a dozen or so children peeking over your shoulder as you stoop to look in at it every little while."
— John Gould

"From Sea to Shining Sea"

7
Beverages

The clear sparkling waters of the American continent were traditionally used to make a variety of beverages. Native people drank *powhicora*, a mixture of crushed fresh corn mixed with the milk from boiled hickory nuts and chestnuts, flavored with the ashes of different wood. Spanish colonists also enjoyed nut milks, bringing over with them almonds. In the English colonies, beer arrived with the *Mayflower* and, along with ale, served as a staple for several generations. Tea arrived with Dutch traders in 1670, and the British custom of drinking black tea quickly swept the colonies. Duties on tea sparked the Boston Tea Party, setting off the American Revolution and reducing the popularity of this beverage on American shores ever since.

In the nineteenth century, homemade or store-bought root beers, ginger beers (made from ginger root or powdered ginger), and spruce beers could be obtained from coast to coast. In New England, spruce beer was made from black spruce branches or birth sap. In the middle states, it was made from hemlock or sassafras, and in the South from sassafras or sarsaparilla. Coffee, a tropical bean that originated in Ethiopia and was transplanted to Central and South America, remained expensive during America's early years. In Kansas, Nebraska, and other pioneer territories, families customarily drank grain coffee made from roasted rye, barley, or chickory.

"On this day more than 120 canoes came to the ships, all being full of people, and they all brought something, especially their bread and fish, and water in small earthenware jars, and seeds of many kinds . . . They threw a grain into a mug of water and drank it, and the Indians, whom the Admiral carried with him, said that it was a most healthy thing."
— **Las Casas, from Columbus' Journal**

Fruit-based party drinks were known by many colorful names, including punches, toddies, shrubs, orgeats, ratifias, bounces, flips, and fools.

The Standard Macrobiotic Diet recommends various beverages for daily use and for occasional or less frequent consumption. The amount of beverage intake varies according to the individual's needs, the climate and environment, season and daily weather. Beverage consumption should comfortably satisfy the desire for liquid in terms of kind, volume, and frequency of intake.

Bancha tea is the staple beverage in most macrobiotic homes around the world. Bancha is made from the twigs or stems of the tea plant, while black tea and green tea are made from the leaves. In macrobiotic parlance, bancha is more yang—more balanced—than either black or green tea. Bancha also contains no caffeine which remains in the leaves and gives black and green tea their stimulating effect.

We have been drinking bancha tea as our main beverage for many years and find it soothing, peaceful, and thirst-quenching. It is suitable for children as well as adults and is customarily taken plain. Occasionally, we will mix it with half grain coffee, half apple juice, or other beverage for variety or a more relaxing drink. We also enjoy roasted grain teas, including brown rice tea, millet tea, and barley tea.

In the spring or summer, we enjoy carrot juice, mixed vegetable juice, or other vegetable juice once or twice a week in small volume. In the fall, we like apple cider and other juices from time to time. We are careful with juices because they are very concentrated. A half dozen apples can easily go into making one glass of apple juice.

Bancha Tea

Bancha is made from the mature leaves, twigs, and stems of the tea bush. It is also commonly called kukicha tea. The twigs are usually sold dry-roasted and should be kept in an air-tight jar.

2 tablespoons of roasted twigs
5 cups spring water

Add twigs to pot of water and bring to a boil. Lower flame and simmer for several minutes. Place bamboo tea strainer in cup and pour out tea. Twigs in strainer may be returned to teapot.

Roasted Barley Tea

Barley tea is slightly more relaxing than bancha tea and is especially enjoyable in the spring and summer. It is available already roasted in the natural foods store (sometimes under its Far Eastern name, mugi cha*).*

2 tablespoons barley tea
1 quart spring water

Add twigs to pot of water and bring to a boil. Lower flame and simmer for 10 to 15 minutes. Place bamboo tea strainer in cup and pour out tea. Twigs in strainer may be returned to teapot.

Brown Rice Tea

Brown rice makes a strong, centering tea.

2-3 tablespoons of roasted rice
1 quart spring water

Dry-roast uncooked rice over medium flame for 10 minutes or until a fragrant aroma develops. Stir and shake pan occasionally to prevent burning. Add roasted rice to pot of spring water. Bring to a boil, reduce flame, and simmer 10 to 15 minutes.

• Tea may also be made from millet, barley, oats, buckwheat, quinoa, and other grains in this way.

Grain Coffee

There are a variety of grain coffees available in the natural foods store. Some of them contain molasses, figs, dates, honey, and other ingredients not usually eaten in the macrobiotic diet. George Ohsawa made a cereal grain coffee which he called yannoh. *It is very delicious and can be made at home or obtained ready-made in many stores.*

3 cups uncooked brown rice
2 1/2 cups wheat berries
1 1/2 cups aduki beans
2 cups chickpeas
1 cup chicory root

Cooking Tip
Glass, ceramic, or enamel containers are best for making tea.

"Each preparation of the leaves has its individuality, its special affinity with water and heat, its hereditary memories to recall, its own method of telling a story. . . East and West have met in the tea-cup."
— Kakuzo Okakura, The Book of Tea

Health Note
Chemicals from pesti-cides and fertilizers, industrial production, and from additives to muncipal tap water are associated with a wide variety of sick-nesses including Alz-heimer's Disease.

In macrobiotic cooking and eating, good quality spring or well water is highly recommended.

Health Note
If you're feeling tense and agitated, you can relax with a cup of shiitake mushroom tea, ginger tea, or hot apple juice or apple ci-der.

Roast ingredients until dark brown, then mix together, and grind into a fine powder in a grain mill. For a coffee-like drink, use 1 tablespoon per cup of water. Bring to a boil, lower flame, and simmer for 5 to 10 minutes.

Corn Silk Tea

Native peoples traditionally enjoyed a beverage made from the golden silk strands of fresh corn. It is good in hot weather and especially beneficial to the heart and kidneys.

1/2 cup fresh corn silk
1 quart spring water

Place corn silk in water and bring to a boil. Reduce heat and simmmer several minutes. Strain into cup and serve.

Mu Tea

Mu tea is a tea made with a variety of herbs that was also de-veloped by George Ohsawa. It is sold prepackaged in many nat-ural foods stores and comes in several varieties. It was popular in the '60s and early '70s because of its association with mu—a central concept in Zen meaning nothingness—and the Beatniks.

1 mu teabag
1 quart of spring water

Place teabag in water and simmer for 10 minutes and strain into cup.

Umeboshi Tea

Umeboshi tea has a nice sour taste. It helps cool the body in summer and prevent loss of minerals through perspiration. It is usually served cool, and the taste should not be salty.

2-3 pitted umeboshi plums
1 quart spring water

Boil the umeboshi plums in the water, reducing the heat, and simmering for about 20 minutes. A few shiso leaves, which come with umeboshi plums, may be added to enhance flavor.

Amasake

*Amasake, a sweet, delicious beverage made from fermented
sweet rice, is a universal favorite of macrobiotic women and
children. (It is too yin for men except on special occasions!) It
may be made at home or obtained ready-made in many natural
foods stores. In addition to a beverage, amasake may be used
as a natural sweetener for making cookies, cakes, pies, or other
desserts.*

4 cups sweet brown rice
8 cups spring water
1/2 cup koji (inoculated grain starter)

Wash rice, drain, and soak in 8 cups of water overnight. Place
rice in pressure-cooker and bring to pressure. Reduce heat and
cook for 45 minutes. When cool enough, mix koji into rice by
hand and allow to ferment for 6 to 8 hours. During fermentation, place mixture in a glass bowl, cover with wet cloth or towel, and place near oven, radiator, or other warm place. During
fermentation period, stir the mixture occasionally to melt the
koji. After fermenting, place ingredients in a pot and bring to
boil. When bubbles appear, turn off heat, allow to cool, and refrigerate in a glass bowl or jar.

To use as a beverage, first blend the amasake and place in a
saucepan with a pinch of sea salt and spring water in volume to
desired consistency. Bring to boil and serve hot or allow to cool
to room temperature.

Raspberry Shrub

*Shrub comes from the Arabic word for "drink," and is a punch-
made with a fruit base and diluted with wine, water, cider, or
brandy. This recipe, served at the reception at the Executive
Mansion in Philadelphia on July 4, 1776, makes a nice punch—
once every 200 years.*

1/2 cup lime juice
1 cup raspberry syrup
3 cups ginger wine
2 cups apple wine
ginger root, grated the size of an egg

Mix all ingredients. Makes 10 punch-cup servings.

*"I never before knew
the virtue of Sequoia
juice. Seen with sun-
beams in it, its color is
the most royal of all
royal purples. No
wonder the Indians
instictively drink it
for they know not
what. I wish I was so
drunk & Sequoical
that I could preach
the green brown woods
to all the juiceless
world, descending
from this divine wil-
derness like a John
Baptist . . . crying,
Repent for the King-
dom of Sequoia is at
hand."*
*— John Muir,
founder of the Sierra
Club*

Birch Beer

Before the era of soft drinks and store-bought liquor, fermented beverages made of tree saps, herbs, and roots were popular in American history. This is a traditional Appalachian recipe for birch beer.

1/2 gallon birch sap
1/2 gallon spring water
1/2 gallon cornmeal

Tap a birch tree and collect the sap. Mix the sap with spring water and cornmeal and put in a warm place to ferment. After about 3 weeks, drain off the liquid, cool, and serve.

Ecology Note
The production of animal foods uses nearly 80 percent of all piped water in the United States and is chiefly responsible for pollution of two-thirds of U.S. basins and for generating over half of the pollution burden entering the nation's lakes and streams.

Part III

Special Cooking

1
Holiday Food

In addition to national holidays, there are religious celebrations; birthdays, anniversaries, and other family occasions; balls, picnics, barbeques, cookouts, and other social gatherings; and various regional and cultural festivals at which special food is prepared. Macrobiotic households in the United States and Canada are no exception, and many superb party foods are served that are not eaten on a daily basis. At the Kushi Institute in Becket, we customarily have large Thanksgiving and Christmas banquets in the Main House for up to a hundred staff, teachers, students, and friends. Smaller celebrations are held on the Lunar New Year in February, Earth Day in May, Peace Day in August, and other special occasions. Below are menus for seven holidays drawn from recipes in this book.

Oriental New Year's

The Lunar New Year begins on February 4. At home we usually celebrate it with an Eastern-style macrobiotic diiner

Miso Soup with Mochi
Red Rice (Brown Rice with Aduki Beans)
Sushi Rolls
Squash and Onion Nishime
Hiziki with Vegetables
Daikon Pickles
Amasake Pudding
Sake, Beer, Bancha Tea

Regional North American Festivals and Celebrations

House-Raising
Log-Rolling
Barn-Raising
Corn-Husking
Quilting Bee
Nutting Party
Apple-Picking
Taffy Pull
Baked Bean Supper
Church Social
Skating Party
Country Fair
Sugarin' Off Party
Sleigh Ride
Wedding
Christening
Bar Mitzvah
Debutante Ball
Square Dance
Sporting Event
Election Rally
Peace March
Clambake
Chili Cookout
Salmon Roast
Oktoberfest
Potlatch
Luau Feast

Earth Day

Earth Day is observed around the world on April 22. This recipe has a West Coast accent and, in terms of energy, pollution, cost, and health, is beneficial to the world as a whole.

Creamy Leek Soup with Barley
Pressure-Cooked Brown Rice
Stir-Fry Vegetables
Sea Palm
Miso Pickles
Apple Compote
Grain Coffee, Bancha Tea

Independence Day

America celebrates the nation's birthday on July 4th with picnics, barbeques, and other family and social gatherings. Here is a healthful alternative to the hamburgers, frankfurters, and sugary desserts.

Corn Chowder
Tempeh Kebabs with Soy-Ginger Kuzu Sauce
Boiled Carrots and Onions
Arame
Watermelon Pickles
Tofu Lemon Creme Pie
Umeboshi Tea, Raspberry Shrub, Birch Beer

Peace Day

International Peace Days are celebrated on August 6 and August 9, the anniversary of the atomic bombing of Hiroshima and Nagasaki.

Carrot Soup
Wild Rice Croquettes with Miso-Tahini Sauce
Corn on the Cob
Wakame-Cucumber Salad
Fresh Lotus Root
East West Bread
Strawberry Kanten
Spring Water

Thanksgiving

The first Thanksgiving meal featured a variety of dishes made with corn, squash, and beans—the Indians' traditional staples—and wild game and seafood. This menu is adapted from one we celebrated in Dallas, with each guest bringing a different dish.

Smooth Red Lentil Soup
Stuffed Squash Turkey with Mushroom Seitan Sauce
Rice with Sweet Rice and Slivered Almonds
Cranberry Applesauce
Succotash
Mustard Greens
Plimouth Plantation Boiled Salad
Deep Purple Dulse
Squash or Pumpkin Pie
Apple Couscous Cake
Apple Cider, Bancha Tea

Christmas or Hanukkah

This is usually the most joyful season of the year, and we like to celebrate the midwinter holidays with tree-trimming, carol singing, and candle lighting.

Creamy Squash Soup
Brown Rice with Millet
Vegetable Tempura
Tofu Cheese
Tender Collard Greens
Sauerkraut
Heavenly Gingerbread
Hot Amasake with Ginger
Bancha Tea

*A chimney where all
  Winter long
The logs give back the
  wild bird's song.
The wind that cools
  my hidden spring
And sets my corn-field
  whispering.
And shakes with Autumn breath for me
Late apples from the
  apple-tree.
The shy paths darting
  through the wheat,
Marked by the prints
  of little feet.*
— *Edwin Markham*

Kwaanza

Kwaanza is a year-end cultural festival celebrated by many African-Americans from December 26-31. It customarily features story-telling, music, dance, and other artistic expression, as well as food from Africa, the Caribbean, and American South. Here is just one delicious, healthful macrobiotic Kwaanza menu.

Parsnip Soup
Hoppin' John (Brown Rice and Black-Eyed Peas)
Vegetable Kinpira
Steamed Kale
Soy Sauce Pickles
Millet Cornbread
Mochi Waffles with Apricots
Grain Coffee

"By the time we had placed the cold, fresh-smelling little tree in a corner of the sitting-room, it was already Christmas Eve. After supper, we all gathered there, and even grandfather, reading his paper by the table, looked up with friendly interest now and then. The cedar was about five feet high and very shapely. We hung it with the gingerbread animals, strings of popcorn, and bits of candle which Fuchs had fitted into pasteboard sockets."
— Willa Cather, My Antonia

2
Medicinal Food

On one of his voyages to the New World, Columbus abandoned a group of desperately ill sailors on a Caribbean island without any provisions. On his return to Europe, he stopped and discovered that the dying men had miraculously returned to health. Inquiring about their recovery, they told him that they had eaten the natural foods that grew wild. Ever since, the island has been known as Curacao, meaning "the place of cures" in Portuguese.

Native peoples commonly used food as medicine. From New England to the Southwest, wild and domesticated grains, vegetables from land and sea, and roots and tubers continued to be used by American families as they settled the land. On his death bed, George Washington was given a wheat bran poultice to reduce his suffering. National abundance, however, brought new sicknesses and treatments. Early observers of American cultural life frequently commented on how quickly Americans ate, gobbling their food down, and eating huge quantities. Dyspepsia—indigestion, constipation, and other intestinal ills—became known as the archetypal American affliction. Drugs, chemicals, and a variety of patent medicines were devised for these afflictions.

The early health reformers of the nineteenth century such as Mary Gove Nichols and Dr. William Alcott, a member of the famous Alcott family, encouraged orderly eating and eating in small volume. Their mostly vegetable-quality diet met approval among all segments of society. *The White House Cookbook*, the nearest thing to an authoritative food guide, originally published in 1887, popularized simple foods and the use of food as medicine. In the early twentieth century, Horace Fletcher, a pro-

"Many seem to have no idea that there are established laws with respect to life and health, and that the transgression of these laws is followed by disease."
— *Mary Gove Nichols, Lectures to Women on Anatomy and Physiology 1846*

fessor of nutrition at Yale, popularized thorough chewing, recommending that each mouthful be chewed at least 50 times. "Fletcherizing"—as chewing was called—spread through all segments of the American population but proved to be short-lived experiment. After "Wheatless" and "Meatless" meals during World War I, the country entered the Roaring '20s, meat consumption spread (especially of sirloin and other cuts of beef), and the modern epidemics of heart disease, cancer, and other degenerative disease began. Following World War II, and the explosion of antibiotics and chemical fertilizers and drugs, the use of foods in the home medicine chest all but disappeared.

Rice Cream

Early American cooks and cookbook writers often recommended soft rice or rice milk as a healing food, especially for children. In macrobiotic homes today, rice cream is the principal home remedy used for sickness, loss of appetite, difficulty swallowing, and other special medicinal conditions.

This is sometimes called genuine rice cream in contrast to the ready-made rice creams you find in the natural foods store. It is made fresh—and takes some effort—but the results are worth it. The soft, creamy texture and strong nourishing energy make this a perfect food for people who are sick, for nursing mothers, and for anyone else who needs easily digestible food and extra vitality. Everyone who eats this special dish will feel the love you put into it all day long.

1 cup short-grain brown rice
5 cups spring water
pinch of sea salt or 1-inch piece of kombu

Dry-roast 1 cup of brown rice in a stainless steel skillet until golden in color. Place in pressure cooker. Add water and a pinch of sea salt or the kombu. Salt may be eliminated if cooking this dish for someone over sixty. Bring to pressure and cook for one hour.

Let rice cool slightly. Then place about a cup of rice in a cheesecloth or unbleached muslin cloth, and tie and squeeze out the liquid with a wooden spoon or your hands. Alternately, you may use a pestle to press the rice through a strong strainer. The holes should be large enough to let the "cream" through while keeping the bran out.

"Her heart was beating loudly. She drew the blanket over him and kissed his forehead. In the kitchen she slowly stirred the spoon in the barley. She returned to the sick room with the pewter bowl.

"Thank you, Stacey," he said for the first time. She had brought a small saucer of gruel for herself.

"Are you eating this stuff, too?"

"Oh, I often steal a bit. It's good for everybody."
— Thorton Wilder, The Eighth Day

Soft Rye

Soft grains such as barley porridge, cornmeal porridge, oatmeal, and arrowroot gruel were recommended by Grahamites, vegetarians, homeopaths, Adventists, and other early dietary pioneers. In Domestic Cookery, *published in 1853, Quaker author Elizabeth Ellicott Lea recommended Rye Mush as a nourishing and light diet for the sick. "Nervous persons who sleep badly rest much better after a supper of corn, or rye mush, than if they take tea or coffee," she observed.*

4 tablespoons rye flour
pinch of sea salt
2 cups spring water

Mix the rye flour in water, stir in a pint of boiling water, and boil 20 minutes, stirring frequently.

Arrowroot Gruel

Before going to Japan and becoming the best known interpreter of East West culture, Lafcadio Hearn worked as a journalist in New Orleans and other cities and towns across America. In one of his first books, La Cuisine Créole, *he includes a recipe for arrowroot gruel for the sick or invalided.*

1 tablespoon of arrowroot powder
spring water
salt to season

Mix the arrowroot with cold water, stir in half a pint of boiling water, and season to taste. For an infant, use half a tablespoon.

Kuzu Drink

Kuzu, or kudzu as it is known in America, is a starchy root that strengthens digestion, increases vitality, and relieves general fatigue. At our home, kuzu is one of the main foods in our medicine chest.

1 teaspoon kuzu
1 cup spring water
1/2 to 1 teaspoon soy sauce

"If we eat bad food, we make bad blood . . . Such blood cannot make good bone, good muscle, good brain and nerve matter. . . . When the matters which should be cast out of the body are retained to poison the blood, every kind of acute or chronic disease is of easy production. Men may be poisoned to death by bad air. Thousands are poisoned to death by bad food."
— Dr. William Alcott, The Diet Cure 1838

Dissolve kuzu powder in a little cold water, than add to 1 cup of cold water. Bring the mixture to a boil, reduce the heat, and simmer, stirring constantly until the liquid becomes transparent. Stir in soy sauce to taste and drink while hot.

• To strengthen digestion even more, add 1/2 to 1 umeboshi plum and 1/8 teaspoon of fresh grated ginger.

Ginger Compress

The medicinal properties of ginger were appreciated by early colonists and homemakers. In her book of Quaker recipes, Elizabeth Ellicott Lea advised, "A piece of ginger root, kept about the person to chew, is good for a tickling in the throat, which many persons are subject to, when sitting in close heated apartments, in lecture rooms, or places of worship."

In macrobiotic households, ginger compresses are often used to stimulate blood and body fluid circulation, help loosen and dissolve stagnated toxic matter, and relieve pain and blockages. For example, a ginger compress is placed over the kidneys to relieve tightness and pain in this region. (In the nineteenth century, a common remedy for kidney pain was an onion compress made from softly boiled and mashed onions.)

1 ounce grated ginger
1 gallon water

To prepare a ginger compress, place a handful of grated ginger in a cheesecloth and squeeze out the ginger juice into a pot containing 1 gallon of very hot water. Do not boil the water or you will lose the power of the ginger. Dip a cotton hand-towel into the ginger water, wring it out tightly and apply, very hot but not uncomfortably hot, to the area of the body to be treated. A second, dry towel can be placed on top to reduce heat loss. Apply a fresh hot towel every 2 to 3 minutes until the skin becomes red. (Do not press the towel against the skin with your hands.)

Lily Root Poultice

Like ginger compress, a lotus root plaster is a traditional Far Eastern remedy used in many contemporary macrobiotic homes, especially for lung and chest conditions. A traditional North American cousin of the lotus, the lily root, was featured in native and pioneer healing. As Elizabeth Lea noted, "This is

"Irish bartenders in some New York pubs soak Irish moss in whiskey and offer it as a cough cure."
— Thomas Lee, The Seaweed Book

a most valuable poultice for a gathering and has given relief in many instances where the suffering was great."

sweet white water lily root
spring water
flour or bread crumbs

Pound the root of the sweet white lily and boil in water or rice milk. When soft, thicken with flour or bread crumbs.
   • Kuzu or arrowroot may be used instead of flour.

Spiral Wrack Compress

Seaweed figured prominently in early American medicinal preparations. Spiral wrack (*fucus spiralis*), a seaweed found from New York to Newfoundland, was used externally to help heal corns and other inflammations. This remedy was made by taking the "jelly bags" or receptacles of the spiral wrack, crushing then, and adding them to salt water. The affected part was soaked in the mixture.

Bancha Tea with Umeboshi

Umeboshi plums, salted and aged for a year or more, are wonderful for neutralizing extreme foodstuffs and restoring balance. Originally cultivated in the Orient, they are now produced in California and other parts of this country.

1/2 to 1 umeboshi plum
1 cup bancha tea

For medicinal purposes, take 1/2 to 1 plum in 1 cup of hot bancha tea.
   • To strengthen the blood and circulation, add 1 teaspoon of soy sauce to this drink.
   • To neutralize an acidic condition and relieve intestinal problems, including those caused by microorganisms, bake the umeboshi plum before adding it to tea.

"The bear is the only animal which eats roots from the earth and is also especially fond of acorns, June berries, and cherries. These three are frequently compounded with other herbs in making medicine, and if a person is fond of cherries we say he is like a bear. We consider the bear as chief of all animals in regard to herb medicine, and therefore it is understood that if a man dreams of a bear he will be expert in the use of herbs for curing illness."
— Siyaka, Sioux Medicine Man

Mugwort Tea

Mugwort, a medicinal herb used around the world, was a favorite of the Chippewas in the Great Lakes region and present-day Canada. It was used for female afflictions, hemorrhage, dystentery, and tonics and remedies for the hair. In the Far East, mugwort is commonly used as moxa, an herbal application that is burned on pressure points and meridians to stimulate energy flow. We enjoy mugwort in mochi. Here is a trecipe for mugwort tea adapted from traditional North American herbal use.

3 tablespoons dried mugwort
2 cups spring water

Steep mugwort in boiling water for about 10 minutes. Let partially cool and give 1/2 cup to the person and have him or her recline. Repeat at half hour intervals until relief is experienced.

3
Children's Food

In North America, native people traditionally brought up their infants and children on a sweet beverage made from corn and fresh corn stalks. The first Europeans also used grains, beans, seeds, and nuts to feed their offspring. The Pilgrims made milk from crushed fresh corn mixed with the juice from boiled hickory nuts and chestnuts or almonds. This drink was heated for babies and served at room temperature to older children. The first dairy food did not appear until later. In the South, where rice was the staple, rice milk was given to infants and children up until about a century ago.

In macrobiotic households today, a grain-based milk known as *kokkoh* is usually given to babies after about six months of nursing. In addition to this recipe, we include a few traditional American recipes for children and suggested foods for children to take to school. Generally, because they are small, compact, and active—more yang—children require less salt, soy sauce, and other seasoning than adults. Buckwheat often is too yang for children (see poem in margin). Usually, the food for the whole family is prepared with milder seasoning suitable for the children, and older family members and adults can strengthen the flavor and taste of the meal with condiments at the table.

There are many wonderful items that can be made for the macrobiotic school lunchbox, including grainburgers, pita bread sandwiches, and other foods that look and taste like conventional foods. However, we have found that children, like adults, do best on whole grains. At every meal, even when veggie burgers and seitan cutlets are served, some whole rice, millet, barley, or other grain should be included.

A little boy named Thomas ate Hot buckwheat cakes for tea— A very rash proceeding, as We presently shall see.

He went to bed at eight o'clock, As all good children do, But scarce had closed his little eyes, When he most restless grew. . . .

— Eugene Field, The Remorseful Cakes

God bless the master of this house,
God bless the mistress too,
And all the little children
That 'round the table go.
— Traditional Grace

Baby Food

Kokkoh is made by combining brown rice and aduki beans with sweet rice and barley. This gives a nice sweet taste and is easy for the infant or toddler to digest.

1 1/2 cups brown rice
1/2 cup sweet rice
1/4 cup barley
1/4 cup aduki beans
5 cups spring water

Pre-soak the aduki beans and then pressure cook with grains in the usual manner. For toddlers, you may wish to purée the cereal in a food mill before serving. To use as a substitute for mother's milk, purée and add a little barley malt. Give as milk in a bottle.

Arrowroot Tea

This traditional Southern recipe is adapted from Lafcadio Hearn's Creole cookbook, substituting a grain-based sweetener for sugar and spices.

1 tablespoon arrowroot
spring water
barley malt or rice syrup

Mix arrowroot in a little cold water and stir it into boiling spring water. Season to taste and serve.
   • For an infant, use half a tablespoon of arrowroot.

Irish Moss Tea

This is adapted from another traditional recipe collected by Lafadio Hearn. He notes, "Delicate infants may be fed on it when they will take no other nourishment."

1 tablespoon Irish moss
1 cup spring water
barley malt or rice syrup

Wash Irish moss and put it in a saucepan. Pour over it a cup of boiling water and let it simmer for a short time. When it is all dissolved, add sweetener to taste and serve.

Grainburger

1 1/2 cup rice cooked with millet or other grain
1/4 cup grated carrots
1/4 cup onions, minced and boiled
whole wheat or oat flour
sesame oil

Mix grain, carrots, and onions with a little whole wheat or oat flour and form into croquettes. Pan-fry on each side until brown. Serve on whole wheat bread with lettuce and sprouts.

Children's Lunch Menus

Most of the time a simple, nourishing lunch can be prepared from food cooked the night before. However, from time to time, a few dishes can be prepared especially for the children's lunches to balance their condition. It's important to give them what they need for their health and development and not what they want to fulfill their sensory desires. If the food you prepare is tasty and attractive, your children will be happy to share it with their friends. Here are several menu suggestions.

Rice Balls
Tempeh Stew
Boiled Collards
Pickle

Ohagi Rolls
Tofu with Vegetables
Sauerkraut
Fruit Kanten

Udon Noodles Water-Sautéed with Vegetables
Sushi Rolls
Steamed Squash

Brown Rice with Chestnuts
Boiled Kale and Carrots

"It was the summer when I was nine years old, and our people were moving slowly towards the Rocky Mountains.

"We camped one evening in a valley beside a little creek just before it ran into the Greasy Grass, and there was a man by the name of Man Hip who liked me and asked me to eat with him in his teepee.

"While I was eating, a voice came and said, 'It is time; now they are calling you.'"
— Black Elk, Black Elk Speaks

Arame with Corn and Onions

Squash Soup
Brown Rice Cooked with Aduki Beans
Seitan Sandwich with Lettuce and Sprouts

Golden Millet Stew
Black Beans with Carrots
Boiled Salad

Grainburger
Steamed Cabbage or Fresh Salad

Brown Rice Salad
Rice Cakes with Hummus
Amasake Pudding

4
Travel Food

Eating well on the road takes some planning and ingenuity. Native peoples and the early colonists lived on parched corn, Johnnycakes, *arepas*, and other whole corn preparations that transported well, stored easily, and could be made quickly. Rice balls are the standard travel food for most macrobiotic friends today, though a wide variety of grainburgers, sandwiches, and other items may also be prepared.

Since Duncan Hines' travel advisory in the mid-1950's (*see quote in margin*), eating out has become increasingly safer. In addition to natural foods restaurants and health food stores, most ordinary eating establishments now serve salads, whole wheat or pita bread, fish and seafood, steamed vegetables, and sometimes rice, pasta, grits, oatmeal, or other grain. We are happily surprised at how many Chinese and Japanese restaurants now serve brown rice.

Compared to other places, America has the most natural food and most organically grown food of any country in the modern world. As Michio and Aveline often say, the most difficult country to eat healthfully in is modern Japan, where polished rice is the rule and everything is cooked in sugar and chemicals. Japan, the Kushis explain, is the last country where macrobiotics will spread, and it will likely do so in an American form. For harmonious East West relations, it is up to us to develop a delicious, healthful North American cuisine that can successfully cross the Pacific.

"I've run more risk eating my way across the country than in all my driving."
— Duncan Hines, Adventures in Good Eating

Rice Balls

Rice balls are the macrobiotic travel food par excellence. They are easy to make, light and transportable, don't require any utensils, and keep for several days. They are also energizing. Two rice balls will usually satisfy the most demanding traveler for the rest of the morning or afternoon. We take them on short trips, long trips, airplane rides, to the ball park, the concert hall, on picnics, and just about everywhere else you can think of. There are numerous variations with wonderfully different shapes, sizes, and ingredients.

Rice balls are special because they retain a natural balance of yin and yang and elevate cooked rice to a still higher level of energy. And while most rice will begin losing its ki once it has been served, the rice ball continues to gather ki and will be stronger the day after it is made or even two or three days later than when it is freshly made. This feature makes it a valuable mainstay of lunch boxes and a special food for on the road.

The rice ball is an accurate reflection of the cook's condition. Keep practicing until you perfect them. You'll be greatly rewarded for the time and energy you put into making rice balls by the health and peaceful energy of those who eat them.

1 handful cooked rice
1 sheet of nori
umeboshi plums

Toast nori by waving it gently a few inches above a medium high flame with the shiny side up. Fold and cut or tear into quarters. Wet hands and take about one-half cup of rice and form into a ball or triangle. Press a hole in the center and add about a quarter of an umeboshi plum inside. Pack the ball again to close the corners. Don't be in a hurry. Take time to turn the rice slowly in your hand so that it is well pressed and will stay together.

Then place one-quarter sheet of nori on top of the ball and fold down the corners. Turn the ball over and add a second piece of nori in such a way that the corners fit in between the corners of the first piece and all of the rice is covered. Press ball again. The moisture from the rice will make the nori stick.

• Alternatively, you can dip your hands in a little soy sauce to form the rice ball and roll in roasted, ground sesame seeds.

Johnnycakes

Journey cakes, the traditional travel food of England and the British Isles, were grilled over the open hearth. Made of wheat, barley, oats, rye, or other grains, they were available at inns and pubs and served as standard fare of travelers for many centuries. In America, they became known as Johnnycakes and were made from cornmeal. They are also known as Shawnee cakes after a traditional native corn cake. This basic recipe makes about 16 cakes.

2 cups cornmeal
2 cups boiling spring water
sea salt to taste

Combine ingredients, pour enough batter to make a 3-inch cake on a hot griddle or oiled skillet. Let cook about 5 to 7 minutes, turn over and brown the other side.

Moistening Powder

This is the traditional Native American travel food. Across the continent travelers, messengers, traders, and scouts carried moistening powder in travel pouches for breakfast, lunch, and dinner. In the late 1880s, six Zuni elders journeyed across the country to visit Boston, living on this preparation, known in Zuni as tchu-k'ia-na'owe. At the Palmer House, Boston's fanciest restaurant and hotel, the Zunis became sick eating standard fare and resorted to their time-honored food.

1 bushel of white or yellow corn on the cob

Boil corn on the cob in wood ashes until the hulls can be removed. Dry corn for a day or two and then roast well and grind into coarse meal or *samp*. Toast again and grind into a very fine flour. Once more toast or roast, and then carefully sift.

In this process, a bushel of corn is reduced to a few quarts of flour. A single teaspoon of this moistening flour, mixed in a pint of water, makes a thick batter which is drunk. Just a few sips quench a strong appetite. Dry, the mixture keeps readily throughout the year and can be eaten without fire or further cooking.

Silvertip sat down cross-legged and began to eat his supper. [The two men] could have offered him some of their food, when they saw that he was chewing parched corn only.. . .
"Maybe a sage hen could live on that dead feed," said one of the bearded men. "It don't look human nor right nor nacheral to me."
"It takes some chewing," said Silvertip. "That's all it needs . . . A man can travel a lot better light than he can loaded," answered Silvertip. "I'll stick to the corn till I catch my horse."
— Max Brand, The Stolen Stallion

"The Zunis brought a liberal supply of this favorite lunch-material in the belief that where such armies of Americans dwelt as they had been told inhabited the 'Land of Sun-rise' one might find a scarcity of provisions."
— Frank Cushing, Zuni Breadstuffs

Glossary

Aduki bean   A small, dark, red bean originally from Japan but now also grown in the United States.

Agar agar   A white gelatin processed from a sea vegetable into bars, flakes, or powder, and used in making kanten and vegetable aspics.

Alaria   A sea vegetable found in the North Atlantic, similar to wakame.

Amaranth   A small whole grain, staple in ancient Mexico.

Amasake   A sweet, creamy beverage made from fermented sweet rice that can be served as a drink, hot or cold, or used as a natural sweetener in puddings and other dishes.

Arame   A thin, wiry black sea vegetable similar to hiziki.

Arepa   An oval-shaped corn ball or cake made from whole corn dough and baked or fried.

Arrowroot   A starch flour processed from the root of an American plant used as a thickening agent in cooking.

Ashcake   Cornbread baked in hot ashes.

Bancha tea   The twigs, stems, and leaves from mature tea bushes.

Barley   A whole grain that is used in soups and stews, served as a staple dish or combined with rice or other grains, made into flour and baked, and malted to make a sweetener or beer.

Barley malt   A natural sweetener made from malted barley.

Bennes   Original African-American name for sesame seeds.

Boiled salad   Salad whose ingredients are lightly boiled or dipped in hot water before serving.

Bok choy   A leafy green and white vegetable that originally came from China.

Brown rice   Whole unpolished rice, containing an ideal balance of nutrients.

Buckwheat   A hardy cereal grass eaten in the form of kasha (whole groats) or soba noodles.

Bulgur   A form of whole wheat that has been cracked, partially boiled, and dried.

Burdock   A wild hardy plant whose long, dark root is valued in cooking for its strengthening qualities.

Chica   Corn that has been chewed thoroughly and allowed to ferent and used in traditional cooking of Mexico and the desert Southwest.

Corn   A whole grain traditionally eaten by native peoples throughout North America. Varieties of corn include dent, flint, flour, and sweet. Non-hybridized corn is available in natural foods as open-pollinated or standard corn.

Couscous   Partially refined cracked wheat, served as a grain side dish, in salad, and with fruit or sweetener in a cake and other desserts.

Cracked wheat   Whole wheat berries that have been processed and cut into small pieces.

Daikon   A long, white radish used in many types of dishes and for medicinal preparations.
Dried tofu   A type of tofu that has been dried and is beige in color and very light.
Dry-roast   To toast a grain, seed, or flour in an unoiled skillet, stirring gently until brown or golden and a nutty aroma is released.
Dulse   A red-purple sea vegetable used in soups, salads, and vegetable dishes or as a garnish.

Fu   Dried wheat gluten cakes or sheets.

Ginger   A spicy, pungent, golden-colored root used in cooking and for medicinal purposes.
Gomashio   Sesame seed salt made from dry-roasting and grinding sea salt and sesame seeds and crushing them in a *suribachi*.
Gluten   The protein factor in grain. The higher the gluten, the lighter the bread. In making seitan, gluten is the sticky substance that remains after the bran has been separated from whole wheat flour.
Grits   Dried corn that has been cut and ground into a fine yellow or white meal; usually served as a hot morning cereal.
Groats   A hulled, usually crushed grain such as buckwheat or oats.
Gumbo   Original African name for okra; later identified with a fish-based vegetable soup or stew in the South.

Hiziki   A dark brown sea vegetalbe that when dried turns black.
Hoecake   Cornbread that is baked on a hoe or other farm implement.
Hoppin' John   Rice cooked with black-eyed peas; a traditional Carolina dish and one enjoyed on New Year's throughout the South.
Hominy   Coarsely ground corn, commonly prepared and served as a hot morning cereal.
Hush puppies   Deep-fried corn balls, customarily served with fish in the South.

Irish moss   A sea vegetable found in the Atlantic and Gulf of Mexico and valued for its natural gelatinous properties.

Johnnycake   A small griddle cake made of cornmeal.

Kanten   A jelled fruit dessert made with the sea vegetable agar-agar.
Kasha   Roasted groats, usually of buckwheat, but also of millet or other grain.
Kelp   A large family of sea vegetables similar to kombu.
Ki   Natural electromagnetic energy circulating between heaven and earth; the vital life energy of any person, food, or other phenomenon.
Kimpira   A style of cooking root vegetables by first sautéing, then adding a little water, and seasoning with soy sauce at the end of cooking.
Kinako   Roasted soybean flour.
Koji   A grain inoculated with bacteria and used in making fermented foods such as miso, soy sauce, amasake, natto, and sake.
Kokkoh   A cereal grain porridge or beverage that is customarily given to macrobiotic babies and infants after weaning.

Kombu   A wide, thick, dark green sea vegetable that grows in deep ocean water. Used in making soup stocks and condiments, and cooked as a separate dish or with vegetables, beans, and grains.

Kuzu   A white starch made from the root of a prolific wild vine. Used in thickening soups, gravies, sauces, desserts, and for medicinal beverages; also known as kudzu.

Laver   A sea vegetable, similar to nori.

Lentils   Small green or red beans used in soups, stews, and other dishes.

Limpin' Susan   Rice cooked with kidney or other colorful red beans; traditionally served in Louisiana and other parts of the South.

Lotus root   Root of the water lily, brown-skinned with a hollow, chambered, off-white inside, used in many dishes and for medicinal preparations.

Macrobiotics   From the traditional Greek words for "Long Life." The way of life according to the longest, largest possible view, the infinite order of the universe. The practice of macrobiotics includes the understanding and practical application of this order to daily life, including the selection, preparation, and manner of cooking and eating, as well as the orientation of consciousness and the realization of a healthy, peaceful world.

Marinate   To let foods such as vegetables soak in seasoning.

Masa   Dough made from whole corn, used in making arepas, tortillas, and other traditional dishes.

Millet   A small, yellow grain that can be prepared whole and be added to soups, salads, and vegetable dishes.

Mirin   A sweet cooking wine made from sweet rice.

Miso   A fermented paste made from soybeans, sea salt, and usually rice or barley. Used in soups, stews, spreads, baking, and as a seasoning. Miso gives a nice sweet taste and salty flavor.

Mochi   A cake or dumpling made from cooked, pounded sweet rice.

Moors and Christians   Rice cooked with black beans; a traditional Spanish dish from the Middle Ages popular in the South.

Natto   A lightly fermented soybean dish with sticky, long strands and a strong odor.

Natural food   Whole foods that are unrefined and untreated with artificial additives or preservatives.

Nigari   Hard crystallized salt made from liquid droppings of dampened sea salt; used in making tofu.

Nishime   Long, slow style of boiling in which vegetables or other ingredients cook primarily in their own juices, giving strong, peaceful energy.

Nori   Thin sheets of dried sea vegetable, black or dark purple in color, that turn green when roasted; used as a garnish, to wrap rice balls, in making sushi, or cooked with soy sauce as a condiment.

Oats   A whole grain that is eaten in whole form or rolled into common oatmeal or roughly cut into Scotch Oats.

Ocean ribbons   A sea vegetable harvested along the West Coast of the Pacific.

Ohagi   A rice cake made from cooked pounded sweet rice and coated with aduki beans, chestnuts, sesame seeds, roasted soybean flour, and other preparations.

Organic foods   Foods grown without the use of chemical fertilizers, herbicides, pesticides, or other artificial sprays and additives.

Pan-fry   To sauté with or without a little oil over a low to medium heat, stirring or turning occasionally but not so often as stir-frying.

Pearl barley   A small white barley valued for its cosmetic properties, also known as *hato mugi*.

Pearled barley   A polished form of barley.

Pickle press   A small enclosed glass or plastic container with a screw-plate for making pressed salad or light, quick pickles.

Piki bread   Traditional wafer-thin cornbread of the Hopi Indians.

Pilaf   Flully rice or rice served with vegetables.

Poi   Hawaiian name for taro potato.

Polenta   A casserole made with corn and often beans and vegetables.

Pressed salad   Salad prepared by pressing sliced vegetables and sea salt in a small pickle press or an improvised weight on a plate.

Pressure cooker   An airtight metal pot that cooks food quickly by steaming under pressure at high temperatures. Used primarily in macrobiotic cooking for whole grains and occasionally for beans and other dishes.

Purée   To mash food in a *suribachi*, bowl, mill, or food processor until smooth and even in consistency.

Quinoa   Ancient grain of the Incans traditionally grown in the high mountains of Peru and Bolivia and now grown in North America.

Red rice   Rice cooked together with aduki beans and having a nice red color.

Rice cake   A light, round cake made of puffed brown rice enjoyed as a snack.

Rice syrup   A natural sweetener made from malted brown rice.

Rolled oats   Oats that have been rolled and flattened; common oatmeal.

Rye   A whole grain traditionally used in making bread and other baked goods and combined with rice and other grains.

Samp   Whole corn that has been pounded coarsely and used in various dishes.

Sauté   To fry lightly in a skillet or shallow pan.

Sea palm   A mild green sea vegetable harvested in Pacific waters.

Sea salt   Salt obtained from the ocean. Unrefined sea salt is high in trace minerals and contains no chemicals, sugar, or added iodine.

Seasoning   Something used to flavor food such as salt, soy sauce, miso, or vinegar.

Sea vegetable   An edible seaweed such as kombu, wakame, arame, hiziki, nori, or dulse.

Seitan   A whole wheat product cooked in soy sauce, kombu, and water; used for stews, croquettes, grainburgers, and many other dishes; high in protein and gives a strong, dynamic taste; also called wheat gluten or wheat meat.

Shiitake   A mushroom used, fresh or dried, for soups and stews and for medicinal purposes.

Shiso   Leaves usually pickled with umeboshi plums; also known as beefsteak leaves.

Soba   Noodles made from buckwheat flour or buckwheat combined with whole wheat.

Sorghum   Grain native to Africa that is grown in the South and also used to make molasses.

Sourdough bread   Bread made with a sour starter of whole wheat flour and water or other sour food that has naturally fermenting properties.

Soy sauce   Traditionally, naturally made soy sauce as distinguished from refined, chemically processed soy sauce; also known as natural *shoyu* or organic *shoyu.*

Steam   To cook by exposing to hot steam.

Stir-fry   To quickly cook food in a wok or skillet using a small amount of oil, high heat, and stirring continuously.

Stoneground   Unrefined flour that has been ground in a stone mill that preserves the germ, bran, and other nutrients.

Succotash   A traditional native dish made of corn, beans, and squash.

Suppone   Traditional porridge made from whole corn.

Suribachi   A serrated, glazed clay bowl or mortar, used with a pestle for grinding and purée-ing foods.

Sushi   A traditional Japanese-style dish consisting of rice served with various vegetables and usually cut into spiral rounds.

Sweet kombu   A variety of kelp harvested off the West Coast that is sweet and tender.

Sweet rice   A glutinous type of rice that is slightly sweeter to the taste and used in making mochi, amasake, and various dishes.

Tahini   A thick, smooth paste made from ground sesame seeds.

Tamari   A stronger, wheat-free soy sauce sometimes called real or genuine tamari, a by-product of making miso, used for special dishes.

Teff   A grain traditionally used in Ethiopia in whole or baked form.

Tempeh   A traditional Southeast Asian soy product made from split soybeans, water, and a special bacteria; high in protein with a rich, dynamic taste, tempeh is used in soups, stews, sandwiches, casseroles, and other dishes.

Tempura   A style of cooking in which vegetables and other foods are dipped in batter, deep-fried in oil, and served with a dipping sauce; also the food cooked in this way.

Tofu   Soybean curd made from soybeans and *nigari*; high in protein and prepared in cakes, it is used in soups, vegetable dishes, salads, sauces, dressings, and other dishes.

Tortilla   Traditional flat bread of the Southwest made from whole corn dough.

Udon   Oriental-style whole wheat noodles.

Umeboshi   A salted pickled plum that has aged, usually for several years. Its nice zesty sour taste and salty flavor go well with many foods, and it is used as a seasoning, in sauces, as a condiment, in beverages, and in medicinal preparations.

Unrefined oil   Vegetable oil that has been naturally processed to retain its natural color, taste, aroma, and nutrients.

Wakame   A long thin, green sea vegetable used in making miso soup, as well as salads and other dishes.

Water-sauté   To cook in a skillet or saucepan with a small volume of water, like ordinary sautéing but without the oil.

Whole foods   Foods in their natural form that have not been refined or processed, such as brown rice or whole wheat berries.

Whole grains   Unrefined cereal grains to which nothing has been added or subtracted in milling except for the inedible outer hull. Whole grains include brown rice, millet, barley, whole wheat, oats, rye, buckwheat, corn, amaranth, teff, and quinoa.

Whole wheat   A whole cereal grain that may be prepared in whole form or made into flour. Whole wheat products such as noodles, seitan, fu, bulgur, couscous, and cracked wheat make a variety of dishes; in whole form, referred to as whole wheat berries.

Wild rice   Aquatic seed-bearing grass that grows in the Great Lakes region and prized for its smoky aroma and fruity taste; prepared as a side dish, cooked with other grains, and used in salads and other dishes.

Wok   A deep round Chinese-style skillet that is excellent for stir-frying and tempura.

Wood ashes   Residue of burnt hardwood traditionally used to soften and flavor corn.

Yang   One of the two fundamental energies of the universe. Yang refers to the relative tendency of contraction, centripetality, density, heat, light, and other qualities. Applied to foods, yang items include sea salt, most condiments, fish and seafood, sea vegetables, pressure-cooked brown rice, and buckwheat, millet, and hardier grains and styles of cooking that involve heavier ingredients, stronger seasoning, and longer cooking. Excessively yang items include eggs, meat, poultry, hard, salty cheese, and other animal food.

Yin   One of the two fundamental energies of the universe. Yin refers to the relative tendency of expansion, centrifugality, growth, diffusion, cold, darkness, and other qualities. Applied to foods, yin items include oil, most leafy vegetables, nuts and seeds, fruit, desserts, and beverages and styles of preparation that involve lighter ingredients, milder seasoning, and quicker cooking. Excessive yin items include polished grains, tropical fruits and vegetables, coffee and black tea, other aromatic and fragrant beverages, milk, yogurt, and other light dairy products, sugar, honey, and other simple sugars, and alcohol.

Resources

One Peaceful World

One Peaceful World is an international information network and friendship society of macrobiotic friends and families devoted to the realization of one healthy, peaceful world. Activities include educational and spiritual tours, assemblies and forums, international food aid and development, and publishing. For membership information and a current catalog of books, contact:

One Peaceful World
Box 10
Becket, MA 01223
(413) 623-2322

The Kushi Institute

The Kushi Institute is a center for macrobiotic studies located in the Berkshire mountains of western Massachusetts with affiliates in Europe and extension programs in various North American cities. The seven-day Macrobiotic Residential Program offers instruction in hands-on macrobiotic cooking, and there are cooking classes and demonstrations at the annual Macrobiotic Summer Conference. For information, contact:

Kushi Institute
Box 7
Becket, MA 01223
(413) 623-5741

George Ohsawa Macrobiotic Foundation

G.O.M.F. is a center for macrobiotic publishing and education located in northern California. Founded by Herman and Cornelia Aihara, it offers year-round seminars and classes, publishes books by George Ohsawa and other authors, circulates *Macrobiotics Today*, a monthly magazine, and holds an annual summer camp. For information, contact:

George Ohsawa Macrobiotic Foundation
1511 Robinson Street
Oroville, CA 95965
(916) 533-7702

Kusa Research Foundation

Traditional varieties of rice, millet, wheat, corn, and other grains are available to organic farmers and gardeners from Kusa, a seed bank founded on macrobiotic principles and whose name comes from the Sanskrit term for "sacred grass."

Kusa Society
Box 761
Ojai, CA 93023

Regional Macrobiotic Centers

Macrobiotic Center of Middletown
214-400 Plaza Middlesex
Middletown, CT 06457
(203) 344-0628

Macrobiotic Center of Philadelphia
243 Dickenson St.
Philadelphia, PA 19147
(215) 551-1430

East West Center of Cleveland
Suite 536, 2800 Superior Ave.
Cleveland, OH 44144
(216) 696-0146

Macrobiotic Center of Knoxville
7469 Highway 70 East
Lenoir City, TN 37771
(615) 986-9711

Macrobiotic Center of South Carolina
814 Queens St.
Columbia, SC 29205
(803) 765-1400

Macrobiotic Foundation of Florida
3291 Franklin Ave.
Coconut Grove (Miami), FL 33133
(305) 448-6625

Macrobiotic Center of Dallas
850 South Glenville Ave. #110
Richardson, TX 75081
(214) 669-8328

East West Center of Austin
3904 Avenue D
Austin TX 78751
(512) 467-1700

East West Center of Los Angeles
11215 Hannum Ave.
Culver City CA 90230
(310) 398-2228

Recommended Reading

Albanese, Catharine L. *Nature Religion in America from the Algonkian Indians to the New Age.* Chicago: University of Chicago Press, 1990.

Belasco, Warren J. *Appetite for Change: How the Counter-Culture Took on the Food Industry 1966-1988.* New York: Pantheon, 1989.

Brewster, Letitia, and Michael F. Jacobson, *The Changing American Diet.* Washington, D.C.: Center for Science in the Public Interest, 1978.

Columbus, Christopher. *The Journal of Christopher Columbus,* translated by Cecil Jane. New York: Bonanza, 1960.

Cushing, Frank Hamilton. *Zuni: The Selected Writings of Frank Hamilton Cushing.* Lincoln: University of Nebraska Press, 1979.

Densmore, Frances. *How Indians Use Wild Plants for Food, Medicine, and Crafts.* Mineola, N.Y.: Dover, (1928), 1974.

East West Foundation, with Ann Fawcett and Cynthia Smith. *Cancer-Free: 30 Who Triumphed Over Cancer Naturally.* Tokyo and New York: Japan Publications, Inc., 1992.

Esko, Edward, editor. *Doctors Look at Macrobiotics.* Tokyo and New York: Japan Publications, Inc., 1988.

Esko, Edward and Wendy Esko. *Macrobiotic Cooking for Everyone.* Tokyo and New York: Japan Publications, Inc., 1980.

Esko, Wendy. *Aveline Kushi's Introducing Macrobiotic Cooking.* Tokyo and New York: Japan Publications, Inc., revised edition, 1987.

Fischer, David Hackett. *Albion's Seed: Four British Folkways in America.* New York: Oxford University Press, 1989.

Jack, Alex, and Gale Jack, *Promenade Home: Macrobiotics and Women's Health.* Tokyo and New York: Japan Publications, Inc., 1988.

Jack, Alex, *Let Food Be Thy Medicine.* Becket, Mass.: One Peaceful World Press, 1991.

----- *The New Age Dictionary.* Tokyo and New York: Japan Publications, Inc., 1990.

Jack, Alex, and Aveline Kushi. *Aveline Kushi's Complete Guide to Macrobiotic Cooking.* New York: Warner Books, 1985.

-----*Aveline: The Life and Dream of the Woman Behind Macrobiotics Today.* Tokyo and New York: Japan Publications, Inc., 1988.

Jack, Alex, and Michio Kushi. *The Book of Macrobiotics.* Tokyo and New York: Japan Publications, Inc., revised edition, 1987.

-----*The Cancer-Prevention Diet.* New York: St. Martin's Press, 1983; revised edition 1993.

-----*Diet for a Strong Heart.* New York: St. Martin's Press, 1985.

-----*The Gospel of Peace: Jesus's Teachings of Eternal Truth.* Tokyo and New York: Japan Publications, Inc., 1992.

-----*One Peaceful World*. New York: St. Martin's Press, 1987.

Jack, Alex, with Aveline and Michio Kushi. *Macrobiotic Diet*. Tokyo and New York: Japan Publications, Inc., 1986; revised edition 1993.

-----*Food Governs Your Destiny: The Teachings of Namboku Mizuno*. Tokyo and New York: Japan Publications, Inc., 1991.

Kushi, Aveline, and Wendy Esko. *Aveline Kushi's Wonderful World of Salads*. Tokyo and New York: Japan Publications, Inc., 1990.

-----*Changing Seasons Cookbook*. Garden City Park, N.Y.: Avery Publishing Group, 1985.

-----*The Good Morning Breakfast Book*. Garden City Park, N.Y.: Avery Publishing Group, 1991.

-----*Macrobiotic Family Favorites*. Tokyo and New York: Japan Publications, Inc., 1988.

-----*The New Pasta Cuisine*. Tokyo and New York: Japan Publications, Inc., 1992.

Kushi, Michio. *The Book of Do-In: Exercises for Physical and Spiritual Development*. Tokyo and New York: Japan Publications, Inc., 1979.

-----*How to See How Health: The Book of Oriental Diagnosis*. Tokyo and New York: Japan Publications, Inc., 1980.

-----*Standard Macrobiotic Diet*. Becket, Mass.: One Peaceful World Press, 1992.

Kushi, Michio, and Edward Esko. *Forgotten Worlds*. Becket, Mass.: One Peaceful World Press, 1992.

-----*Nine Star Ki*. Becket, Mass.: One Peaceful World Press, 1991.

Levenstein, Harvey. *Revolution at the Table: The Transformation of the American Diet*. New York: Oxford University Press, 1988.

Mintz, Sidney. *Sweetness and Power: The Place of Sugar in Modern History*. New York: Viking Press, 1985.

Schwartz, Hillel. *Never Satisfied: A Cultural History of Diets, Fantasies, and Fat*. New York: Doubleday, 1986.

Shurtleff, William, and Akiko Aoyagi. *The Book of Miso*. Berkeley: Ten Speed Press, 1976.

-----*The Book of Tofu*. New York: Ballantine, 1980.

Wood, Peter. *Black Majority*. New York: Alfred Knopf, 1974.

Periodicals

One Peaceful World Newsletter, Becket, Massachusetts
Macro News, Philadelphia, Pennsylvania
Macrobiotics Today, Oroville, California

General Index

Recipe Index

About the Authors

Alex Jack has served as editor-in-chief of the *East West Journal*, director of the Kushi Institute of the Berkshires, and global coordinator of One Peaceful World. With Michio Kushi, he is the co-author of *The Book of Macrobiotics, Macrobiotic Diet, The Cancer-Prevention Diet, Diet for a Strong Heart, One Peaceful World, Food Governs Your Destiny,* and *The Gospel of Peace.* With Aveline Kushi, he is the co-author of *Aveline Kushi's Complete Guide to Macrobiotic Cooking* and *Aveline: The Life and Dream of the Woman Behind Macrobiotics Today.* He is also the editor of *Let Food Be Thy Medicine* and *The New Age Dictionary.* Alex has traveled and taught in many countries and organized an airlift of macrobiotic food to Russia. He is presently teaching at the Kushi Institute in Becket, Massachusetts, and directing One Peaceful World Press.

Gale Jack is a homemaker, professional counselor, and certified cooking instructor. With Alex, she is the co-author of *Promenade Home: Macrobiotics and Women's Health,* the story of her childhood growing up in Oklahoma and Texas, her teaching and counseling career in Houston and Dallas, and her healing adventures with macrobiotics. Gale has taught cooking in Dallas, at the Kushi Institute, and elsewhere around the country. Gale and Alex live in the Berkshires with their daughter, Masha, and frequently visit their son, Jon, in Dallas.

Alex and Gale maintain an active teaching and counseling schedule and offer cooking classes, seminars, and private instruction. Comments or suggestions about *Amber Waves of Grain* are welcomed. Their address is:

Alex and Gale Jack
P.O. Box 487
Becket, MA 01223

Rod House, the illustrator, has served on the faculty of the Massachusetts College of Art and the Kushi Institute, managed Ghinga Japanese Macrobiotic Restaurant in Stockbridge, Massachusetts, and presented many exhibits and shows of his original paintings and drawings. He lives with his wife, Gloria, in Lee, Massachusetts.